W9-DEI-006

The War on Terror

The War on Terror

The Legal Dimension

James P. Terry

ROWMAN & LITTLEFIELD PUBLISHERS, INC.
Lanham • Boulder • New York • Toronto • Plymouth, UK

Published by Rowman & Littlefield Publishers, Inc.
A wholly owned subsidiary of The Rowman & Littlefield Publishing Group, Inc.
4501 Forbes Boulevard, Suite 200, Lanham, Maryland 20706
www.rowman.com

10 Thornbury Road, Plymouth PL6 7PP, United Kingdom

British Library Cataloguing in Publication Information Available

Library of Congress Cataloging-in-Publication Data

Terry, James P., (lawyer)
The war on terror : the legal dimension / James P. Terry.
p. cm.
Includes bibliographical references and index.
ISBN 978-1-4422-2242-7 (cloth : alk. paper) -- ISBN 978-1-4422-2244-1 (electronic)
1. War on Terrorism, 2001-2009. 2. Terrorism--Prevention. 3. Terrorism--United States. 4. Terrorism--Government policy--United States. I. Title.
KZ6795.T47T47 2013
344.7305'325--dc23

                                                                    2013004659

™ The paper used in this publication meets the minimum requirements of American National Standard for Information Sciences Permanence of Paper for Printed Library Materials, ANSI/NISO Z39.48-1992.

Printed in the United States of America

For Michelle

Contents

Foreword

Retired Marine Colonel James Terry is an extraordinary human being—a Marine warrior who almost lost his life in the service of his country during the Vietnam War and spent months in military hospitals recuperating from his battle wounds. When the Marine Corps decided to discharge him because of his battle wounds, he persuaded them instead to send him to law school—which began a process that ultimately produced a superb national security law scholar who continues to make important contributions in diverse areas of this important new field of study.

His distinguished career as a Marine Judge Advocate (JAG) officer culminated in arguably the most important position to which a military lawyer can aspire, Legal Counsel to the Chairman of the Joint Chiefs of Staff, under both General Colin Powell and General John Shalikashvili. In his spare time he earned three master's degrees and a rare earned academic law doctorate (SJD), degrees often granted "with distinction" or "highest honors." After retiring from the Corps, he continued his distinguished career as a public servant in a variety of new assignments, including as Principal Deputy Assistant Secretary of State for Legislative Affairs and as the Senate–confirmed Chairman of the Board of Veterans Appeals.

Not satisfied with more than four decades spent serving his country, in his latest "retirement" he has become a prolific scholar and author—talents developed and honed during decades of writing and lecturing beyond the normal requirements of his various jobs. Now a Senior Fellow with the Center for National Security Law at the University of Virginia School of Law, Dr. Terry has within less than two years produced two excellent book manuscripts, one on the powers of the commander-in-chief and this quite excellent volume on legal dimensions of the war on terror.

The tragic events of September 11, 2001, shocked most of the nation and created a growth industry of often newly minted "experts" on the subject of terrorism. That was a good thing, because prior to those attacks too few Americans were seriously focused upon threats that had been building for decades. For many of us who were working in the field decades before 9/11, the issue was not *whether* America would experience terrorist attacks, but rather *when* and *where* those attacks would occur.

More than fifteen years before the 9/11 "wake-up call" focused public attention in America on the dangers of terrorism, the Naval War College awarded its prestigious Captain Hugh Nott Prize to then Lt Col James Terry for an outstanding essay that was published in the *Naval War College Review* under the title "An Appraisal of Lawful Military Response to State-Sponsored Terrorism." Put simply, Dr. Terry is no newcomer to the field addressed by this excellent volume.

War is the ultimate political instrument. Americans have found it necessary to engage in war far too often in our history, both to secure and maintain our own freedom and to protect the people of other nations from international tyranny. To our credit, the United States has played a prominent role in promoting the growth of legal regimes governing both the initiation of hostilities (*jus ad bellum*) and the conduct of wars once begun (*jus in bello*). The 1863 "Lieber Code," issued as General Order 100 by President Lincoln during the Civil War, was the first effort to codify the "law of war" (often referred to today as the "law of armed conflict," or LOAC), and the United States played an active role in securing international agreement on a series of Hague and Geneva Conventions seeking to regulate the conduct of war and to protect innocent noncombatants and military personnel who, because of injury, shipwreck, detention, etc., were no longer able to protect themselves.

But the conflict that Congress authorized following the 9/11 attacks raised a variety of important legal issues that had not been adequately addressed by the LOAC treaties of the nineteenth and twentieth centuries. To be sure, some issues inherent in fighting a non-State actor were confronted during the Vietnam War, when often part-time guerrillas, covertly doing the bidding of the Communist regime in North Vietnam, failed to comply with established LOAC principles and often made civilians the targets of terrorist attacks. Although (like al Qaeda and Taliban forces in the current conflict) the so-called Viet Cong were clearly not protected by most of the provisions of the 1949 Geneva Convention Relative to the Treatment of Prisoners of War, in an attempt to maintain the high moral ground, General William Westmoreland in 1966 established a policy that captured Viet Cong combatants would be given the full protections of the 1949 convention—with but one exception: when they were apprehended while engaged in acts of terrorism.

The current struggle against al Qaeda, the Taliban, and their radical Islamist allies did not, of course, start on September 11, 2001. Two hundred and forty Marines were killed by a terrorist truck bomb on October 23, 1983, and subsequent attacks were made against the *USS Cole*, American embassies in Kenya and Tanzania, and elsewhere. But most Americans did not realize there was a war going on until they watched their television monitors in horror as hijacked commercial airplanes flew into the twin towers and the Pentagon that September morning.

Three days after the 9/11 attacks, with but a single dissenting vote, Congress invoked the 1973 War Powers Resolution and authorized the president to use armed force against those "nations, organizations, or persons" he concluded were complicit in those attacks. While some have sought to dismiss this conflict as more akin to the "war on poverty" than a legitimate armed conflict, the Supreme Court has repeatedly sided with Congress and both Presidents Bush and Obama in holding that America is engaged in an armed conflict in which the law of armed conflict sets most of the relevant legal rules.

Sadly, perhaps because this is an unusual type of conflict to most Americans, there has been a great deal of ignorance and misinformation about the governing legal rules. American high school students are taught that the government may not generally detain suspected criminals without charging them with a specific crime, giving them access to legal counsel, and taking them before a judge or magistrate to determine if there is sufficient "probable cause" to detain them further or bring them to trial. Thus, when it was reported that detainees captured in foreign lands in the current conflict were being held in a military detention facility without being formally charged or (initially) given access to legal counsel, there was a public outcry. It is to our credit that our citizens are so committed to the rule of law that they would demand fair process even for foreign nationals who if given the chance would kill them. But few Americans understood that detaining captured enemy combatants for the duration of hostilities was a well-established principle of LOAC, or knew that during World War II more than 400,000 German POWs were held in camps spread across more than forty American states without access to courts or lawyers.

Mistakes were also made by the government. Just as in their determination to prevent another "Pearl Harbor," civil libertarians like President Franklin Roosevelt, California Attorney General (later Supreme Court Chief Justice) Earl Warren, and a majority of the U.S. Supreme Court approved the apprehension and detention of more than 100,000 Americans along the West Coast simply because they were descendants of Japanese ancestors; government officials following the 9/11 attacks made some serious mistakes. Some of these, no doubt, were motivated by a determination to avoid "another 9/11," but others resulted because not enough people in the decision-making process were trained in this important but somewhat esoteric area of national security law. Some of the nation's foremost authorities in the field were military JAG officers, who sadly were often excluded from the process.

It is important that the American people understand the legal dimensions of this ongoing armed conflict, and few people are better qualified to address them than Dr. Jim Terry. Not all of the issues have clearly agreed-upon answers, even among experts, and debates will continue with able and honorable people on different sides. In that spirit, not everyone will agree with all of the conclusions of this volume. But it is an excellent overview and a valuable contribution to the important goal of producing an informed nation committed both to protecting its people against terrorism and upholding the rule of law. It is a book that will be of value both to experts in the field and ordinary citizens who wish to better understand the legal dimensions of a conflict that may be with us for some years to come.

I am pleased to give it my enthusiastic recommendation.

Robert F. Turner
Co-Founder (1981)
Center for National Security Law
University of Virginia School of Law
Charlottesville, Virginia

Preface

It has been more than ten years since the world was required to focus its attention on the terrorist violence perpetrated by al Qaeda in New York and Washington. The major nations, and most significantly the United States, realized immediately that the international regime established to regulate armed conflict between states, the Hague and Geneva law, was simply ineffective and irrelevant to this genre of violence. Spawned within the Muslim world and justified by claims of Palestinian injustice, the two campaigns marked by Operation Enduring Freedom in Afghanistan and Operation Iraqi Freedom in Iraq have offered legal challenges unlike any other within the history of modern warfare.

Instead of reflecting rights vis-à-vis national or state interests, the current combatants, represented by al Qaeda in Afghanistan and state-sponsored agents in Iraq, operate with impunity outside any recognized legal regime. The legal issues that have arisen in addressing these irregular and unlawful belligerents are not only complex and diverse but exceedingly challenging to our federal court system.

In the twenty chapters that follow, the genesis of the United States' approach to terror violence is explored, as is the legal development that creates the predicate for our response to the current conflicts in Kabul and Baghdad. The historical underpinning of the Palestinian claim in Gaza and the West Bank is reviewed in chapter 3 as a focus to the al Qaeda justification for the precipitating attacks of September 11, 2001. The law of self-defense as applied to the terrorist threat is then dissected and carefully related to our operational approach to the continuing crisis.

The text addresses terror violence within a conjoined operational and legal framework. In nearly every case, they are inextricably intertwined. The international law of self-defense forms the underpinning for U.S. rules of engagement and the operational context in which the president has directed the application of U.S. military force. The resulting flood of detainees and captured enemy combatants has raised questions of detainee rights and the obligations of their captors. Interrogation and venue issues have unduly burdened the federal court system.

The war on terror is far broader than the national concerns related to the terrorist group or the individual terrorist, however. The spill-over issues of media coverage, demands for application to the International Criminal Court, and serious concerns related to protection of critical national infrastructure abound.

In this treatise on the legal dimension of the war on terror, the author carefully explores the myriad juridical concerns that must be addressed in prosecuting a war with few established legal boundaries.

Chapter One

War on Terror

The Legal Dimension

THE THREAT OF TERRORISM IN PERSPECTIVE

In addressing the postconflict terrorist threat in Afghanistan and Iraq, and the earlier terrorist attacks directed from al Qaeda in September 2001, the United States was not addressing a new phenomenon, but certainly a level of violence unusual to that genre. In fact, the crisis emanating from al Qaeda and the earlier hostage taking by militants in Iran in 1979–1980 have provided cogent lessons. Nor have they been the first such incidents. During his presidency, James Monroe established the right to enter the territory of another state to prevent terrorist attacks, where the host is unable, or unwilling, to quell a continuing threat to ordinary citizens. The Seminole Indians, in Spanish Florida, had demanded "arms, ammunition and provisions or the possession of the garrison at Fort Marks."[1] President Monroe directed General Andrew Jackson to proceed against the Seminoles, with the explanation that the Spanish "were bound by treaty to keep their Indians at peace, but were incompetent to do so."[2]

During the Canadian insurrection of 1837, the standard for justifiable anticipatory self-defense that could legally be exercised by the commander-in-chief during terrorist threats was more clearly established.[3] Anti-British sympathizers gathered near Buffalo, New York. A large number of Americans and Canadians were similarly encamped on the Canadian side of the border, with the apparent intention of aiding these rebels. The *Caroline*, an American vessel which the rebels used for supplies and communications, was boarded in an American port, at midnight, by an armed group, acting under orders of a British officer, who set the vessel on fire and let it drift over

Niagara Falls. The United States protested the incident, which had claimed the lives of at least two American citizens. The British government replied that the threat posed by the *Caroline* was established, that American laws were not being enforced along the border, and that the destruction was an act of necessary self-defense to terrorist violence.

In the controversy that followed, the United States did not deny that circumstances were conceivable that would justify this action, and Great Britain admitted the necessity of showing circumstances of extreme urgency. The two countries differed only on the question of whether the facts brought the case within the exceptional principle. Charles Cheney Hyde summed up the incident by saying that "the British force did that which the United States itself would have done, had it possessed the means and disposition to perform its duties."[4] Secretary of State Daniel Webster, in formulating an oft-cited principle of self-defense, said that there must be a demonstrated "necessity of self-defense, instant, overwhelming, leaving no choice of means and no moment of deliberation."[5] It is clear, however, that the Webster formulation was *not* applied by the British in the decision to destroy the *Caroline*, at least with respect to the element requiring "no moment of deliberation." The U.S. Department of State has properly criticized Secretary Webster's formulation as follows: "This definition is obviously drawn from consideration of the right of self-defense in domestic law: the cases are rare indeed in which it would fit an international situation."[6] Today, when terrorists and their sponsors possess weapons with rapid delivery capabilities, any requirement that a nation may not respond until faced with a situation providing no moment of deliberation is unrealistic.[7]

In the modern era, four presidents have faced major incidents of terrorist violence that have impacted the vital national interests of the United States. The November 1979 seizure of U.S. diplomats by Iranian militants protected by the Iranian government and the Carter Administration's ineffective response, was likely responsible for President Carter's defeat by Ronald Reagan in the 1980 election. In 1986, President Reagan's second administration acted forcefully to address the threat by Kaddafi's Libyan terrorist organization after an attack on U.S. citizens in then West Germany. This military action against Kaddafi followed precisely the articulation of presidential prerogatives set forth earlier by President Reagan in National Security Decision Directive (NSDD) 138. While President Clinton took no direct action after attacks on two of our embassies and on the *USS Cole*, he did reorganize our internal policy-making bodies responsible for counter terrorism.

In responding forcefully and effectively to the al Qaeda 2001 attacks on the Trade Center and the Pentagon, President George W. Bush properly viewed the attacks not as terrorist violence, per se, but as a military attack upon America that demanded the full weight of US response. It was his careful articulation of a new policy toward the threat of terrorism in the two

National Security strategies issued at the beginning of his first and second terms, respectively, that have provided the roadmap for future response to terrorist violence.

PRESIDENT CARTER AND THE IRANIAN HOSTAGE CRISIS

President Jimmy Carter faced an administration-altering terrorist incident in the waning days of his tenure in office. The 1979 attacks on the United States Embassy in Tehran and the Consulates at Tabriz and Shiraz followed by one week the entry of the Shah into the United States for medical treatment.[8] On November 4, 1979, approximately three hundred militant demonstrators overran the U.S. Embassy compound in Tehran and took fifty-two U.S. citizens hostage for a period of 444 days.

As in most developing countries, there were few internal constraints—whether from opposition parties, a critical press, or an enlightened public—to pressure Khomeini, the Iranian leader, to uphold the law. In the atmosphere of fervent nationalism that accompanied Khomeini's sweep to power, forces for moderation were depicted as tools of foreign interests. In such an atmosphere, the militant supporters of the clerical leadership fomented domestic pressure to violate other recognized norms as well—in areas such as property ownership, religious freedom, and judicial protection. This combination of revolution and nationalism yielded explosive results—a re-ordering of both Iranian domestic society and its approach to foreign affairs.

It was President Carter's lack of resolve in addressing the crisis that proved costliest to his administration, however. While the United Nations Security Council, at the behest of the United States, unanimously adopted Resolution 457 on December 4th, 1979, calling upon the Government of Iran "to release immediately the personnel of the Embassy of the United States of America being held in Tehran, to provide them protection and allow them to leave the country,"[9] this was not accompanied by any threat of imminent military action on the part of the United States. Resolution 457 also requested that the Secretary General lend his good offices to the immediate implementation of the resolution and that he take all appropriate measures to that end.

While the United States, through Secretary of State Cyrus Vance, was able to secure repeated Security Council measures requiring Iran to comply with its international obligations, there were no sanctions included, as a result of a Soviet veto.[10] In the subsequent U.S. application to the International Court of Justice[11] the Court on December 15, 1979, unanimously ruled that Iran should release the American hostages and restore seized premises to exclusive American control.[12] This ruling was ignored by Iran.

When diplomatic efforts at securing the hostages' freedom via diplomacy failed in the United Nations and through legal means in the International

Court of Justice, President Carter banned United States' purchases of Iranian oil under the Trade Expansion Act.[13] He did so to make clear that the United States would not be blackmailed because of oil requirements.[14] The United States then learned that Iran planned to withdraw all assets held in American banking institutions. The removal of funds would have jeopardized billions of dollars in American claims against those assets—debts owed to both government and private enterprise.[15] The ripple effect of a mass withdrawal would have threatened the entire international financial system.

The president acted quickly to protect the interests of American creditors by blocking the removal of the Iranian funds. In order to do this, the president invoked the provisions of the International Emergency Powers Act of 1977.[16] This act permits the freezing of foreign assets when there exists "an unusual and extraordinary threat to the national security, foreign policy, and economy of the United States."[17] The Secretary of the Treasury implemented the President's executive order on November 14, 1979, with a series of Iranian assets control regulations.[18]

A month later, the United States informed the Iranian Chargé d'Affaires in Washington that personnel assigned to the Iranian Embassy and consular posts in the United States would be limited to fifteen at the embassy and five per consulate.[19] From January to March 1980, the United States exercised restraint in generating additional pressure in order to allow the initiatives of UN Secretary General Waldheim to work as well as those of intermediaries. Factional disputes prevented Bani-Sadr and Iranian authorities from honoring their pledges regarding the authority of the United Nations Commission in Iran and this in turn stifled Waldheim's diplomatic initiatives.

President Carter then moved to impose unilateral sanctions on Iran, and in April 1980 all financial dealings and exports to Iran except food and medicine were prohibited.[20] On April 17, 1980, the Carter Administration imposed additional prohibitions on imports, travel, and financial transfers related to Iran.[21] This executive order also restricted travel under the Immigration and Nationality Act.[22] Finally, in April 1980, the United States broke diplomatic relations with Iran and ordered the Iranian Embassy in Washington closed.

While these unilateral measures were being implemented, our allies in Europe, Japan, and Canada were imposing economic and diplomatic sanctions against Iran in an effort to maintain a common front. At the April 21, 1980, meeting of the leaders of the European Community, nine allied nations reaffirmed their support for severe sanctions against Iran and stated they would seek legislation enabling them to join the effort to isolate Iran internationally in the event the hostage crisis had not been resolved by May 17, 1980.[23] When no progress had been made by that date, these allies moved to accommodate the United States' request that no new contracts be entered into with Iran and that all contracts negotiated between these nations and Iran after November 4, 1979, be disavowed.[24]

Unfortunately, several European states—Great Britain included—were unable to gain parliamentary support for the entire package of sanctions promised. Thus the impact, while significant, failed to isolate Iran completely from a vital source of imports—Europe. The then–Soviet Union compounded the problem of incomplete support when it announced that if Iranian ports were blockaded or primary commodities became unavailable from the West, the Soviet Union would neutralize the impact of such measures by providing all necessary assistance. Specifically, the Soviet Union offered its roads and railway system to move goods if Iran's harbors should be blocked.[25] It also promised to supply Iran with primary foodstuffs if these became unavailable from customary sources.[26]

The economic measures adopted by the Western nations, while psychologically satisfying, proved singularly ineffective. In fact, the only noticeable impact was a rallying of Iranians behind Khomeini and the diversion of Iranian attention from internal difficulties to the foreign challenge. These measures tended to fragment international support for the United States while making it politically difficult for the Iranians to back down. In short, economic pressures, although perhaps politically expedient as a means to demonstrate presidential resolution, had the counterproductive effect of unifying Iranian opposition without coercing cooperation.

Concurrent with its judicial, diplomatic, and economic initiatives, in November 1979 the United States began planning a military operation to rescue the hostages. Citing the same legal justification claimed by Israel in rescuing its citizens from terrorists at Entebbe, Uganda, and by then–West Germany in a similar successful rescue at Mogadishu, Somalia, in 1977,[27] the United States entered Iran during the night of April 24, 1980. A team of approximately ninety American servicemen departed the aircraft carrier Nimitz by helicopter for a remote, deserted airstrip in southern Iran, approximately three hundred miles from Tehran. There they rendezvoused with a C-130 transport aircraft for refueling. The plan then called for a flight from this rendezvous to Tehran.[28] However, when three of the eight RH-53 helicopters were disabled by mechanical failures resulting from sand intake,[29] the mission was aborted and the remaining aircraft departed Iran, but not before a helicopter and transport collided and exploded.[30]

With respect to the Americans held, the 1961 Vienna Convention on Diplomatic Relations[31] obligated Iran to treat each American diplomat with "due respect," to take "all appropriate steps to prevent any attack on his person, freedom, or dignity," and to ensure that diplomatic personnel were not subjected to "any form of arrest or detention." Article 37 of this Convention extends these same privileges and immunities to members of the administrative and technical staffs as well as to their families.[32] These protections embody "the oldest established and the most fundamental rule of diplomatic law,"[33] a point repeatedly emphasized by the International Court of Justice in its December 15, 1979, order discussing provisional measures with respect to the American hostages.[34] In addition to its obligation to protect diplomatic personnel, Iran also had a duty to bring the attacking militants to justice. Its failure to take either step laid the groundwork for subsequent American claims for reparations.[35]

In retrospect, certain implications of the 444-day Iranian hostage crisis are now clear. The continued vitality of mutual world values depends on much more than a search for national catharsis. The American public's penchant for gestures, such as candlelight vigils and yellow ribbons, was matched by the Carter Administration's tendency to confuse symbol with substance and to adopt pose in the name of policy. Time was perceived as being on the side of the Iranians. It appeared that the crisis controlled Carter rather than him controlling the crisis.

In the longer term, the attempt by President Carter to embrace all options other than the direct use of military force resulted in a settlement favorable to Iran. A country that confuses catharsis with defense of its interests is a nation uncertain of its values, and President Carter's effort to eschew the military instrument in favor of all others proved to be counterproductive. President Reagan's pledge during the 1980 campaign of "swift and effective retribution" in case of further threats to Americans abroad was clearly meant to deter future attacks as well as reassure a concerned nation. It also assured his election.

Upon his inauguration and the release of the hostages, President Reagan found himself bound by the terms of the Carter Administration's negotiated settlement, terms which the Supreme Court upheld as legal, if not wise.[36] Certain terms, such as the requirement to return unencumbered Iranian financial assets, did no more than honor a pre-existing obligation. Other commitments which pertained directly to the official relationship between the United States and Iran, such as the formation of a Joint U.S.–Iranian Claims Tribunal, were also honored as positive contributions to community values.

Some parts of the agreement, however, were legally unenforceable. One such provision was the requirement that the United States "order all persons within U.S. jurisdiction to report to the U.S. Treasury, within 30 days, for transmission to Iran, all information known to them, as of Nov. 3, 1979 . . . with respect to the property and assets of the former Shah. Violation of the requirement will be subject to civil and criminal penalties described by U.S. law."[37] No such order was ever issued, nor could it have been enforced if it had been.

PRESIDENT RONALD REAGAN'S RESPONSE TO
INTERNATIONAL TERRORISM: THE CASE OF LIBYA

One of President Ronald Reagan's strongest attributes was his direct approach in responding to threats to the American people. When he took office, he engaged scholars at the war colleges to begin a review of available options to address the increased incidence of terrorist violence worldwide. Early in 1984, the president issued the seminal "preemption" doctrine addressing response to terrorist violence. In the words of former Defense Department official Noel Koch, President Reagan's NSDD 138, issued April 3, 1984[38] "represent[ed] a quantum leap in countering terrorism, from the reactive mode to recognition that pro-active steps [were] needed."[39] Although NSDD 138 remains classified to this day, Robert C. McFarlane suggested at the Defense Strategy Forum on March 25, 1985, that it included the following key elements: The practice of terrorism under all circumstances is a threat to the national security of the United States; the practice of international terrorism must be resisted by all legal means; the United States has the responsibility to take protective measures whenever there is evidence that terrorism is about to be committed; and the threat of terrorism constitutes a form of aggression and justifies acts in self-defense.[40]

It is the linkage between the terrorist and the sponsoring state which is crucial to providing the United States, or any nation, with the justification for response against a violating state. Covert intelligence operatives are necessary for identifying and targeting terrorist training camps and bases, and for providing an effective warning of impending terrorist attacks. Unfortunately, as noted by former Secretary of State George Shultz in 1984, "we may never have the kind of evidence that can stand up in an American court of law."[41]

Although no U.S. administration official, past or present, has been able to define adequately, "how much evidence is enough," the demand for probative, or court-sustainable evidence affirming the complicity of a specific sponsoring state is an impractical standard that contributed to the impression—prior to the articulation of NSDD 138 in 1984—that the United States was inhibited from responding meaningfully to terrorist outrages. This view was certainly reinforced in 1979, as addressed above, when the United States government allowed 52 American citizens to remain hostage to Iranian militants for more than four hundred days. Hugh Tovar has correctly noted: "There is a very real danger that the pursuit of more and better intelligence may become an excuse for non-action, which in itself might do more harm than action based on plausible though incomplete intelligence."[42]

True to his commitment under NSDD 138, and consistent with his 1980 campaign pledge to effect "swift and effective retribution" in case of further threats to Americans abroad, President Reagan directed military force against Libyan terrorists on April 15, 1986. On that date, the United States launched defensive strikes on military targets in Tripoli and Benghazi, Libya. The use of force was preceded by conclusive evidence of Libyan responsibility for prior acts of terrorism against the United States, with clear evidence that more were planned. The final provocation occurred in West Berlin, on April 5, when two U.S. citizens were killed and seventy-eight others were injured by an explosive device detonated in a discotheque. [43]

Eleven days earlier, on March 25, a cable from Tripoli directed the Libyan People's Bureau, in East Berlin, to target U.S. personnel and interests. On April 4, a return message was intercepted, which informed Colonel Kaddafi's headquarters that a terrorist attack would take place the next day. On April 5, the same People's Bureau reported to Colonel Kaddafi that the attack was a success and "could not be traced to the Libyan people." [44] On the next day, Tripoli exhorted other People's Bureaus to follow East Berlin's example. [45]

The April 1986 response used F-111 bombers from an American air base in Great Britain and A-6 fighter-bombers from two aircraft carriers in the Mediterranean Sea to strike five Libyan bases. The United States responded only after it was determined that the Libyan leader was clearly responsible for the April 5 bombing, that he would continue such attacks and, after an assessment that the economic and political sanctions imposed after the Rome and Vienna airport bombings had been unsuccessful, that our West European allies were unwilling to take stronger joint steps against Kaddafi. A clear linkage existed between the threat perceived and the response directed against Libyan military targets.

President Reagan summed up the U.S. view of Kaddafi's complicity in supporting international terrorism when he spoke to the nation immediately following the April 15, 1986, defensive response by U.S. warplanes:

> Colonel Kaddafi is not only an enemy of the United States. His record of subversion and aggression against the neighboring states in Africa is well documented and well known. He has ordered the murder of fellow Libyans in countless countries. He has sanctioned acts of terror in Africa, Europe and the Middle East as well as the Western Hemisphere. [46]

The United States directed its response to continuing Libyan violence at military targets only. The objective was to strike at the military "nerve center" of Kaddafi's terrorist operations and limit his ability to use his military power to shield terrorist activities, thus "raising the costs" of terrorism in the Libyan leader's eyes and "deterring" him from future terrorist acts. [47] Press Secretary Larry Speakes advised that the American raids on Libya "were justified on grounds of 'self-defense' to preempt further Libyan attacks." [48]

In an August 21, 1986, meeting in Luxembourg that followed, the foreign ministers of twelve European states reflected the profound effect the defensive raid had on inspiring allied efforts to resist terrorism. The foreign ministers approved a package of diplomatic sanctions, aimed at limiting Libya's ability to sponsor terrorist attacks, which had been rejected only a week earlier.[49] These sanctions were endorsed and refined during the Tokyo Economic Summit in May 1986, when President Reagan met with the leaders of Britain, Canada, France, Italy, Japan, and West Germany, as well as other representatives of the European Community. It is worthy of note that the United States essentially had to act alone against Libya, following Kaddafi's implication in the 1985 Vienna and Rome airport bombings. In April 1986, however, the United States' use of force suddenly spurred more active support among the allies.

This allied support, even though offered only after the fact, suggested that the allies viewed the April 15, 1986, U.S. actions to be proportional to the perceived threat. Proportionality in the Libyan case could be assessed from a dual perspective. First, this element of self-defense required that U.S. claims, in the nature of counterterrorist goals, be reasonably related to the existing terrorist threat to U.S. national interests. Second, proportionality mandated that the United States, and other offended states, use only such means in addressing terrorist violence as were required to induce termination of the offending course of conduct. In the first sense of proportionality, the U.S. actions in 1986 sought only to neutralize the broad effort to overthrow the power balance in the Mediterranean region through terrorist violence. The U.S. response did not seek to create a new alignment of that balance in North Africa. In the second sense of proportionality, the defensive strikes, directed at targets in Tripoli and Benghazi, were restricted to military installations behind which Kaddafi's terrorist infrastructure was concealed.

Response to terrorism, like response to other forms of armed conflict, has as its principal purpose termination of hostilities under favorable conditions. Having forcefully demonstrated that the United States would respond to weaken Libya's military support for terrorist violence, President Reagan's follow-on moves were clearly appropriate. The president, through his support for coordinated diplomatic and economic sanctions at the April 21, 1986, European Community ministerial session, and his plea for concerted action at the follow-on Economic Summit in Tokyo, emphasized that nonmilitary coercive measures against a pariah state are only effective if all major free nations participate. If the April 15, 1986, blow against Libya was to do more than reestablish the credibility of U.S. forces, an integration of strategies involving those nations trading with Libya was imperative.

The Libyan incident just cited does not suggest the lack of international law restraints upon the determination of necessity for preemptive action. Rather, it affirms that a self-defense claim must be appraised in the total context in which it occurs. One aspect of this contextual appraisal of necessity, especially as it relates to responding after the fact to terrorist violence, concerns the issue of whether force can be considered necessary if peaceful measures are available to lessen the threat. To require a state to tolerate terrorist violence without resistance, on the grounds that peaceful means have not been exhausted, is absurd. Once a terrorist attack has occurred, the failure to consider a military response would play into the hands of aggressors who deny the relevance of law in their actions. The legal criteria for the proportionate use of force are established once a state-supported terrorist act has taken place. No state is obliged to ignore an attack as irrelevant, and the imminent threat to the lives of one's nationals requires consideration of a response.

THE CLINTON RESPONSE TO TERROR-VIOLENCE: NAIROBI, DAR ES SALAAM, AND THE *USS COLE*

Although the United States under the Clinton Administration suffered three significant attacks against U.S. facilities abroad—the U.S. Embassies in Nairobi and Dar es Salaam in 1998, and the attack in Yemeni waters against the *USS Cole* in 2000—President Clinton never responded directly to these attacks. His administration did, however, do much to address the terrorist threat through development of a comprehensive counterterrorism structure. When the former president signed Executive Order (EO) 13010 on July 15, 1996, he established the President's Commission on Critical Infrastructure Protection (CCIP). The then-president declared that certain designated "national infrastructures are so vital that their incapacity or destruction . . . would have a debilitating impact on the defense or economic security of the United States."[50] The eight categories of critical infrastructure designated in the EO as requiring the development of a national strategy for protection included: continuity of government; telecommunications; transportation; electric power systems; banking and finance; water supply systems; gas and oil storage and transportation; and emergency services (medical, police, fire and rescue).

Initially chaired by Robert T. Marsh, a retired Air Force General, the CCIP was tasked with developing a comprehensive national strategy for protecting critical infrastructures from electronic and physical threats. On October 13, 1997, the CCIP issued the unclassified version of its report entitled "Critical Foundations: Protecting America's Infrastructure." In addition to recognizing the challenge of adapting to a changing culture, the report found that the existing legal framework was inadequate to deal with threats to critical infrastructure. Although the report itself provided few specifics, on May 22, 1998, the Clinton Administration issued Presidential Decision Directives (PDD) 62 and 63 in implementation of its policy framework.

PDD 62, *Combating Terrorism,* was the successor to National Security Decision Directive (NSDD) 138, which determined that the threat of terrorism constitutes a form of aggression and justifies acts in self-defense.[51] PDD 62 was more expansive in its coverage than NSDD 138 and addressed a broad range of unconventional threats, to include attacks on critical infrastructure, terrorist acts, and the threat of the use of weapons of mass destruction. The aim of the PDD was to establish a more pragmatic and systems-based approach to protection of critical infrastructure and counterterrorism, with preparedness the key to effective consequence management. PDD 62 created the new position of National Coordinator for Security, Infrastructure Protection and Counter-terrorism, which would coordinate program management through the Office of the National Security Advisor.[52]

PDD 63, *Critical Infrastructure Protection,* mandated that the National Coordinator, established in PDD 62, initiate immediate action between the public and private sectors to assure the continuity and viability of our political infrastructures. The goal established within PDD 63 was to significantly increase security for government systems and a reliable interconnected and secure information system. A National Plan Coordination staff integrated the plans developed by the various departments of government which served as lead agencies within their respective areas of responsibility into a comprehensive National Infrastructure Assurance Plan. The Assurance Plan is overseen by the National Infrastructure Assurance Council. The Council includes representation from both the public and private sectors. Under the PDD, the Federal Bureau of Investigation's National Infrastructure Protection Center, established in February 1998, would continue to provide a control and crisis management point for gathering information on threats to critical infrastructure and for coordinating the federal government's response.[53]

Together, these measures and the structure created, if implemented, would be invaluable in addressing current threats to the United States. Unfortunately, when, in the summer of 1998, two U.S. embassies were attacked, and in the fall of 2000 when the *USS Cole* was the target of terrorist violence, implementation by the Clinton Administration was totally lacking.

THE RESPONSE BY PRESIDENT GEORGE W. BUSH TO THE AL QAEDA ATTACKS IN NEW YORK AND WASHINGTON

The attacks by the al Qaeda terrorists on the World Trade Center in New York and on the Pentagon in Washington, DC, on September 11, 2001, presented new challenges to the presidency and the effective exercise of the commander-in-chief powers. Following the September 11, 2001, attacks, the rapid U.S. response by the Bush Administration was only possible because of the clear linkage established between bin Laden's organization and the assault on U.S. personnel and property. The thrust of the U.S. strategy by President Bush, first outlined in NSDD 138, and reflected in Operation Enduring Freedom in Afghanistan, was to reclaim the initiative lost when the U.S. pursued a reactive policy toward unconventional threats and attacks, as represented by the inaction in response to the attacks on our embassies in Nairobi and Dar es Salaam, and on the *USS Cole* under President Clinton.

To counter the worldwide al Qaeda threat, President Bush implemented the proactive policies later incorporated in the critically important 2006 National Security Strategy.[54] When President George W. Bush released the National Security Strategy for his second term on March 16, 2006, his administration continued the emphasis on preemption articulated in his 2003 speech at West Point and included the points made earlier in the National Security Strategy announced for his first term in 2002.[55]

In the *Washington Post*'s review of the 2006 Strategy, Peter Baker, like other writers around the country, suggested that this security framework had been developed by the Bush Administration in 2002, prior to our invasion of Iraq. Baker wrote on March 16:

> The strategy expands on the original security framework developed by the Bush Administration in September 2002, before our invasion of Iraq. That strategy shifted U.S. foreign policy away from decades of deterrence and containment toward a more aggressive stance of attacking enemies before they attack the United States.[56]

The Doctrine of Preemption was certainly put in context for the current terrorism threat in the 2002 National Security Strategy, just as it was updated in 2006 for the second term. The language in the current version clearly relates the doctrine to events in Afghanistan and elsewhere that are creating current threats. For example, one section is entitled "Prevent Attacks by Terrorist Networks before They Occur."[57] In another section, the text claims: "We are committed to keeping the world's most dangerous weapons out of the hands of the world's most dangerous people."[58] A further section states: "[w]e do not rule out the use of force before attack occurs, even if uncertainty remains as to the time and place of the enemy's attack."[59] The Doctrine of Preemption, or Anticipatory Self-Defense, as it is otherwise known, was clarified in terms of its use by the Bush Administration, just as it had been by the Reagan Presidency, which was the first to formally adopt this venerable legal principle as an administration policy.

These policies required that we make the fullest use of all the weapons in our arsenal. These include not only those defensive and protective measures which reduce U.S. systems vulnerability, but also new legal tools and agreements on international sanctions, as well as the collaboration of other concerned governments. While we should use our military power only as a last resort and where lesser means are not available, there will be instances where the use of force is the only alternative to eliminate the threat to critical civil or military infrastructure. The response to al Qaeda posed such a requirement.

In the chapters that follow, the various challenges encountered by nations fighting terrorist violence are carefully addressed. The contours of the international and operational law framework and its various options are examined from both legal and policy perspectives. The various actors and their standing are reviewed and their rights under domestic law as well as international convention circumscribed. The unforeseen consequences of aggression, such as the environmental terrorism reflected in the First Gulf War, are likewise dissected. Finally, post conflict considerations and peripheral issues not directly related to war fighting, but no less important, such as the outsourcing of activities previously thought central to a nation's military effort are engaged.

Chapter Two

Legal Requirements for Unconventional Warfare

The Operational Context

The Global War on Terror was clearly not contemplated when the four Geneva Conventions, addressing wars between national entities, were signed in 1949.[1] The violence in Afghanistan currently perpetrated by al Qaeda and its Taliban associates is being spearheaded by individuals under no known national authority, with no command structure that enforces the laws and customs of warfare, with no recognizable, distinguishing military insignia, and who don't carry arms openly. More importantly, they represent no identifiable national minority in Afghanistan, but rather largely draw their support from sponsors outside the Afghan borders. Their attacks have injured and killed civilians of all ethnic groups, as well as more than one thousand U.S. military personnel attempting to assist the fledgling, democratic government in Kabul to succeed. The terrorists' use of young people and women as human couriers for explosive devices[2] is reminiscent of the U.S. experience in Vietnam and raises serious questions about the status of those individuals when they are acting on behalf of terrorist elements in Afghanistan. The lack of legal status of the terrorists and their surrogates as other than common criminals is seldom, if ever, acknowledged publicly by unbiased news services, and this raises serious concerns for the military in their efforts to assure the public of their adherence to the law of war.

The U.S. military participation on the ground in Afghanistan was dictated by approved rules of engagement (ROE), which are a direct reflection of the law of war in its application to this specific conflict. This chapter addresses the legal considerations that must be part of our thinking when developing the rules of engagement that will both protect those lawful participants (U.S., coalition, and Afghan) in the conflict and those who are innocent civilians, while denying any but required minimal legal protections accorded common criminals for the unlawful belligerents represented by al Qaeda and their outside sponsors.

THE LEGAL STATUS OF AL QAEDA AND OTHER TERRORIST ELEMENTS

It is important to understand that terrorist violence provides no legal gloss for its perpetrators. The critical international law principles applicable to the violence in Afghanistan are found in the 1949 Geneva Conventions in Common Article 3 relating to internal armed conflicts and the principles enunciated in the two additional protocols to these conventions negotiated in 1977.[3] The minimal protections afforded by Common Article 3, for example, include prohibitions on inhumane treatment of noncombatants, including members of the armed forces who have laid down their arms. Specifically forbidden are "murder of all kinds, mutilation, cruel treatment and torture; taking of hostages; outrages upon personal dignity, in particular, humiliating and degrading treatment," and extrajudicial executions. Provision must also be made for collecting and caring for the sick and wounded.

The 1977 Geneva Protocols had their roots in wars of national liberation following World War II. Colonial powers, to include the United States, Great Britain, and the Netherlands, had engaged these liberation movements militarily often with little regard for the law of armed conflict. In the 1974 Conference hosted by the Swiss government in Geneva, the need to address conflicts of a noninternational character was addressed in Article 96(3) of Protocol I and in Protocol II. At the Conference, the Swiss government invited members of National Liberation Organizations to participate, but not vote.

The participation of nonstate actors helped shape the drafting of Article 96, Paragraph 3 of Protocol I. This section provides that a party to a conflict against a state army can unilaterally declare it wants the 1949 Geneva Conventions and the 1977 Protocols to apply. This would, of course, offer greater protection for members of National Liberation movements. Under Article 96, however, parties authorized to make such a declaration had to establish that they were involved in "armed conflicts in which people are fighting against colonial domination and alien occupation and against racist regimes in the exercise of their right of self-determination."[4] In Afghanistan, however, terrorists are trying to unseat the government that has been approved by the people. Moreover, al Qaeda has made no statement that it desires the Geneva Conventions to apply in Afghanistan.

These terrorists, or unlawful combatants, however described, have no juridical existence other than as common criminals. Protocol I, Article I conflicts, or those between a nation and a recognized insurgency seeking a legal status, differ from the present terrorist violence in that participants in Article I conflicts opposing government forces are required to meet certain minimum requirements. These are: (1) that they operate under responsible command and are subject to internal military discipline; (2) that they carry their arms openly; and (3) that they otherwise distinguish themselves clearly from the civilian population.[5] In return they are accorded certain protections when captured. Those perpetuating violence in Afghanistan today do not meet these criteria, and they are viciously exploiting every ethnic group for their own ends, without regard for these requirements.

TERRORISM AND THE APPLICATION OF INTERNATIONAL LAW

The basic provision restricting the threat or use of force in the Middle East and Southwest Asia, including restrictions on support for terrorist violence, is Article 2, Paragraph 4, of the United Nations Charter. That provision states: "All Members shall refrain in their international relations from the threat or use of force against the territorial integrity or political independence of any state, or in any manner inconsistent with the Purposes of the United Nations."[6]

The underlying purpose of Article 2, Paragraph 4, to regulate aggressive behavior in international relations, is identical to that of its precursor in the Covenant of the League of Nations. Article 12 of the Covenant stated that League members were obligated not "to resort to war."[7] This terminology, however, left unmentioned hostilities which, although violent, could not be considered war. The drafters of the UN Charter wished to ensure that the legal characterization of a conflict's status did not preclude cognizance by the international body. Thus, in drafting Article 2, Paragraph 4, the term "war" was replaced by the phrase "threat or use of force." The wording was interpreted as prohibiting a broad range of hostile activities including not only "war" and equally destructive conflicts, but also applications of force of a lesser intensity or magnitude such as observed in Afghanistan today.[8]

The United Nations General Assembly has clarified the scope of Article 2 in two important resolutions, adopted unanimously.[9] Resolution 2625, the Declaration on Friendly Relations, describes behavior that constitutes the unlawful "threat or use of force" and enumerates standards of conduct by which states and their surrogates must abide.[10] Contravention of any of these standards of conduct is declared to be in violation of Article 2, Paragraph 4.[11]

Resolution 3314, the Definition of Aggression, provided a detailed statement on the meaning of "aggression," and defined it as "the use of armed force by a state against the sovereignty, territorial integrity, or political independence of another state, or in any manner inconsistent with the Charter of the United Nations."[12] This resolution contains a list of acts which, regardless of a declaration of war, qualify as acts of aggression.[13] The resolution provides that a state that commits an act of aggression through surrogates violates international law as embodied in the UN Charter.[14]

The actions of states supporting terrorist activities, such as Iran and Syria, when interpreted in light of these resolutions, clearly fall within the scope of Article 2, Paragraph 4. The illegality of aid to terrorist groups has been well established by the UN General Assembly. Both resolutions specifically prohibit the "organizing," "assisting," or "financing" of "armed bands" or "terrorists" for the purpose of aggression against another state.

With respect to the terrorists themselves, they seek on the one hand to achieve *ad hoc* protected status by blending in with the civilian populace, while violating the law of war in terms of those they target on the other (civilians and other noncombatants). In wars involving nation-states, all lawful combatants can be targeted (to include those sleeping, unarmed, etc.) until or unless they achieve Protected Status as POWs, sick, or wounded under the Geneva Conventions. Similarly, lawful belligerents have immunity under the criminal law for warlike acts that do not violate the law of war. Terrorists, on the other hand, want it both ways. They seek the protection of civilians until they attack, then seek to be treated as combatants with all the protections of POWs when captured. Fortunately, the recent *Jose Padilla* case and others are carefully differentiating their status as unlawful combatants based on their actions.

Chapter Three

State-Sponsored Terrorism

The International Political Context

Just as the community of nations has had occasion to study the causes and to alleviate the impact of racism, there has been a continuing requirement to examine and deal with repressive state practices justified by recourse to pleas of "internal security" and protection against external subversion. The policies of incumbent regimes that seek to suppress legitimate opposition through extralegal means have actually tended to create international violence, not limit it. The Western view has always been that acts of government ought not be included within proscriptions against terrorism because they are already subject to international control.[1] This view has been unrealistic, in light of the clash between policy considerations and legal precepts, particularly when the states in which the brutal practices are alleged to have occurred are perceived to be important in the international struggle between the major powers. This chapter comments on the methodology available to the world community to ensure renewed respect on the part of states for the shared values of dignity and self-determination.

ORIGINS, CAUSES, AND GOALS

Strategies to facilitate suppression of minorities with interests at odds with that of the ruling government are not a product of the period following World War II or even of the last century. The word "terrorism" originated during the era of the French Revolution and the Jacobin Reign of Terror. It was first identified with state action wherein terror was used as an instrument of political repression and social control. "As the Revolutionary Government

became established and grew stronger, the (Jacobin) terror was institutional-
ized and legalized."[2] Government or state terrorism became an integral part
of recorded governmental processes almost two centuries ago. Ever since,
terror violence from above has remained as much a part of the terrorist
process as terrorism from below.

The word "totalitarianism" was added to the litany of terrorism during the
last century as a result of Nazi barbarism and Stalinist despotism. Both
systems relied upon organized, systematized, discriminate terror to create a
bondage of the mind as well as the body. "If lawfulness is the essence of
tyranny, then terror is the essence of totalitarian domination."[3]

The obsession of Third World governments with governmental or state
terrorism is evidenced by the report of the 1973 UN *Ad Hoc* Committee on
International Terrorism.[4] While their concern is very real, a significant portion of that brand of terrorist activity is of their own making. It is hard to
disagree with the observation of Third World states, however, that "violence
(on the part of states) breeds violence, so terrorism begets counter-terrorism,
which in turn leads to more terrorism in an ever increasing spiral."[5] Nor can
one disagree with Third World sentiment that repressive regimes have been
more deadly than individual or group actors in the last century, and they have
not diminished in the decades following the end of the Second World War.[6]
This is especially true in the early twenty-first century where control of land,
who can use it, and who is denied its use are at the heart of the world's most
difficult conflicts. One only has to look at Darfur, Rwanda, Nigeria, and the
West Bank and Gaza as prime examples.

CAUSES OF STATE TERRORISM

The causes of state terrorism appear to center on the perceived need for
greater control of national functions thought to be unavailable through normal governmental processes. That coercion applied by regimes to enforce
policies not in accord with humanitarian principles can be thought of as
authorized terror. State terror is also the means by which those in control of
society seek to maintain their authority. Felix Gross claims that state terror
upon a minority is caused by a desire to keep the majority in line. He posits
that the ruling group coerces the manipulable crowd by preying upon the
opposition, either organized or unorganized.[7] Political scientist Paul Wilkinson describes state terrorism in terms of effects as well as causes. Wilkinson
concludes: "First, authorized terrorism is highly unpredictable in its effects;
and second, that terroristic violence can escalate until it is uncontrollable
with terrible results for society."[8]

GOALS OF STATE AUTHORIZED TERRORISM

State terrorism has been observed to be a mix of personality and ideology. Nazism and Stalinism, for example, both personified the misguided genius of their leaders but they could not have succeeded without a disoriented, controlled citizenry. "Isolation and impotence," writes Hannah Arendt in her authoritative study of totalitarian terror, "have always been characteristic of tyrannies."[9] State-authorized terror aims not merely at the transformation of society, but at "the transformation of human nature itself."[10] The common goal of criminally repressive regimes is mass disorientation and mass anxiety.[11] Contemporary terroristic governments have employed terror-violence as an integral part of the governing process. With these regimes and others of their kind—either of the Left or of the Right—to quote the Marxist French philosopher Maurice Merleau-Ponty: "Humanism is suspended and Government is terror."[12]

While state-sponsored repressive measures require a strong psychological impact upon a vast audience to achieve their immediate goals of increasing state authority or implementing state policy, the propaganda value of mass communication is a two-edged sword. While individual or group terrorism is a totally impotent force when deprived of the benefit of mass communication, overexposure of state-authorized repressive practices can assist the mobilization of counterterrorist activity from within and sharp criticism from without. In fact, the strict control of dissemination of information is required for a repressive government to effectively control opposition.

OPTIONS FOR CONTROL OF STATE TERRORISM

One central theme must be pursued throughout. In attempting to define and formulate effective proposals to reduce the destruction of human and material values as a result of state repression, emphasis must be placed on the fact that sanctioning alternatives have long been available.[13] They have simply not been applied because of the lack of support from the major nations. In the remaining part of this chapter, emphasis will be placed on the greater need for states to examine possible solutions in terms of the relationship of those solutions to causes and not merely to existing symptoms.

In the early 1970s, the Sixth Committee of the United Nations General Assembly conducted a study for the Secretary General entitled *Measures to Prevent Terrorism and Other Forms of Violence which Endanger or Take Innocent Lives or Jeopardize Fundamental Freedoms*.[14] A contingent of nations, through their spokesman Ambassador Baroody of Saudi Arabia, successfully moved to amend this title to include the significantly revealing phrase:

and study of the underlying causes of those forms of terrorism and acts of violence which result in misery, frustration, grievance and despair and which cause some people to sacrifice human lives, including their own, in an attempt to effect radical change. [15]

This obvious attempt to link repressive policies of states with the effect those policies generate was adamantly but unsuccessfully resisted by the United States. Then–Secretary of State William Rogers, before the General Assembly, stated:

The issue is not war—war between states, civil war, or revolutionary war. The issue is not the striving of people to achieve self-determination and independence. . . . We are all aware that, aside from the psychotic and purely felonious, many criminal acts of terrorism derive from political origins. We all recognize that issues such as self-determination must continue to be addressed seriously by the international community. But political passion, however deeply held, cannot be justification for criminal violence against innocent persons. [16]

Without the support of the major nations, real efforts to implement and support the purposes of resolution 3034 are nearly impossible. [17] While no one can argue with the major nations' (including the United States) position that the legitimacy of a cause does not in itself legitimize the use of certain forms of violence, especially against the innocent, the failure of these states to accept the solution as one ultimately tied to causes is unfortunate. To underestimate the significance of the causal factors in favor of unilateral preventative measures directed toward individual incidents is "not only a failure of moral perspective, it is a serious miscalculation in the one area which should be paramount, the effectiveness of any proposed solution." [18]

The limitations inherent in this sort of unilateral effort has prompted the United States historically to spearhead the ratification of multilateral and bilateral agreements through the auspices of the International Civil Aviation Organization, the Organization of American States, and the various Economic Conferences initially sponsored by the Group of 7 and now by the Group of 8. [19] Even if the convention approach does attract a significant number of ratifications, this approach is always limited by its acceptability among those nations most crucial to effective measures—those nations that have endured colonialism and oppression and now tolerate, support and harbor the guerrilla and political organizations that the United States government has labeled "terrorists." These emerging nations find the American initiatives unacceptable and unrealistic. Terrorism, from the point of view of the developing nations of the world, is more likely to be employed by governments than against governments, especially those of totalitarian, [20] primitive, [21] or colonial powers. [22]

The United States and other major nations recognize that while a just cause may not legitimize acts of individual or group violence, a study of the causes of this violence is not thereby made irrelevant. Such an examination reveals that most such acts spring from a frustration of legitimate means, caused in turn by policies of governmental repression. The truism that the causes of individual and group terrorism often represent the effects of repressive state practices is nowhere better represented than in Gaza today. The frustration of the Palestinians who perceive themselves as unjustly victimized by the Israelis is understandable, but there seems to be no hope for resolution unless an effective and honest dialogue between the parties can be developed, and restraint employed on both sides.

The current crisis between the Israelis and Palestinians can be briefly summarized as follows. On December 27, 2008, Israel launched a major military campaign named Operation Cast Lead against Hamas in the Gaza Strip. The offensive came in response to a marked increase in Palestinian rocket fire into Israeli communities following the end of a six-month cease fire on December 19, 2008. This (the increased rocket firing by Gaza residents) was precipitated in large measure by the closure of border crossings and the elimination of commerce in and out of Gaza. On January 3, 2009, Israel began a ground offensive into Gaza which was followed by international pressure to stop the fighting. On January 8, 2009, the Security Council, by a 14–0 vote (the United States abstained), called on both sides to terminate hostilities in Resolution 1860. The operation nevertheless continued until January 18, 2009, when Israel unilaterally declared a ceasefire. Hamas also ceased firing a short time later. The cost to the Palestinian population was 1,440 dead, half of whom were civilians. The Israelis sustained thirteen dead (including four civilians). The officially stated Israeli goal of Operation Cast Lead was to diminish the security threat to its citizens in southern Israel by steeply reducing rocket fire, weakening Hamas, and by restoring Israeli deterrence. Following the ceasefire, Israel implemented a blockade of the Gaza coastline to decrease the rearmament capacity of Hamas and other Palestinian militants. It also did not reopen the border crossings from the Gaza Strip, thus precluding commerce to outside areas. This decision alone ensured that the crisis environment and the physical deprivation in Gaza would continue. Israel similarly refused to consider a UN peace enforcement operation.

The current conflict has exacerbated tensions between countries in the region with a pro-Western orientation like Egypt, Jordan, Saudi Arabia, and Turkey, and those with a historical pro-Palestinian posture like Iran and Syria. The United States has been the greatest loser, as efforts to address the conflicts in Iraq and Afghanistan require cooperation from certain of these states for transshipment, over-flight rights, and logistics support. The good will generated by the United States in assisting the new legitimate Muslim governments in Kabul and Baghdad has been largely squandered within the region as a result of the view by many that the United States has a one-sided approach when it comes to Israel and the Palestinian people.

Nor is this the first occasion where the government in Tel Aviv has spawned violence by the repression of its own indigenous population. Abuses with respect to the inhabitants' property rights in the occupied areas include illegal Israeli settlements, the involuntary resettlement of the Gaza population, and the refusal to permit the return of Palestinians who were displaced during the 1967 war. Since the Israeli occupation began in 1967, approximately sixty thousand Israeli citizens have settled in some one hundred locations in the West Bank and Gaza.[23] This despite the provision that prohibits such actions in Article 49(6) of the Fourth Geneva Convention of 1949 (Civilians Convention). The government of Israel justifies its policies of annexation and settlement with arguments related to internal security, and with claims of the basic right of Israeli citizens to settle anywhere in the occupied territories.[24]

It is clear, however, that these settlements are not temporary features designed to serve a security function. Former Prime Minister Rabin stated that no settlement had been set up in order to be taken down again, and Mr. Allon, former Foreign Minister, stated the settlements had not been established in order to be abandoned.[25] What is most startling has been the passage of domestic legislation by Israel to facilitate the takeover of Palestinian-owned land by Israeli settlers. Dr. A. Barkejian, former UN Area Officer for Jerusalem, has estimated that these laws have permitted Israelis to render 25 percent of the land in the West Bank inaccessible to Palestinians.[26]

The problem is one of fostering an understanding within U.S. administrations that long-term security for governments is only possible when they adhere to law and where they accord basic inalienable rights to those over whom they rule. The total withdrawal of foreign assistance by the major powers to repressive regimes will certainly not produce such an understanding. The result of the denial of economic assistance is greater political repression to maintain order in the face of worsening economic conditions. What is required on the part of the United States and other major states is not an idealistic foreign policy that requires in every instance fundamental reform as a condition for aid, nor a security oriented foreign policy that subordinates all other values to the maintenance of a regional power balance. What is required is a realistic approach to repressive regimes to determine the most appropriate response in each instance in light of the scope of values sought to be developed.

While it is certainly beyond human powers for the United States or any nation to enforce its values upon all delinquent regimes, the opportunities that do arise, such as on a vote on the Palestinian issue in Security Council Resolution 1860 in 2009, *cannot* be squandered. The major nations must consider the available means for effective action as well as the possible undesired side effects. The most important thing that can be done to suppress repressive practices by states is for the economically and militarily powerful nations not to be selectively indifferent to their professed moral and political values and to their obligations under the UN Charter. While there is no question that there will be repressive state practices that cannot be easily influenced, the U.S. failure to recognize such practices for what they are does violence to the sense Americans have of themselves and destroys a principal source of U.S. power in the world. When, for example, the United States passes comprehensive foreign assistance legislation with included human rights provisions and then subsequently ignores these restrictions by providing ever-increasing aid to certain of the violating states, U.S. credibility and ability to influence change are irreparably damaged. When the United States is seen to be concerned only with the enforcement of rights for its own citizens and entirely willing to selectively ignore similar claims abroad, it is understandable that regimes engaging in repressive practices feel little pressure to change.

Chapter Four

The Law of Self-Defense as Applied to the Terrorist Threat

Historically, rules on the lawful use of force have developed within a framework of state-to-state relationships. Little doubt exists, however, concerning their applicability in the terrorist arena where actors are surrogates or agents of state sponsors. The Long Commission, for example, in commenting upon the devastating 1983 terrorist attack on the U.S. Marine Headquarters in Beirut, concluded:

> [S]tate sponsored terrorism is an important part of the spectrum of warfare and . . . adequate response to this increasing threat requires an active national policy which seeks to deter attack or reduce its effectiveness. The Commission further concludes that this policy needs to be supported by political and diplomatic actions and by a wide range of timely military response capabilities. [1]

When the UN Charter was drafted in 1945, the right of self-defense was the only included exception to the prohibition of the use of force. Customary international law had previously accepted reprisal, retaliation, and retribution as legitimate responses as well. Reprisal allows a state to commit an act that is otherwise illegal to counter the illegal act of another state or its surrogate. Retaliation is the infliction upon the delinquent state of the same injury that it or its surrogate has caused the victim. Retribution is a criminal law concept, implying vengeance, that is sometimes used loosely in the international law context as a synonym for retaliation. While debate continues as to the present status of these responses with respect to terrorist violence, the United States' position has always been that actions protective of U.S. and Afghan interests, rather than punitive in nature, offer the greatest hope for of securing a lasting, peaceful resolution of the crisis. [2]

The right of self-defense was codified in Article 51 of the Charter. That article provides: "Nothing in the present Charter shall impair the inherent right of individual or collective self-defense if an armed attack occurs against a Member of the United Nations . . ."[3] The use of the word 'inherent' in the text of Article 51 suggests that self-defense is broader than the immediate Charter parameters. During the drafting of the Kellogg-Briand Treaty, for example, the United States expressed its views as follows:

> There is nothing in the American draft of an anti-war treaty
> which restricts or impairs in any way the right of self-defense.
> That right is inherent in every sovereign state and is implicit in
> every treaty. Every nation is free at all times and regardless of
> treaty provisions to defend its territory from attack or invasion
> and it alone is competent to decide whether circumstances
> require recourse to war in self-defense.[4]

Because self-defense is an inherent right, its contours have been shaped by custom and are subject to customary interpretation. Although the drafters of Article 51 may not have anticipated its use in protecting states from the effects of terrorist violence, international law has long recognized the need for flexible application. Former Secretary of State George Shultz emphasized this point when he said: "The U.N. Charter is not a suicide pact. The law is a weapon on our side and it is up to us to use it to its maximum extent. . . . There should be no confusion about the status of nations that sponsor terrorism."[5] The final clause of Article 2, Paragraph 4, of the Charter supports this interpretation and forbids the threat or use of force "in any manner inconsistent with the Purposes of the United Nations."[6]

The late Professor Myres McDougal of Yale University has placed the relationship between Article 2, Paragraph 4, and Article 51 in clearer perspective:

> Article 2(4) refers to both the *threat* and the use of force and commits the
> Members to refrain from the "threat or use of force against the territorial
> integrity or political independence of any state, or in any manner inconsistent
> with the Purposes of the United Nations"; the customary right of self-defense,
> as limited by the requirements of necessity and proportionality, can scarcely be
> regarded as inconsistent with the purpose of the United Nations, and a decent
> respect for balance and effectiveness would suggest that a conception of im-
> permissible coercion, which includes threats of force, should be countered
> with an equally comprehensive and adequate conception of permissible or
> defensive coercion.[7]

Significant in Professor McDougal's interpretation is the recognition of the right to counter the imminent threat of unlawful coercion as well as an actual attack. This comprehensive conception of permissible or defensive coercion, honoring appropriate response to threats of an imminent nature, is merely reflective of the customary international law. It is precisely this anticipatory element of lawful self-defense that is critical to an effective policy to counter terrorist violence in Iraq and Afghanistan.

IMPLEMENTATION OF THE LAW IN PRESIDENTIAL INITIATIVES

Early in 1984, President Reagan issued the seminal *modern* "preemption" doctrine[8] addressing legal response to terrorist violence. President Reagan's National Security Decision Directive (NSDD) 138, issued April 3, 1984,[9] "represent[ed] a quantum leap in countering terrorism, from the reactive mode to recognition that pro-active steps [were] needed."[10] Although, as noted earlier, NSDD 138 remains classified to this day, National Security Advisor Robert C. McFarlane suggested at the Defense Strategy Forum on March 25, 1985, that it includes the following key elements:

> The practice of terrorism under all circumstances is a threat to the national security of the United States; the practice of international terrorism must be resisted by all legal means; the United States has the responsibility to take protective measures whenever there is evidence that terrorism is about to be committed; and the threat of terrorism constitutes a form of aggression and justifies acts in self-defense.[11]

Similarly, in 1998, as addressed previously in a different context, the Clinton Administration determined the existing legal framework was inadequate to deal with threats of terrorism to critical infrastructure. On May 22, 1998, the president signed Presidential Decision Directives (PDD) 62 and 63 in implementation of his new counterterrorism policy framework. PDD 62, *Combating Terrorism*, was the successor to National Security Decision Directive (NSDD) 138, which determined that the threat of terrorism constitutes a form of aggression and justifies acts in self-defense.[12] PDD 62 was more expansive in its coverage than NSDD 138 and addressed a broad range of unconventional threats, to include attacks on critical infrastructure, terrorist acts, and the threat of the use of weapons of mass destruction. The aim of the PDD was to establish a more pragmatic and systems-based approach to protection of critical infrastructure and counterterrorism, with preparedness the key to effective consequence management. PDD 62 created the new position of National Coordinator for Security, Infrastructure Protection and Counterterrorism, which would coordinate program management through the Office of the National Security Advisor.[13]

To counter the worldwide al Qaeda threat, President George W. Bush implemented the proactive policies in 2002 later incorporated in the critically important 2006 National Security Strategy.[14] When President Bush released the National Security Strategy for his second term on March 16, 2006, his administration continued the emphasis on preemption articulated in his 2003 speech at West Point and included the points made earlier in the National Security Strategy announced for his first term in 2002.[15]

The language in the 2006 version clearly related the doctrine to events in Iraq, Afghanistan, and other areas currently experiencing terrorist violence. For example, one section is entitled "Prevent attacks by terrorist networks before they occur."[16] In another section, the text claims: "We are committed to keeping the world's most dangerous weapons out of the hands of the world's most dangerous people."[17] A further section states: "[w]e do not rule out the use of force before attack occurs, even if uncertainty remains as to the time and place of the enemy's attack."[18] The Doctrine of Preemption, or Anticipatory Self-Defense, as it is otherwise known, was clarified in terms of its use by the Bush Administration, just as it had been by the Reagan Presidency, which was the first to formally adopt this venerable legal principle as an administration policy.

These policies required we make the fullest use of all the arrows in our quiver. These include not only those defensive and protective measures which reduce U.S. systems vulnerability, but also new legal tools and agreements on international sanctions, as well as the collaboration of other concerned governments. While we should use our military power only as a last resort and where lesser means are not available, there will be instances where the use of force is the only alternative to eliminate the threat to critical civil or military infrastructure. The response to al Qaeda poses such a requirement.

Full implementation of the National Security Strategy, as in that articulated by President Reagan, has led to increased planning for protective and defensive measures to address this challenge to our national security, and where deterrence fails, to respond in a manner that eliminates the threat, rather than, as prior to the articulation of NSDD 138 by President Reagan, treating each incident after the fact as a singular crisis provoked by international criminals. By treating terrorists and others attempting to destroy our critical infrastructure as participants in international coercion where clear linkage can be tied to a State actor or its surrogates, the right of self-defense against their sponsor is triggered, and responding coercion (political, economic or military) may be the only proportional response to the threat.

This proactive strategy to the threat posed by attacks on our critical national security interests embraces the use of legal, protective, defensive, nonmilitary, and military measures. The Bush Doctrine attempted, as did the Reagan initiative, to define acts designed to destabilize our national interests in terms of "aggression," with the concomitant right of self-defense available as a lawful and effective response. The use of international law, and more specifically, the Law of Armed Conflict, has not only complemented the prior criminal law approach, but should give pause to those who would target vital U.S. and allied interests in the future.

Chapter Five

The Development of Rules of Engagement

Operational planning, while classified for each military operation, provides the legal and operational road map for our military's response to an attack by terrorists and/or their surrogates. The operational planning cycle, in each of our unified commands, first addresses *legal and international considerations*. That is, the operational planners must consider whether the operation is UN sanctioned, whether it has been approved by the relevant regional organization, whether a strong legal rational can be articulated publicly, whether there is allied political support, and whether the operation can be justified under the customary international law principles of necessity and proportionality. *Geography* is also a critical element of an operation's development, with topography, avenues of approach, delimiting mountain ranges and rivers, and legally prohibited and politically sensitive areas accounted for (e.g., dams, dikes, power plants, etc.). The *civilian populace* must be addressed in terms of location, involvement, and commitment to the opposing forces. The selection of *weapons systems* is dictated by the capability of the opposing force and by the opposing force size and makeup, as well as the political impact the use of certain weapons may have on nations supporting the terrorist force. In this regard, we must consider the use of available special weapons, laser guided munitions, and conventional weapons. *Targeting* considerations are a key element in operational planning, with authorized military targets, targets requiring prior approval, high value targets, economic targets, and intelligence-related targets all to be considered.

In addition, *operational considerations* include tactical concerns, intelligence matters, and opposing force information. As an example, planners must address choice and mix of forces, allied participation, aviation/ground relationships and deconfliction, weapons restrictions for political reasons, availability of lift, fuel, food, ammunition concerns, and resupply planning. *Tactical considerations* include determining whether the ingress will involve clandestine entry or open entry, force sizing, access to critical targets, transportation requirements, time constraints, and weapons selection. *Intelligence considerations* address overhead requirements and capabilities, available human intelligence (humint) assets, ability to monitor enemy communications, security of friendly communications, and our ability to neutralize enemy computer systems. *Opposing force* considerations include size, capability, support of populace, available weaponry, delivery capability, communications, will and training, intelligence capability, aviation assets, artillery, hardened transportation capability, communications jamming capacity, logistics, and WMD (weapons of mass destruction). Finally, every planning evolution addresses an *exit strategy.*

Rules of engagement (ROE), a subset of the planning process, effectively "operationalize" the national security directives executed by recent presidents within the parameters of international law for each military campaign. The customary international law requirements of *necessity of military action* and *proportionality in response to enemy attack* are given operational significance in the terrorist scenario through ROE. Rules of engagement, in their simplest terms, are directives that a government has established to define the circumstances and limitations under which its forces will initiate and continue engagement with terrorist forces. In the United States' context, this ensures that the National Command Authority's (President and Secretary of Defense) guidance for handling crisis responses to terrorist violence and other threats is provided, through the Joint Chiefs of Staff, to deployed forces during armed conflict.

ROE reflect both domestic law requirements and U.S. commitments to international law. They are impacted by political and operational considerations. Captain J. Ashley Roach, USN (Retired), has noted that ROE "should never substitute for a strategy governing the use of deployed forces, in a peacetime crisis or in wartime."[1] For the military commander concerned with responding to a terrorist threat, ROE represent limitations or upper bounds on the disposition of forces and the designation of weapons systems, without diminishing the commander's authority to effectively protect his own forces from attack.

Terrorist violence against U.S. and allied forces in Afghanistan today represent hostile acts that trigger the applicable standing ROE. The first standing rules of engagement applicable worldwide were promulgated in 1980, as a result of a USCINCPAC (Commander in Chief, United States Pacific Command) initiative under Admiral Long, and were denominated the "JCS Peacetime ROE for U.S. Seaborne Forces."[2] These ROE, which served as the bases for all commands' subsequent standing ROE, were designed exclusively for the maritime environment. More comprehensive national

ROE for sea, air, and land operations were promulgated by Secretary of Defense Weinberger in June 1986.[3]

The 1986 ROE were designated the "JCS Peacetime ROE for U.S. Forces." These ROE provided the on-scene commander with the flexibility to respond to the hostile intent of terrorists with minimum necessary force and to limit the scope and intensity of the terrorist threat. The strategy underlying the 1986 rules sought to terminate violence quickly and decisively, and on terms favorable to the United States.[4]

In October 1, 1994, President Clinton's first Secretary of Defense, Les Aspen, approved the Standing Rules of Engagement for U.S. Forces (SROE), which significantly broadened the scope of the national ROE.[5] As established in the SROE, U.S. policy, should deterrence fail, provides flexibility to respond to crises with options that are proportional to the provocation, are designed to limit the scope and intensity of the conflict, discourage escalation, and achieve political and military objectives. The inherent right of self-defense, as in prior national ROE, establishes the policy framework for the SROE. These SROE, which remain in effect, although with certain amendments to accommodate specific new threats,[6] are intended to provide general guidelines on self-defense and are applicable worldwide to all echelons of command, and provide guidance governing the use of force consistent with mission accomplishment. These SROE are to be used in operations representing the spectrum of conflict (i.e., operations other than war) during transition from peacetime to armed conflict or war, and during armed conflict, to include response to terrorist violence, in the absence of superseding guidance.[7]

The expanded national guidance represented in the SROE has greatly assisted in providing both clarity and flexibility for combatant commanders. The approval of amendments by the Secretary of Defense and promulgation by the Chairman, Joint Chiefs of Staff, has ensured consistency in the way all military commanders, wherever assigned, address unconventional threats such as posed by terrorist elements in Southwest Asia, supported clandestinely by regional adversaries.

Chapter Six

Use of Force by the President

Defensive Uses Short of War

The military operations in Afghanistan, and Iraq previously, follow a long pattern in United States history and practice. The Congress has exercised its prerogative and declared war as provided in the Constitution on only five occasions: the War of 1812; the War with Mexico in 1846; the 1898 Spanish-American War; the First World War in 1917; and the Second World War in 1941.[1] In all other military engagements, including the current conflicts, the president has exercised his independent executive responsibility as commander-in-chief pursuant to the authority set forth in Article II, Section 2 of the Constitution to deploy military force on behalf of this nation and in its defense.

While the president has often sought Congressional authorization to ensure a consistent funding stream, no congressional declaration of war was requested by the commander-in-chief in the more than two hundred military responses beyond the five mentioned above. In this period of terrorist violence, we can expect this trend to continue, as the necessity of immediate action in response to terrorist planning often requires preemptive measures which cannot await the outcome of congressional debate. It is to that commander-in-chief authority, its history, its development, its present use, and the efforts by Congress to rein in this power, that this chapter is addressed.

DEFENSIVE USES OF MILITARY FORCE BY THE PRESIDENT

Under the Constitution, Congress alone has the power to declare war.[2] It is the president, however, who is recognized as the authority within the Executive Branch to respond to imminent threats to the United States and its citizens as commander-in-chief of all U.S. armed forces.[3] In fact, most Constitutional scholars recognize the president's broad power to use the armed forces short of all-out war in defense of national interests without formal authorization from Congress.[4] As Professor Edward Corwin has eloquently stated:

> Under the constitutional scheme, the President needed no specific authorization to use force to defend against a military threat to the United States or to faithfully execute the laws or treaties of the nation in circumstances under which the law of nations would not require a formal declaration.[5]

Therefore, if the president considered military action essential for the enforcement of an act of Congress, or to ensure adherence to a treaty, or to protect citizens and territory of the United States from a foreign adversary, he would be obliged by the Constitution itself to use his power as commander-in-chief to direct our military forces to that end. As this duty rests in the Constitution, it cannot be removed or abridged by an act of Congress. President Howard Taft made that point quite succinctly:

> The President is made Commander-in-Chief of the Army and Navy by the Constitution for the purpose of enabling him to defend the country against invasion, to suppress insurrection and to take care that the laws be faithfully executed. If Congress were to attempt to prevent his use of the army for any of these purposes, the action would be void.[6]

In practice, then, the president's discretion to authorize the use of military force is exceedingly broad. As stated by Professor Corwin, the president needs "no specific authorization to use force to defend against a military threat to the United States or to faithfully execute the laws or treaties of the nation in circumstances under which the law of nations would not require a formal declaration."[7] Unique opportunities have presented themselves throughout this nation's history for expansion and refinement of this presidential authority. These were notably evident in not only the declared wars identified above, but in the presidential determinations to use force in defense of U.S. interests. The status of the United States as a world power and guarantor of the peace has also operated to expand the powers of the president and to diminish Congressional powers in the foreign relations arena. Thus it was that President Truman never sought Congressional authorization before dispatching troops to the Korean peninsula (believing the "Uniting for Peace" Resolution of the General Assembly was enough); President Eisenhower likewise acted on his own in putting troops in Lebanon and the Dominican Republic; and most significantly, President Kennedy eschewed asking for any guidance in sending thousands of "advisors" into Vietnam in

1962,[8] although President Johnson did secure passage of the Gulf of Tonkin Resolution in 1964 before introducing significant ground forces.[9]

The doctrine of inherent presidential powers to use troops abroad outside the narrow compass traditionally accorded those powers is actually more vibrant than many realize. As President Truman's Secretary of State, Dean Acheson explained Truman's decision not to seek Congressional authorization to send troops into Korea:

> His great office was to him a sacred and temporary trust, which he was determined to pass on unimpaired by the slightest loss of power or prestige. This attitude would incline him strongly against any attempt to divert criticism from himself by action that might establish a precedent in derogation of presidential power to send our forces into battle. The memorandum that we prepared listed eighty-seven instances in the past century in which his predecessors had done this. And thus another decision was made.[10]

An even more extensive list of military interventions where the president had not invoked Congressional authority was detailed in a 1967 study by the Department of State.[11] In that review, the great majority of the instances where the president acted without Congressional authority involved the policing of piracy, landings of small naval contingents to protect commerce, and dispatch of army forces across the Mexican border to control banditry. Some incidents, however, involved the significant exercise of presidential power. Three are of considerable historic interest: President Polk's use of troops to precipitate war with Mexico in 1846; President Grant's attempt to annex the Dominican Republic; and President McKinley's dispatch of forces into China during the Boxer Rebellion.[12]

Similarly, the early years of the twentieth century witnessed repeated U.S. incursions, authorized by the president, in Central America and the Caribbean in furtherance of national interests, in many instances significant commercial interests. In Panama, for example, the United States intervened on three separate occasions prior to entry to remove Manuel Noriega in 1989 in Operation Just Cause.[13]

In each of the instances above, the federal courts largely upheld the expansive nature of the president's authority as commander-in-chief. In fact, it has been the courts that have carefully shaped the president's authority with respect to the nature and scope of that power under Article II, both in terms of the president's inherent authority and the authority to wage and fund armed conflicts, which are interests shared with the Congress. For example, the Supreme Court has clearly stated the president possesses all the power and authority accorded by customary international law to a supreme commander in the field. "He may invade the hostile country, and subject it to the sovereignty and authority of the United States."[14] He may establish and prescribe the jurisdiction of military commissions, unless limited by the Congress, in territory occupied by American forces.[15] He may insert covert agents behind enemy lines and obtain valuable information on troop dispositions and strength, planning, and resources.[16] Within the theater of operations, he may requisition property and compel services from American citizens and friendly foreigners, although the United States is required to provide "just compensation."[17] He may also bring an armed conflict to a conclusion through an armistice, and stipulate conditions of the armistice.[18] The president may not, however, acquire territory for the United States through occupation,[19] although he may govern recently acquired territory until Congress provides a more permanent governing regime.[20]

In addressing direct threats to the United States, then, there has been little historical opposition to the president's unilateral decision making and, in fact, it has been recognized as essential. As former Supreme Court Justice Joseph Story has succinctly stated:

> Unity of plan, promptitude, activity, and decision, are indispensable to success; and these can scarcely exist, except when a single magistrate is entrusted exclusively with the power. Even the coupling of the authority of an executive council with him, in the exercise of such powers, enfeebles the system, divides the responsibility, and not unfrequently defeats every energetic measure.[21]

PRESIDENTIAL RESPONSE TO POLITICAL-MILITARY CRISIS

It is in the realm of the political-military crisis, where foreign policy *and* national defense are intertwined in a decision to use military force, that Congress has exercised its prerogative most effectively vis-à-vis the president's authority. That has not always been the case, however. In fact, the traditional power of the president to use U.S. forces without consulting Congress was the subject of debate on the Senate floor in 1945. Senator Connally of Texas remarked at that time:

> The historical instances in which the President has directed Armed forces to go to other countries have not been confined to domestic or internal instances at all. Senator Milliken pointed out that in many cases the President has sent troops into a foreign country to protect our foreign policy . . . notably in Central and South America. This was done, he continued, in order to keep foreign countries out of there—was not aimed at protecting any particular American citizen. It was aimed at protecting our foreign policy.[22]

This view that the president could exercise his constitutional authority to deploy forces absent congressional blessing continued even after U.S. ratification of the UN Charter. Despite the fact it could be argued that after ratification, the UN Charter provisions *did become our foreign policy,* this was clearly not the view of the U.S. Senate. They continued to espouse an independent authority resident in the president to enforce the laws and found his constitutional power to be impaired in no way. Senator Wiley stated the position most succinctly:

> But outside of these agreements, there is the power in our Executive to preserve the peace, to see that the "supreme laws" are faithfully executed. When we become a party to this Charter, and define our responsibilities by the agreement or agreements, there can be no question of the power of the Executive to carry out our commitments in relation to international policing. His constitutional power, however, is in no manner impaired. [23]

This was buttressed by the statement of Senator Austin, who claimed:

> So I have no doubt of the authority of the President in the past, and his authority in the future, to enforce peace. I am bound to say that I feel that the President is the officer under our Constitution in whom there is exclusively vested the responsibility for maintenance of peace. [24]

It is with respect to this inherent power in the Executive that President Eisenhower sought to engage the Congress and gain their support, not because he needed it, but because the political will resident in a united front with that body would be persuasive to any adversary in removing any doubt concerning our readiness to fight. The president was nevertheless careful to point out that

> authority for the actions which might be required would be inherent in the authority of the Commander-in-Chief. Until Congress can act I would not hesitate, so far as my Constitutional powers extend to take whatever emergency action might be forced upon us in order to protect the rights and security of the United States. [25]

He clearly believed that the Chinese government would be influenced by a united presidential-Congressional initiative clearly indicating our intent to defend Formosa (now Taiwan) from PRC aggression. In the Joint Congressional Resolution that followed, the Congress gave the president authority "to employ the Armed Forces of the United States as he deems necessary for the specific purpose of protecting Formosa and the Pescadores against armed attack." [26] Eisenhower followed the same process in addressing the 1958 crisis in Lebanon and President Kennedy did the same during the Cuban Missile Crisis. [27]

While Congressional legislation has operated to augment presidential powers in the foreign affairs field much more frequently than it has to curtail them, disillusionment with presidential policy in the context of the Vietnamese conflict led Congress to legislate restrictions, [28] not only with respect to the discretion of the president to use troops abroad in the absence of a declaration of war, but also limiting his economic and political powers through curbs on his authority to declare national emergencies.[29]

THE USE OF THE POWER OF THE PURSE TO RESTRICT PRESIDENTIAL PREROGATIVES

It has been the congressional power and authority to fund military activities under Article I of the Constitution that has been one of the major factors in shaping and restricting presidential decision making with respect to the commitment of forces abroad. It is for this pragmatic reason that presidents have sought to keep the Congress engaged and involved with the Executive Branch in joint decisions to commit forces to combat. In Vietnam, for example, President Johnson gained Congressional approval and funding for the war through the 1964 Gulf of Tonkin Resolution,[30] which was approved unanimously (414–0) by the House and by a margin of 88–2 in the Senate.[31] Coupled with this Congressional imprimatur was parallel funding for the war—$400 million initially although Johnson only requested $125 million to implement the Resolution.[32]

As criticism of the war in Vietnam grew, however, the Johnson Administration, concerned that the Gulf of Tonkin Resolution could be rescinded at any time, argued that the president had full authority to authorize "the actions of the United States currently undertaken in Vietnam."[33] The Administration also claimed a second prong of authority to respond to the threat to Saigon: that it was

> not necessary to rely on the Constitution alone as the source of the President's authority, since the SEATO [Southeast Asia Treaty Organization] treaty— advised and consented to by the Senate and forming part of the law of the land—sets forth a United States commitment to defend South Vietnam against armed attack, and since the Congress—in the Joint Resolution of August 10, 1964, and in the authorization and appropriation acts for support of the U.S. military effort in Vietnam—has given its approval and support to the President's actions.[34]

In December 1972, a bombing campaign north of the 17th parallel was initiated by President Nixon to drive the North Vietnamese to the negotiating table.[35] It was successful and on January 23, 1973, the president announced the signing of the Paris Peace Accords to end U.S. involvement in the Vietnam War. When attacks by the Khmer Rouge in Cambodia continued, however, the United States responded by a resumption of bombing in that nation, arguing that it must retain freedom of action if it was to preclude the North Vietnamese or its Communist allies from violating the Accords.[36]

Despite the president's strong opposition, the Congress, after the resumption of bombing in Cambodia, passed amendments to pending Defense funding legislation which had the effect of cutting off funds, after August 15, 1973, for any combat activities by U.S. military forces in, over, or from off the shores of North Vietnam, South Vietnam, Laos, or Cambodia.[37] With no American forces to contend with, the North Vietnamese then sent their entire army, absent one division reserved to protect Hanoi, into Laos, Cambodia, and South Vietnam. During the next two-year period in which Hanoi's forces established military and political control over previously non-Communist Indochina, more people were killed by the new Communist regimes in these three countries than in the entire period of U.S. involvement in Southeast Asia.[38]

The congressional actions vis-à-vis Southeast Asia were followed in 1974 by Congress's placing restrictions on U.S. funding provisions of the 1972 trade agreement with the former Soviet Union, leading to Soviet disavowal of the agreement. This was followed in 1976 by congressional curtailment of funds (Clark Amendment) for Angolan factions fighting Cuban troops supported by Soviet training and equipment. In 1983, Congress limited President Reagan's authority to fund intelligence activities in support of the Anti-Sandinistas and in 1987, after the Central American governments signed a peace accord, it cut off all military aid to the Nicaraguan Contras.[39]

These lessons were not lost on President George H.W. Bush when Iraq invaded Kuwait in August 1990.[40] Although his advisors urged that he was not required to obtain congressional authorization to assist the UN in implementing UN Security Council Resolution (UNSC) 678, which called upon member states to use all necessary means to implement prior Security Council Resolutions,[41] President Bush formally requested a resolution of approval from Congress to support the UN call for assistance. In January 1991, the Senate, by the narrow and highly partisan vote of 52–47, gave the president that authority.[42] In doing so, however, Congress refused to authorize President Bush to use force beyond ejecting Iraqi forces from Kuwait. The other provisions of UNSC 678, which United States Ambassador to the UN Kirkpatrick and the administration had supported, "to restore international peace and security in the area," were not supported in the Joint Resolution that passed the Congress and thus President Bush was limited solely to actions designed to restore the *status quo ante* in Kuwait.[43]

President Clinton was even more harshly treated by the Congress in 1993, when the loss of Pakistani lives in Somalia in June 1993 and then the further loss of eighteen American lives in Mogadishu in October 1993[44] delivered the death knell to U.S. support for UN peace operations under Chapter VII of the UN Charter—unless led by U.S. officers and with a preponderance of U.S. forces. In passing the Byrd Amendment[45] to the FY (fiscal year) 1994 Defense Appropriations Act, the Congress sent a strong message that the president's enhanced authorities to deploy forces without congressional approval in circumstances where no vital national interest is implicated were not unlimited. Using the power of the purse, the Congress was quick to limit Defense funding where they determined U.S. interests were not well served. When the Byrd legislation lapsed on September 30, 1994, the Congress quickly passed the Kempthorne Amendment[46] to the FY 1995 Defense Authorization Act, which continued funding limitations.

Congress likewise showed itself entirely willing to dictate to President Clinton when it considered he was not doing enough in a peace enforcement effort. Senator Robert Dole, leading the charge, attempted to legislatively compel U.S. actions to lift the arms embargo unilaterally for the Bosnian Muslims in early 1994 and thus vitiate the UN resolution establishing the arms embargo. Senators Nunn and Mitchell, attempting to moderate this effort through compromise, drafted the Nunn-Mitchell Amendment to the FY 1995 Defense Authorization Act. This provision, which was enacted, did not lift the arms embargo unilaterally, but rather precluded enforcement against the Bosnian Muslims while continuing our obligations as they related to the other parties to the conflict.[47] Even though not as severe as Senator Dole's proposal, this amendment undoubtedly contributed to an earlier-than-planned withdrawal from Bosnia by UNPROFOR (UN Protection Force).

Two other initiatives in 1994, both of which failed passage, were efforts by the Congress to interject itself into military affairs long thought the sole province of the president. In S. 5, the Peace Powers Act[48] and in H.R. 7, the National Security Revitalization Act[49] (NSRA) (part of the Contract with America [CWA] in the House), Congress attempted to restrict the president's authority as commander-in-chief and limit U.S. involvement in future peace operations.

In the Peace Powers Act, Senator Robert Dole's initiative would have prohibited U.S. forces from serving under foreign operational control, even where it might be in the U.S. interest, as in Desert Storm.[50] Similarly, in the National Security Revitalization Act, then-Speaker Gingrich's bill would have limited the use of DoD (Department of Defense) funds for peacekeeping activities and would have restricted the sharing of intelligence with the UN. In each case, had these measures passed, the president's constitutional prerogatives would have been severely impacted. Despite the failure of passage of these measures, there remained a bipartisan concern in the Congress after UNOSOM II (UN Operations in Somalia) that the president (and succeeding presidents) had to exercise greater stewardship with regard to operations managed by the UN.

THE THREAT OF TERRORISM AS COMPLICATING THE PRESIDENT'S COMMANDER-IN-CHIEF AUTHORITY

The attacks by the al Qaeda terrorists on the World Trade Center in New York and on the Pentagon in Washington, DC, on September 11, 2001, presented new challenges to the presidency and the effective exercise of the commander-in-chief powers. Because these attacks or threats of attack are often inchoate and depart significantly from traditional warfare[51] between states adhering to the law of armed conflict, the sharing of information with the Congress and the American people must sometimes be delayed as the release of information prematurely may preclude the effective response to an impending threat.

In light of the significant threat to democratic values represented by this form of nontraditional warfare, several U.S. presidents, most recently President Bush in late 2003, have articulated a right to respond "preemptively" when evidence exists of an imminent threat of terrorist violence.[52] This suggests that prior consultation with congressional leadership may be limited in such circumstances.

As noted previously, the Reagan Administration issued the seminal "preemption" doctrine in 1984. In the words of former Defense Department official Noel Koch, President Reagan's National Security Decision Directive (NSDD) 138, issued April 3, 1984,[53] "represent[ed] a quantum leap in countering terrorism, from the reactive mode to recognition that pro-active steps [were] needed."[54] NSDD 138 included the following key elements: The practice of terrorism under all circumstances is a threat to the national security of the United States; the practice of international terrorism must be resisted by all legal means; the United States has the responsibility to take protective measures whenever there is evidence that terrorism is about to be committed; and the threat of terrorism constitutes a form of aggression and justifies acts in self-defense.[55]

While moral justification for this U.S. policy may be obvious, the problem of defining that state support or linkage that warrants a president's military response, that legal framework supportive of such a proactive policy, and those reasonable force alternatives responsive to the threat, is more difficult. It is the linkage between the terrorist and the sponsoring state which is crucial to providing the president with the justification for response against a violating state. Covert intelligence operatives are necessary for identifying and targeting terrorist training camps and bases, and for providing an effective warning of impending terrorist attacks. Unfortunately, "we may never have the kind of evidence that can stand up in an American court of law."[56]

The question then is how much information is enough, from several perspectives. Former Defense Secretary Caspar Weinberger has underscored the very real and practical difficulties that exist for military planners in attempting to apply a relatively small quantum of force, over great distance, with uncertain intelligence. He has accurately noted the difficulty of ensuring success without accurate information, and has echoed the relationship between public support and demonstrable evidence of culpability in any resort to force by the United States in defending against terrorist attack.[57]

Although no U.S. president, past or present, has been able to define adequately, "how much evidence is enough," the demand for probative, or court-sustainable evidence affirming the complicity of a specific sponsoring state is an impractical standard that contributed to the impression—prior to the articulation of NSDD 138 in 1984—that the United States was inhibited from responding meaningfully to terrorist outrages. This view was certainly reinforced in 1979 when the United States government allowed fifty-two American citizens to remain hostage to Iranian militants for more than four hundred days. Hugh Tovar has correctly noted: "There is a very real danger that the pursuit of more and better intelligence may become an excuse for non-action, which in itself might do more harm than action based on plausible though incomplete intelligence."[58]

An examination of authorized responses to state-sponsored terrorism available to a president requires an understanding that terrorism is a strategy that does not follow traditional military patterns. In fact, a fundamental characteristic of terrorism is its violation of established norms. The conduct of warfare is governed by carefully defined norms that survive despite their frequent violation. The sole norm for terrorism is effectiveness. International law requires that belligerent forces identify themselves, carry arms openly, and observe the laws of war.[59] Principal among the laws of war are the principles of discrimination (or noncombatant immunity) and proportion. Terrorists, however, do not distinguish between the innocent (noncombatants) and the armed forces of the country in which the attack is directed.

Other considerations in addressing terrorist violence include the fact that the real-time relationship between threat and threat recognition is often compressed in the terrorist conflict arena. Strategy development is thus limited with respect to the pre-attack, nonmilitary initiatives that must always be the president's option of choice. Traditional means of conflict resolution, authorized by law and customary practice, are precluded because terrorism by definition is covert in execution, unacknowledged by its state sponsor, and practiced with violent effectiveness. Thus diplomacy and conciliation may be of little utility in responding to a state whose actions are denied and whose practices are ultimately designed to eliminate normal, lawful intercourse between nations.

In a democratic society, then, the range of options open to a president desirous of protecting the nation's citizens and resources from terrorism is limited. One of the best things a democratic government can do is educate the public and its military about the realistic options available in any crisis. Professor Abraham Miller suggests:

> The image of an invincible and omnipotent America that can rescue hostages under any circumstance is patently unrealistic. It is a mindset that comes from a failure to realize how lucky the Israelis were at Entebbe and from the charges and countercharges of the 1980 election campaign, during which the Iranian hostage crisis was played to the hilt. [60]

These valid concerns underscore the need to weigh other long-term values, besides countering the immediate terrorist threat, when determining an appropriate policy. Ronald Reagan's Secretary of State George Shultz was correct when he stated that our policy "must be unambiguous. It must be clearly and unequivocally the policy of the United States to fight back—to resist challenges, to defend our interests, and to support those who put their lives on the line in a common cause." [61]

While the president should use our military power only if conditions justify it and other means are not available, there will be instances, as occurred after September 11, 2001, when the use of force is his only alternative. In that circumstance, President Bush's actions were fully justified as necessary defensive measures to eliminate a continuing threat to the United States.

Causal connectivity or linkage, the most important element in justifying the use of force in response to terrorist violence, can only be established if effective intelligence operatives are positioned to discover who the terrorists are, where they are, and who supports them. While U.S. intelligence did not preclude the attacks on the World Trade Center and the Pentagon, it did quickly establish critical linkages. The perpetrators of the September 11, 2001, violence, the al Qaeda organization, were protected and given safe haven in Afghanistan by the Pushtun Taliban militia. [62]

Nor was September 11, 2001 the first time the United States had been subjected to attack by terrorists so clearly linked to a state sponsor. The 1979 attacks on the United States Embassy in Tehran and the Consulates at Tabriz and Shiraz followed by one week the entrance of the Shah into the United States for medical treatment. [63] On November 4, 1979, approximately three hundred demonstrators overran the U.S. Embassy compound in Tehran and took fifty-two U.S. citizens hostage for a period of 444 days.

As in most developing countries, there were few internal constraints— whether from opposition parties, a critical press, or an enlightened public—to pressure Khomeini, the Iranian leader, into upholding the law. In the atmosphere of fervent nationalism that accompanied Khomeini's sweep to power, forces for moderation were depicted as tools of foreign interests. In such an atmosphere, the militant supporters of the clerical leadership fomented domestic pressure to violate other recognized norms as well—in areas such as property ownership, religious freedom, and judicial protection. This combination of revolution and nationalism yielded explosive results—a reordering of both Iranian domestic society and its approach to foreign affairs. Unfortunately, the situation in Iran has not greatly improved.

President Reagan's pledge upon taking office of "swift and effective retribution" in case of further threats to Americans abroad was clearly meant to deter future attacks as well as reassure a concerned nation. Given the profusion of incidents throughout the world since the hostage taking, however, to include the 1993 World Trade Center bombing and the attacks of September 11, 2001, on the United States, it is clear that President Reagan's warnings have not turned back the tide of disorder.

What is clear, however, is that the painful lessons of the Iranian hostage crisis have spurred subsequent administrations to review the entire range of alternatives available for protecting limited—but highly visible—national interests such as American diplomatic personnel and property. For example, National Security Decision Directives approved in the Clinton Administration clearly identified specific U.S. interests and critical infrastructure for protection in a more defined way than had been done previously. [64] The Bush Administration, after the September 11, 2001, attacks, established the Department of Homeland Security to directly address these threats on an institutional basis. From these actions, it is obvious that there is a greater and heightened sensitivity and increased alertness to the possibility of terrorism against Americans in 2013 than in 1979. These actions will go far in preparing presidents to more effectively address future attacks, while at the same time promoting responsive contingency planning.

The elements of the president's authority as Commander-in-Chief under Article II and the successful exercise of this authority in periods short of declared war have clearly been affected by a continuum of congressional and public influence, dictated by the immediacy of the threat to national security. The intensity of the political, legal, and funding debate concerning a president's decision to commit forces has been directly related to the actual threat to the nation or its people and, conversely, by the level of political discretion the president has sought to inject into the decision to use the military instrument.

When the threat to the United States is clear and immediate, the Congress has expressed no objection to decisive action by the president and placed few restrictions on his use of public funds and the commitment of military forces. It is important to note that actions taken where the nation has been directly subjected to attack, such as after September 11th in Afghanistan, have provided the president the greatest latitude and freedom of action, while those in which a strong policy interest but a more attenuated defensive requirement, such as in Iraq, have offered the president a much narrower opportunity to exercise his discretion as Commander-in-Chief. The debate in the House and

Senate on the situation in Iraq in February 2007 clearly put the president on notice that continued funding was tied to performance in the war on the insurgents, political effectiveness of the Malaki government, and the ability of the Iraqi armed forces to exercise greater responsibility in the fight.

Where the Congress has determined the use of the nation's military power no longer reflects the interests of their constituents, it has *not* been reluctant to terminate that funding. In Vietnam in 1973, the Congress cut off all funding not only for Vietnam, but for Cambodia and Laos as well. This was followed in 1976 by the Clark Amendment cutting off funds for support to forces fighting Cuban troops, supported by the then–Soviet Union, in Angola. In 1983, funding support was cut for the anti-Sandinistas, and in 1987, all support for the Nicaraguan Contras was eliminated. The impact of this use of the authority of the purse has forced presidents to be mindful of congressional interests in each case and recognize that a protracted conflict quickly wears thin with the American people *and* their representatives.

The complexity of addressing the terrorist threat to the United States, beginning with the Iranian hostage crisis and reflected most recently in Afghanistan and Iraq, adds an additional layer of intelligence, training, equipment, and logistics concerns for the president, as Commander-in-Chief, in considering when and how the military instrument should be used. Clearly, military response to terrorist violence against the citizens and the nation has traditionally been strongly supported by both Congress and the American people. Because of the inordinate risk to U.S. forces in these more recent conflicts, however, where the terrorist threat does not directly impact vital national interests, this support, monetary and political, will likely be more difficult to obtain and maintain.

The role of the president as Commander-in-Chief is the most loosely defined section within Article II of the Constitution. In wartime, the Congress has gladly delegated its responsibilities to the president. In periods of conflict or terrorist threats short of declared war, it has retained that level of control, through funding restrictions and other legislative enactments, necessary to ensure that vital national interests *are reflected* in the actions of the Commander-in-Chief.

Chapter Seven

Covert Action and the War on Terror

The War on Terror has many elements, one of the most significant being the extensive use of covert operations to neutralize and destabilize the terrorists' political, paramilitary, communications, and financial infrastructure. The elimination of Osama bin Laden reflects that effort. Covert actions are defined as activities of the United States Government that are not intended to be apparent or acknowledged publicly. Those individuals not in the Central Intelligence Agency (CIA) who participate in such operations in the field while in the military could jeopardize any rights they have under the Geneva Conventions of 1949 as lawful combatants, in that those involved in covert operations normally do not satisfy all requirements of that status, which are that they wear recognizable uniforms, work under an obvious command structure, carry arms openly, and adhere to the laws of war. By contrast, clandestine operations, not defined in statute, are considered to be actions that are conducted in secret by U.S. operatives (usually military) but which constitute "passive" intelligence gathering on terrorists that will assist in planning counterterrorism missions, aid in the preparation for the execution of these operations, and help local forces conduct counterterrorism missions of their own.

There are significant differences in the legal requirements for the conduct of "active" covert operations versus "passive" clandestine operations, as well. As addressed below, covert operations require a presidential "finding" and the notification of the majority and minority leadership of the House and Senate Intelligence Committees. Clandestine operations, primarily planned and executed by the Department of Defense, require no such presidential authority or notification, primarily because of their passive nature and because, if discovered, the United States would have the option of acknowledging such activity, therefore assuring that the military participants are afforded some safeguards under the Geneva Conventions.

In the review that follows, the intelligence community is dissected and its structure assessed, as is the statutory framework for counterterrorism activities of a covert or clandestine nature. This analysis precedes a review of the "findings" process justifying covert operations and an examination of the status of CIA operatives acting pursuant to the statutes addressing intelligence activities. Finally, the current debate on the legal efficacy of CIA agents operating drones from remote locations is reviewed.

THE INTELLIGENCE COMMUNITY AND ITS STRUCTURE

The dual attacks on the Twin Towers in New York and the Pentagon in Washington, DC, on September 11, 2001, not only laid bare the inadequacy of our intelligence gathering and dissemination capability as a nation but forecast the increasing terrorist threat to the United States in the years following. Intelligence capabilities and budgets were among the first tier of concerns following those attacks to be addressed by Congress. The responding, highly increased intelligence budgets were passed in coordination with the negotiation of the Intelligence Reform and Terrorism Prevention Act of 2004 (hereinafter Intelligence Reform Act).[1] This legislation created a new Director of National Intelligence (DNI) who would head the intelligence community,[2] serve as the principal intelligence advisor to the president, and direct the focus of the nation's major collection systems (CIA, Defense Intelligence Agency [DIA], National Reconnaissance Office [NRO], Bureau of Intelligence and Research, Department of State [INR], National Security Agency [NSA], Department of Homeland Security [DHS], and ten other agencies).[3]

The Intelligence Reform Act also responded to the recommendations of the National Commission on Terrorist Attacks on the United States (9/11 Commission) that found the Intelligence Community incapable of serving as an agile information gathering network in the war against international terrorism. The 9/11 Commission Report directly addressed the need for improved coordination of the national intelligence effort, but disagreement subsequently developed in the intelligence committees over the extent of authority the DNI should enjoy in budgeting for technical collection systems managed by Defense Department agencies. Ultimately, a compromise was reached among conferees of the Intelligence Reform Act that allowed department secretaries to implement the Act "in a manner that respects and does not abrogate" their statutory authority.[4]

Under the revised landscape of the Intelligence Reform Act, the CIA remains the cornerstone of the intelligence community, with its all-source capabilities spread throughout the world and beyond U.S. borders. Its studies and analysis on every conceivable subject are supplemented by human intelligence sources and covert operations approved by the president. The intelligence developed at CIA headquarters in Langley, Virginia, and at CIA posts abroad is directly supplemented by the products of three major agencies of the Department of Defense: the National Reconnaissance Office (NRO), headquartered in Virginia; NSA, headquartered at Fort Meade, Maryland; and the National Geospatial-Intelligence Agency (NGA), headquartered in Virginia. The NRO operates sophisticated reconnaissance satellites, the NSA downloads signals intelligence from myriad sources, and the NGA prepares the maps, charts, and sophisticated computerized databases necessary for precision-guided targeting.

Key organs within the intelligence community are also resident in the Departments of State, Justice, and Homeland Security. The Bureau of Intelligence and Research (INR) within the State Department provides a careful analysis function for information received from all other intelligence channels. Although a small organization, its products and analyses are highly regarded, timely, and they carefully integrate information from myriad sources.

The Federal Bureau of Investigation (FBI) within the Department of Justice provides key intelligence gathering and analyses in the counterterrorism and counterintelligence arenas. Firewalls established under President Clinton[5] have now been removed and law enforcement is conjoined with intelligence gathering to ensure an integrated product that can best support an all-source approach. Similarly, the intelligence arms of the four military services, together with the DIA, provide service-specific and defense-related intelligence that supplements and provides greater breadth and depth to the analysis of the CIA.

Finally, DHS and the Departments of Energy and Treasury each address specific areas in the counterterrorism effort. The Office of Intelligence and Analysis in DHS has focused on ensuring that state and local law enforcement officials receive up-to-date information on terrorist threats from national intelligence agencies. The Coast Guard, now part of DHS, addresses terrorist concerns related to maritime security, to include the threat of piracy.[6] The Energy Department is charged with energy security issues, to include foreign nuclear weapons programs, and the Treasury Department covers terrorist financing issues.

The work of these organizations within the intelligence community is further defined by the intelligence discipline they serve. The three major intelligence disciplines are human intelligence (*humint*), signals intelligence (*sigint*), and imagery intelligence (*imint*). These three disciplines absorb the bulk of the annual intelligence appropriation. *Humint*, provided both by CIA operatives and military intelligence specialists, is the most written about discipline and also the oldest. The changing nature of this tradecraft is evident as political and military intercourse at embassy gatherings that facilitated contacts in the past has given way to the more difficult need to infiltrate terrorist organizations and narcotics cartels. The CIA operatives assigned to the station chief at our various embassies are sometimes supplemented by U.S. business personnel serving under "nonofficial cover" in foreign countries. These operatives under nonofficial cover have responsibilities to the parent intelligence agency, but also to their civilian employers. There is an unavoidable risk of conflict of interest, and there can be extreme physical danger to those involved.

The responsibility for signals intelligence (*sigint*) is assigned to the Director of the NSA at Fort Meade, Maryland. While all *sigint* operations and methodologies are classified, the increase in sophistication of available and inexpensive encryption technologies since the end of the Cold War has made the (NSA's) ability to adapt to changed conditions critically important. Since the break-up of the former Soviet Union, the NSA's culture and methods of operation have been adapted to the targeting of terrorist groups and threats.

The third major intelligence discipline, imagery intelligence (*imint*), has had a profound impact on our operations in Afghanistan, especially in the area of targeting. Imagery is collected by satellite, manned aircraft, and unmanned aerial vehicles (UAV). The overarching responsibility for *imint* resides within the NGA.[7] The goal of the NGA is to use imagery to describe, assess, and visually depict physical features, persons, and geographically referenced activities.

THE STATUTORY FRAMEWORK FOR COVERT ACTION

The statutory framework undergirding current covert activities had its genesis in the 1974 Hughes-Ryan Amendment to the Foreign Assistance Act of 1961, passed following revelations of covert operations in Southeast Asia. This amendment required that no appropriated funds be expended by the CIA for covert operations unless the president found that each such operation was important to national security and unless he provided the appropriate committees of Congress with a description and scope of each operation in a "timely manner."[8] In 1980, Congress repealed the Hughes-Ryan Amendment, replaced it with a statutory provision limiting the president's reporting requirement on covert actions to the two intelligence committees,[9] and established procedures for prior notice. The statute further stipulated that if the president determined it critical for national security reasons affecting the vital interests of the United States to limit prior notice to less than the full committees, he could notify the chairmen and ranking members of the intelligence committees, the Speaker and minority leader of the House, and the majority and minority leaders of the Senate (Gang of 8).[10]

Following the mining of Nicaraguan harbors by U.S. operatives in support of the Contras in 1984, the Chairman and Vice Chairman of the Senate Select Committee on Intelligence forced an informal agreement upon then–Director of Central Intelligence (DCI) William Casey (the *Casey Accords*). This agreement established clear procedures for reporting covert actions to Congress.[11] The same parties signed a codicil to the earlier agreement in 1986, in which they agreed that the Senate Committee would receive prior notice if "significant military equipment actually is to be supplied for the first time in an ongoing operation . . . even if there is no requirement for separate higher authority or Presidential approval."[12] The latter agreement was reached several months after President Reagan signed the 1986 Iran finding that authorized the secret transfer of missiles to Iran.[13]

In the wake of Congressional furor over the Iran-Contra revelations, President Reagan issued a National Security Decision Directive (NSDD)[14] that required all findings be in writing and prohibited retroactive findings.[15] This was followed in 1988 by bipartisan legislation in the Senate requiring that the president notify the Intelligence Committees in the House and Senate within forty-eight hours of the implementation of covert action if prior notice had not been provided—thus the Senate was attempting to set a standard for "timely notice." This was never voted on in the House.

In 1990, Congress attempted again to further tighten its oversight of covert action. In a bill passed by both houses of Congress, President George H. W. Bush pocket vetoed the bill, finding the notice provision (to Congress) too restrictive and that language stipulating that a U.S. government request of a foreign government or a private citizen to conduct activities of a covert nature would constitute covert action to be both unnecessary and inaccurate.[16] In 1991, Congress compromised with the president by redrafting the notice provision and eliminating any reference to third–party covert action requests. With these changes, Congress approved and the president signed into law the Intelligence Oversight Act of 1991.[17] These provisions remain in effect today and are outlined below in the discussion of the "findings" process.

Although the covert action requirements in the 1991 Intelligence Oversight legislation remain intact, Congress included a provision in the FY 2004 Defense Authorization Act[18] requiring the Department of Defense to advise Congress of any changes in the Special Operating Forces role in counterterrorism and the implication of those changes. This Act similarly included a provision requiring that any Special Operations Command–led missions be authorized by the president or the Secretary of Defense.[19] The 2004 intelligence authorization legislation further reaffirmed the "functional definition of covert action" and cited the importance of the provisions for approval and notification of covert operations contained in the 1991 Intelligence Oversight Act.[20] In the 2009 Duncan Hunter National Defense Authorization Act, the amount of annually authorized funding available to the Secretary of Defense, with the concurrence of the Ambassador, "to provide support for foreign forces, irregular forces, groups, or individuals supporting or facilitating on-going military operations by United States special operations forces to combat terrorism" was increased from $25 million to $35 million. The 2009 law also extended the Secretary of Defense's authority to expend such funds through fiscal year 2011 and required the secretary to notify the committees within forty-eight hours of the use of such authority. This act further provided that the Secretary of Defense's authority under this legislation does not include the authority to conduct a covert action.[21]

THE "FINDINGS" PROCESS[22]

A "finding" is a written determination by the president that covert action is necessary to support identifiable foreign policy objectives of the United States.[23] The "finding" process is encompassed in the *Casey Accords* previously noted, NSDD 286 issued by President Reagan in 1988, and the Intelligence Oversight Act of 1991.[24] The requirement for a "finding" is embodied in the statutory requirement that "[t]he President shall ensure that the intelligence committees are kept fully and currently informed of the intelligence activities of the United States, including any significant anticipated intelligence activity as required by this title."[25]

The part of the 1991 legislation imposing these requirements on the Executive branch was delineated by the conferees in a Joint Explanatory Statement published on July 25, 1991.[26] The legislation, according to the conferees, imposed the following eight requirements in any finding signed by the president: (1) a finding must be in writing; (2) a finding may not retroactively authorize covert activities which have already occurred; (3) the president must determine that the covert action is necessary to support identifiable foreign policy objectives of the United States; (4) a finding must specify all government agencies involved and whether any third party will be involved; (5) a finding may not authorize any action which violates the Constitution of the United States or any statutes of the United States; (6) notification to the congressional leaders specified in the bill must be followed by submission of the written finding to the chairmen of the intelligence committees; (7) the intelligence committees must be informed of significant changes in covert operations; and (8) no funds may be expended by any department, agency, or entity of the executive branch on a covert action until there has been a signed, written finding.[27]

Section 503(e) of the 1991 act for the first time stated in statute that covert action "means an activity or activities of the United States Government to influence political, economic, or military conditions abroad, where it is intended that the role of the United States Government will not be apparent or acknowledged publicly."[28] Just as importantly, the 1991 legislation carefully defined what activities do not constitute covert action and thus do not require a presidential finding. These include: (1) activities the primary purpose of which is to acquire intelligence, traditional counterintelligence activities, traditional activities to improve or maintain the operational security of United States government programs, or administrative activities;[29] (2) traditional diplomatic or military activities or routine support to such activities;[30] (3) traditional law enforcement activities conducted by United States government law enforcement agencies or routine support of such activities;[31] and (4) activities to provide routine support to the covert activities (other than activities described in paragraph [1], [2], or [3] or other United States Government agencies abroad).[32] Equally important, in their Joint Statement, the conferees stated that covert action does not apply to *acknowledged* U.S. activities which are intended to influence public opinion or governmental attitudes in foreign countries.[33]

STATUS OF INDIVIDUALS ENGAGED IN COVERT OPERATIONS

Operatives within the CIA are subject to personnel requirements unlike those of other federal employees. In light of the unique mission of the Central Intelligence Agency and its absolute requirement of secrecy from its agents, the Director may, in his discretion, terminate the employment of any officer or employee of the Agency whenever he shall deem such termination necessary or advisable in the interests of the United States.[34] In several cases, the DCI's discretionary authority has been upheld.[35] This discretionary authority is required because of the special need for discipline within the intelligence agencies. In the Central Intelligence Agency Act of 1949, the Director is further charged with protecting sources and methods from unauthorized disclosure.[36]

The discipline described above extends in particular to public discourse by intelligence agency employees. All employees are required to sign a standard–form secrecy agreement when they begin employment, to include their consent to submit to periodic polygraph examinations. This agreement, which includes a requirement of pre-publication review of employees' writings, extends to those made after retirement or departure.[37]

Congress embraced these CIA requirements in the Intelligence Authorization Act of 1997 in response to several instances where retired CIA employees accepted jobs in the government or the private sector of countries in which they had served while in the Agency. Section 402 of the act requires that former employees designated by the DCI "not represent or advise the government, or any political party, of any foreign government during the three year period beginning on the cessation of the employee's employment with the Central Intelligence Agency unless the Director determines that such representation or advice would be in the best interests of the United States."[38]

Another facet of covert operations is the legal status of these operations, and the legal status of those engaged in them, under international and domestic law. Espionage or "spying" is as old as warfare itself. When the Congress established the CIA in 1947,[39] it was recognizing that it considers spying against foreign entities to be legal under its laws. It is equally clear that the United States considers espionage and spying against the United States to be illegal and punishable through criminal prosecution. In 1996, Congress formally criminalized the efforts of foreign entities to steal U.S. economic, trade, and military secrets.[40]

The status of espionage under international law is more ambiguous. Always considered an adjunct of the right of self-defense and to be in the interest of states in advancing their own interests, it is nowhere specifically prohibited by treaty or other international agreement.

A RELATED LEGAL ISSUE FOR CIA OPERATIVES

The current operation in Southwest Asia has raised a major issue that has caused considerable debate in international legal circles. This relates to the maneuvering of drones by CIA operatives from areas out of theater (Langley, etc.) and striking hostile targets in Pakistan in villages far removed from the fighting in Afghanistan. The cry of foul has arisen with respect to the charge that these operatives are unlawful belligerents with no authority under the law of armed conflict to undertake, let alone participate, in these operations.[41]

The loudest voices against the Bush and Obama Administrations' policy of using drones in this manner to ferret out and attack terrorists has come from Notre Dame Law School's Professor Mary Ellen O'Connell and retired Lieutenant Colonel Gary Solis, an adjunct professor at Georgetown University Law Center. Speaking on October 21, 2010, while presenting a lecture entitled "International Law and the Use of Drones" at the Royal Institute of International Affairs in London, Professor O'Connell urged that: (1) the so-called Global War on Terror is not an armed conflict; (2) members of the CIA are not lawful combatants and their participation in killing—even in an armed conflict—is a crime; (3) the CIA's intention in using drones is to target and kill individual leaders of al Qaeda or Taliban militant groups; (4)

drones have rarely, if ever, killed just the intended target; and (5) even if the loss of civilian lives is not disproportionate, counterterrorism studies show that military force is rarely effective against terrorism, making the use of drones difficult to justify under the principle of necessity.[42] Lieutenant Colonel Solis has made certain of these same points.[43]

Speaking before the American Society of International Law, State Department Legal Advisor Harold Koh presents a very different view and one supported by the Justice Department and most international lawyers. Koh argues that: (1) the United States is in an armed conflict with al Qaeda, as well as the Taliban and associated forces in response to the horrific 9/11 attacks, and may use force consistent with its inherent right of self-defense under international law; (2) Congress authorized the use of all necessary and appropriate force through the 2001 Authorization for the Use of Military Force (AUMF); (3) this is a conflict with an organized terrorist enemy that does not have conventional forces but that plans and executes its attacks against us and our allies while hiding among the civilian population; (4) this administration has carefully reviewed the rules governing targeting operations to ensure that these operations are conducted consistently with law of war principles, including the principle of distinction and the principle of proportionality; (5) targeting particular individuals serves to narrow the focus when force is employed and to avoid broader harm to civilians and civilian objects; (6) the rules that govern targeting do not turn on the type of weapon used, and there is no prohibition under the laws of war on the use of technologically advanced weapons systems in armed conflict—such as pilotless aircraft and or so-called smart bombs; (7) a state that is engaged in an armed conflict or in legitimate self-defense is not required to provide targets with legal process before the state may use lethal force; (8) our procedures and practices for identifying lawful targets are extremely robust, and advanced technologies have helped make our targeting even more precise; and (9) under domestic law, the use of lawful weapons systems—consistent with the applicable laws of war—for precision targeting of specific high-level belligerent leaders when acting in self-defense or during an armed conflict is not unlawful, and hence does not constitute "assassination."[44]

What Koh has done in his explication is to distinguish and separate the inherent right of self-defense from the narrower principles of the law of armed conflict, which were developed and set forth in the Hague Rules of 1899 and 1907 to prevent perfidy on the battlefields of Europe. The rules, as he points out, were developed to prevent excess carnage in conventional warfare, and "the organized terrorist enemy does not have conventional forces." More importantly he carefully explains that the law of war principles are followed when protection of civilians is at stake and at all other times when permitted in the nonconventional terrorist environment. In his discussion, it is clear that the deployment of weapons systems including pilotless airframes with CIA drone pilots not on scene constitutes weapons not envisioned when the Hague Rules were drafted, and that the methods of their application support rather than denigrate the principles of distinction and proportionality involved.

FINAL WORD

The CIA has a unique role in the War on Terror. Unlike the Cold War years when carefully designed tactics were understood and accepted by both sides, today the agency requires a far more sophisticated and culturally adept agent who can infiltrate and live under deep cover for months on end, often in areas where exposure to extreme danger is constant. The requirements and challenges have also evolved, with a more integrated relationship between the Department of Defense and the CIA critical to the success of each in the current War on Terror. As noted above, these new requirements do not always fit neatly into considerations and rules born of conventional warfare in prior centuries, as reflected in the Hague Rules, but the values do remain. When the values are retained and applied in the context of new challenges, the concerns of thoughtful Americans should be satisfied.

Chapter Eight

Habeas Corpus and the Detention of Enemy Combatants

Like other enemies faced in the past, al Qaeda and its affiliates possess both the ability and the intention to inflict catastrophic harm, if not on the nation, then on its citizens. Considering the nature of this adversary, no one can expect that this conflict will conclude around a negotiating table.

Recognizing this threat and to preclude further attacks on its homeland, U.S. military forces have captured enemy combatants and terrorists on battlefields in Afghanistan, Iraq, and Southwest Asia. Patterning its actions on past conflicts, the United States has determined it necessary to detain these combatants until the conclusion of hostilities, if only to preclude their return to the battlefield. Soon after the September 11, 2001, attacks, the Bush Administration established a detention facility outside United States territory at the U.S. Naval Base at Guantanamo Bay. This would permit effective detention, without the legal requirement to entertain continual court suits by the detainees. While this result was true under the law existing prior to June 12, 2008, the whole equation has now changed.

Prior to this conflict, alien detainees held on foreign soil had been denied access to U.S. federal courts to contest detention (habeas corpus). The lawsuits and legislation arising from the detention of alien combatants at Guantanamo since 2002 have led to refinement in the law regarding detainees and further development of the law of habeas corpus during armed conflict.

THE HISTORICAL ANTECEDENTS

In the nation's history, aliens held by military forces in foreign territory have not been entitled to the civilian remedy of habeas corpus in the United States

Federal Courts, because the courts had no jurisdiction over the land on which they were being held. As the Supreme Court explained over fifty years ago in *Johnson v. Eisentrager*,[1] "[w]e are cited to no instance where a court, in this or any other country where the writ is known, has issued it on behalf of an enemy alien who, at no relevant time and in no stage of his captivity, has been within the territorial jurisdiction. Nothing in the text of the Constitution extends such a right, nor does anything in our statutes."[2] The implementing legislation, 22 U.S.C. 2241, similarly limited access to the courts to those within its jurisdiction.[3]

An underlying concern in granting access to U.S. courts to alien combatants detained abroad during armed conflict, quite apart from the jurisdictional element, relates to the nature of warfare. The witnesses who would be needed to provide personal testimony and rebut the aliens' contentions in a judicial, as opposed to an administrative forum, are engaged in military operations or subject to commitment to combat. Requiring them to leave their units and appear in habeas proceedings would be both disruptive and divisive. The original documents necessary to present the government's position would likely not be available until all hostilities are concluded. Identification and transport of foreign witnesses demanded by the detainees for in-person testimony would often prove infeasible, if not logistically impossible. Moreover, there is no authority over such foreign witnesses and their appearance could not be assured.

In fact, the historical common law underpinnings of the legal right to habeas corpus, and its limitations, reflect many of the tenets of the *Eisentrager* case. The history of habeas corpus as the "symbol and guardian of individual liberty"[4] for English, and now American, citizens is well established. What we know now as the "Great Writ" originated as the "prerogative writ of the Crown,"[5] its original purpose being to bring people *within the jurisdiction* into court, rather than out of imprisonment.[6] By the early thirteenth century, the use of the writ for this purpose (to bring them to court) was a commonly invoked aspect of English law.[7]

The reformation of the writ to one in which freedom from incarceration was the focus can be traced to the fourteenth century, when, as an aspect of the earlier Norman conquest,[8] the French conquerors developed a centralized judicial framework over existing local courts. During this period, prisoners began to initiate habeas proceedings to challenge the legality of their detention.[9] The first such use was by members of the privileged class who raised habeas claims in the superior central courts to challenge their convictions in the local inferior courts. The central courts would often grant such writs to assert the primacy of their jurisdiction.[10]

Thus, the rationale behind the grant of these writs more often focused on the jurisdiction of the particular court than concerns over the liberty of the petitioners.[11]

The availability and meaning of habeas corpus expanded in the fifteenth century. Alan Clarke notes that the writ became a favorite tool of both the judiciary and the Parliament in contesting the Crown's assertion of unfettered power.[12] By the late 1600s, habeas corpus was "the most usual remedy by which a man is restored again to his liberty, if he has been against the law deprived of it."[13] Despite its status, it was not uncommon for the Crown to suspend the right during periods of insurrection, during conspiracies against the King (1688 and 1696), during the American Revolution, and during other periods in the eighteenth century.[14]

In the early American colonies, New Hampshire, Georgia, and Massachusetts adopted provisions in their state constitutions prohibiting suspension of the right of habeas corpus for their citizens under nearly all circumstances.[15] During debate on the U.S. Constitution, some delegates in Philadelphia sought a guarantee of habeas corpus in the federal Constitution.[16] The compromise that emerged forbade the suspension of habeas corpus unless necessary in the face of "rebellion or invasion."[17] Despite the compromise, habeas corpus remains the only writ at common law referenced in the Constitution. In Section 14 of the Judiciary Act of 1789,[18] moreover, the Congress specifically gave authority to the newly created federal courts to issue the writ.

Suspension of the writ had been authorized by the Congress only four times in the nation's history,[19] that is, prior to Congress's and the Court's consideration of the Guantanamo detainees. The first occurred during the Civil War when Congress, after the fact, gave approval to President Lincoln's earlier permission to his Commanding General of the Army, Winfield Scott, to suspend the right between Washington and Philadelphia. This was in response to rioting by southern sympathizers as Union troops moved down the coast.[20] The second occurred after the Civil War in 1871 when Congress, in the Ku Klux Klan Act, gave President Grant authority to suspend the writ in nine South Carolina counties where rebellion was raging.[21] The third and fourth authorizations occurred in 1902 and in 1941, respectively. During the insurrection in the Philippines following the Spanish-American War, President McKinley sought and obtained congressional authorization to suspend the writ.[22] Similarly, in 1941, immediately after the Japanese attacked the U.S. fleet at Pearl Harbor, President Roosevelt asked the Congress to suspend habeas corpus throughout the Hawaiian Islands and that body authorized the territorial Governor of Hawaii to temporarily do so.[23] Unlike the current circumstance involving the Guantanamo detainees, each of the prior suspensions of the right involved "rebellion or invasion," as required by Article I of the Constitution. *But rebellion or invasion has never been required to preclude habeas jurisdiction if the detainee was held outside U.S. territory.*

In each of the four prior instances cited, Congress was authorizing suspension of habeas corpus over territory in which the U.S. was sovereign.

Conversely, in the 1950 *Eisentrager* decision, where the Supreme Court held that the right of judicial access in habeas cases did not extend beyond the territorial jurisdiction of the United States, the part of Germany where Eisentrager was held and the confinement facility in which he was incarcerated were under the complete control and authority of U.S. forces, but it was not U.S. sovereign territory.[24]

The foreign detention in *Eisentrager* had been informed by the government's experience in two principal cases arising from World War II. In *Ex parte Quirin*,[25] a 1942 Supreme Court decision, a team of German saboteurs were captured in the United States and tried before a military commission, similar to that established for the Guantanamo detainees.[26] The presidential proclamation establishing their military tribunal, by its terms, had precluded access to the federal courts.[27] Held in a federal confinement facility in Washington, DC, the saboteurs nevertheless sought relief through a petition for a writ of habeas corpus in the U.S. District Court. The Supreme Court, in rejecting arguments by the Solicitor General that judicial access through a writ of habeas corpus was precluded by the presidential proclamation, stated that "neither the Proclamation nor the fact they are enemy aliens forecloses consideration by the courts of petitioners' contention that the Constitution and laws of the United States constitutionally enacted forbid their trial by military commission."[28]

In 1948 in *Ahrens v. Clark*,[29] the Supreme Court addressed the habeas petitions of 120 German nationals held on Ellis Island in New York awaiting deportation to Germany. Filing their petitions in the U.S. District Court for the District of Columbia, the German petitioners named the Attorney General, located in the District, respondent in their suit under the theory that they were under his control.[30] The Supreme Court dismissed. The Court held that a district court may only grant a writ of habeas corpus to a prisoner confined within its territorial jurisdiction.[31] The Court addressed the "immediate custodian rule," addressed more fully below, only in passing. They stated: "Since there is a defect in the jurisdiction of the District Court that remains uncured, we do not reach the question whether the Attorney General is the proper respondent."[32] The Court's reasoning in *Ahrens* concerning the locus of incarceration would be heavily relied upon by Justice Rehnquist in his decision in *Padilla*, discussed below.[33]

In the current Global War on Terror, the detainees held at Guantanamo are under the complete control of U.S. forces but on territory over which the Republic of Cuba is sovereign.[34] Until 2004, the Bush Administration was successful, as reflected in *Al Odah v. United States*,[35] in precluding access to U.S. federal courts on the part of detainees based on the lack of sovereignty over the Guantanamo Naval facility. This changed with the Supreme Court's decisions in the *Enemy Combatant Cases of 2004*,[36] and in *Boumediene v. Bush*,[37] decided June 12, 2008.

THE 2004 ENEMY COMBATANT CASES

The Enemy Combatant Cases decided by the Supreme Court in 2004, *Rasul v. Bush*, *Padilla v. Rumsfeld*, and *Hamdi v. Rumsfeld*,[38] were collectively interpreted by many as strong judicial direction for the administration on its detainee policies. These cases addressed both foreign detention of enemy combatants and their detention within the United States. In ruling against the government in *Rasul v. Bush*,[39] the Supreme Court, per Justice Stevens, reversed the DC Circuit Court in *Al Odah v. United States*,[40] and held that the federal habeas statute, 22 U.S.C. 2241, extended to alien detainees[41] at Guantanamo. The Court decided "the narrow but important question whether United States courts lack jurisdiction to consider challenges to the legality of detention of foreign nationals captured abroad in connection with hostilities and incarcerated at the Guantanamo Bay Naval Base, Cuba."[42] Although the Guantanamo detainees themselves were held to be beyond the district court's jurisdiction, the Supreme Court determined that the district court's jurisdiction over the detainees' military custodians was sufficient to provide it subject matter jurisdiction over the aliens' habeas corpus claims under Section 2241.[43] The Court also found subject matter jurisdiction over the detainees' non-habeas claims (Fifth Amendment, etc.) because it found that nothing in the federal question statute[44] or the Alien Torts Act[45] excluded aliens outside the United States from bringing these claims in federal court.[46]

In *Padilla v. Rumsfeld*,[47] decided the same day, the Court, per Justice Rehnquist, determined that there was no jurisdiction in a New York District Court to hear the habeas petition of Jose Padilla, a U.S. citizen confined in a Charleston, South Carolina, naval brig after having been transferred from New York as an alleged enemy combatant.[48] The Supreme Court found that the only person who could be named as respondent in the habeas petition was the custodian of the Charleston brig, Commander Marr, as she was the only one of the named respondents who could produce the body.[49] She, however, was not within the jurisdiction of the Southern District of New York. The Court, in dismissing the habeas petition, found that Secretary Rumsfeld, likewise, could not be considered Padilla's custodian or named as respondent of the petition, as he did not qualify as such under the "immediate custodian rule," nor was his Pentagon office within the jurisdiction of the District Court in New York.[50]

In *Hamdi v. Rumsfeld*,[51] the third of the *Enemy Combatant Cases*, the Supreme Court provided clear guidance on the protections to be afforded enemy combatants in custody. From the standpoint of jurisdiction, there were no significant issues raised in Hamdi's habeas petition, and the Supreme Court considered the case upon its merits. The petitioner, Hamdi, a U.S. citizen of Saudi origin, was incarcerated in the brig at the U.S. Naval Base in Norfolk as an alleged enemy combatant serving in Afghanistan.[52] The petition was filed in the Eastern District of Virginia, the locus of Secretary Rumsfeld (the Pentagon is in Arlington, Virginia), and the Commanding Officer of the Norfolk brig, satisfying the "immediate custodian rule."[53] The case is significant in holding that enemy combatants who are U.S. citizens detained by the U.S. military in the United States in furtherance of the Global War on Terror are entitled to due process protections, specifically "notice of the factual basis for the classification, and a fair opportunity to rebut the Government's factual assertions . . ."[54]

THE CONGRESSIONAL RESPONSE TO THE ENEMY COMBATANT CASES

The Congress, at administration urging, responded quickly to the decisions in *Rasul v. Bush* and *Hamdi v. Rumsfeld* with the Detainee Treatment Act (Act) of 2005.[55] This legislation was designed to restore the status quo reflected in *Eisentrager*,[56] at least with respect to Guantanamo detainees. In this act, Congress added a subsection (e) to 28 U.S.C. 2241, the habeas statute. This new provision stated that "[e]xcept as provided in Section 1005 of the Detainee Treatment Act, no court, justice, or judge may exercise jurisdiction over

1. an application for a writ of habeas corpus filed by or on behalf of an alien detained by the Department of Defense at Guantanamo Bay, Cuba; or
2. any other action against the United States or its agents relating to any aspect of the detention by the Department of Defense of any alien at Guantanamo Bay, Cuba, who

   a.) is currently in military custody; or
   b.) has been determined by the United States Court of Appeals for the District of Columbia Circuit . . . to have been properly detained as an enemy combatant."[57]

The act further provided in Section 1005 for exclusive judicial review of Combatant Status Review Tribunal (CSRT) determinations and Military Commission decisions in the DC Circuit.[58] On its face, this legislation appeared to have undone the harm created by *Rasul* and *Hamdi* and restored the delicate balance created years earlier by *Eisentrager*.

In June 2006, however, the Supreme Court, in *Hamdan v. Rumsfeld*,[59] interpreted the Detainee Treatment Act restrictively, finding that the Act only applied prospectively from the date of enactment and did not remove jurisdiction from the federal courts in habeas proceedings pending on that date. The Court pointed to Section 1005(h) of the Act which states that subsections (e)(2) and (e)(3) of Section 1005 "shall apply with respect to any claim . . . that is pending on or after the date of the enactment of this Act," and then compared this with subsection (e)(1). The Court found that no similar provision stated whether subsection (e)(1), the dispositive subsection, applied to pending habeas cases. Finding that Congress "chose not to so provide . . . after having been provided with the option," the Court concluded the "[t]he omission [wa]s an integral part of the statutory scheme."[60]

Frustrated once again, Congress quickly passed the Military Commissions Act of 2006,[61] which, in Section 7, again amended Section 2241(e) (habeas statute) to clearly provide that subsection (e)(1) "shall apply to all cases, without exception, pending on or after the date of enactment."[62] Both the proponents and opponents of Section 7 understood the provision to eliminate habeas jurisdiction over pending detainee cases.[63]

Nevertheless, the detainees in *Hamdan* were undeterred. Despite the fact that anyone who followed the interplay between Congress and the Supreme Court knew full well that the sole purpose of the 2006 Military Commissions Act was to overrule *Hamdan*, the detainees claimed otherwise. In *Boumediene v. Bush*,[64] the same detainees urged the DC Circuit to find that habeas jurisdiction had not been repealed. Arguing that if Congress had intended to remove jurisdiction in their cases, it should have expressly stated in Section 7(b) that habeas cases were included among "all cases, without exception, pending on or after" the Military Commissions Act became law.[65] Otherwise, they argued, the Military Commissions Act did not represent an "unambiguous statutory directive []" to repeal habeas corpus jurisdiction.[66] The DC Circuit, however, made clear in their February 20, 2007, decision in *Boumediene*,[67] that the Military Commissions Act applied to the detainees' habeas petitions.[68]

On June 20, 2007, the Court of Appeals for the DC Circuit further denied the appellant, Boumediene's, motion to hold the collected cases in abeyance and to stay issuance of the mandate.[69] This followed the Supreme Court's April 2, 2007, denial of the appellants' petition for a writ of certiorari.[70] On June 29, 2007, however, the Supreme Court vacated its prior denial and granted the detainees' petition for a writ of certiorari.[71]

BOUMEDIENE V. BUSH (2008): A NEW CHAPTER IN HABEAS PROCEEDINGS

On June 12, 2008, the Supreme Court reversed course in its approach to the Guantanamo detainees. In a 5–4 decision authored by Justice Kennedy, the Court in *Boumediene v. Bush*[72] reversed the Court of Appeals for the DC Circuit and held that aliens detained as enemy combatants at the naval station at Guantanamo Bay, Cuba, were entitled to the right of habeas corpus to challenge the legality of their detention.[73] The Court further held that the provision of the Military Commissions Act denying federal courts jurisdiction to hear habeas corpus suits that were pending at the time of its enactment constituted an unconstitutional suspension of the writ to these individuals.[74] Further, the Supreme Court found that the Suspension Clause had full effect at the naval station at Guantanamo Bay,[75] that the detainees were entitled to prompt habeas corpus hearings,[76] and that they could not be required to exhaust other review procedures prior to filing their habeas petition.[77]

In addressing this complete reversal of precedent by the Court, Chief Justice Roberts, joined by Justices Scalia, Thomas, and Alito, decried the decision as ill-founded and labeled the new approach mandated by the Court's majority as "misguided."[78] In examining what the Court did, Chief Justice Roberts stated that

> [h]abeas is most fundamentally a procedural right, a mechanism for contesting the legality of executive detention. The critical threshold question in these cases, prior to any inquiry about the writ's scope, is whether the system the political branches designed protects whatever rights the detainees may possess. If so, there is no need for any additional process, whether called "habeas" or something else.
>
> Congress entrusted that threshold question in the first instance to the Court of Appeals for the District of Columbia Circuit, as the Constitution surely allows Congress to do. See Detainee Treatment Act of 2005 (DTA), sec. 1005(e)(2)(A, 119 Stat. 2742. But before the D.C. Circuit has addressed the issue, the Court cashiers the statute, and without answering this critical question itself. The Court does eventually get around to asking whether review under the DTA is, as the Court frames it, an "adequate substitute" for habeas, *ante*, at ——, but even then its opinion fails to determine what rights the detainees possess and whether the DTA system satisfies them. The majority instead compares the undefined DTA process to an equally undefined habeas right—one that is to be given shape only in the future by district courts on a case-by-case basis. This whole approach is misguided.[79]

Similarly, Justice Scalia, joined by Chief Justice Roberts and Justices Thomas and Alito, vigorously dissented, the dissenters finding the decision to have been driven by a "notion of judicial supremacy."[80] As succinctly stated by Justice Scalia:

> There is simply no support for the Court's assertion that constitutional rights extend to aliens held outside U.S. sovereign territory, *see Verdugo-Urquidez*, 494 U.S., at 271, 110 S.Ct. 1056, and *Eisentrager* could not be clearer that the privilege of habeas corpus does not extend to aliens abroad. By blatantly distorting *Eisentrager*, the Court avoids the difficulty of explaining why it should be overruled. *See Planned Parenthood of Southeastern Pa. V. Casey*, 505 U.S. 833, 854-55, 112 S. Ct. 2791, 120 L.Ed. 2d. 674 (1992) (identifying

stare *decisis* factors). The rule that aliens abroad are not constitutionally entitled to habeas corpus has not proved unworkable in practice; if anything, it is
the Court's "functional" test that does not, (and never will) provide clear
guidance for the future. *Eisentrager* forms a coherent whole with the accepted
proposition that aliens abroad have no substantive rights under our Constitution. Since it was announced, no relevant factual premises have changed. It has
engendered considerable reliance on the part of our military. And as the Court
acknowledges, text and history do not clearly compel a contrary ruling. It is a
sad day for the rule of law when such an important constitutional precedent is
discarded without an *apologia*, much less an apology.[81]

Despite these criticisms, the law *has changed* and the writ of habeas corpus is
no longer suspended with respect to the alien detainees held at the detention
facility at Guantanamo. It is to the Suspension Clause that we now turn.

THE SUSPENSION CLAUSE AND ITS RELATIONSHIP TO THE GUANTANAMO DETAINEES

Separate from, but related to, the jurisdictional arguments of the detainees in
the *Boumediene* case were their claims under the Suspension Clause[82] of the
Constitution. The Supreme Court had previously held in 2001 that the Suspension Clause protects the writ of habeas corpus "as it existed in 1789,"
when the first Judiciary Act created the federal court system and granted
jurisdiction to those courts to issue writs of habeas corpus.[83] Before the DC
Circuit in the *Boumediene*[84] appeal, however, appellants argued that in 1789,
the privilege of the writ extended to aliens outside the sovereign's territory.[85]

Unfortunately, in none of the cases cited by appellants in the Circuit
Court were the aliens outside the territory of the sovereign.[86] More significantly, the historical antecedents in England upon which U.S. practice is
based show that the writ was simply not available in any land not the sovereign territory of the Crown. As Lord Mansfield explained in *Rex v. Cowle*,[87]
cited with authority by the DC Circuit in *Boumediene*:[88] "To foreign domin-
ions . . . this Court has no power to send any writ of any kind. We cannot
send a habeas corpus to Scotland, or to the electorate; but to Ireland, the Isle
of Man, the plantations [American colonies] . . . we may." Each territory that
Lord Mansfield cited as a jurisdiction to which the writ extended (e.g., Ireland, the Isle of Man, and the colonies) was a sovereign territory of the
Crown at the time.

Given the clear history of the writ in England prior to the founding of the
United States, habeas corpus would not have been available to aliens in the
United States in 1789 without presence or property within its territory. This
is borne out by the Supreme Court's 1950 decision in *Johnson v. Eisentrager*,[89] noted earlier, where the Court said: "Nothing in the text of the Constitution extends such a right, nor does anything in our statutes."[90] Similarly, the

majority in *Boumediene* in 2007 observed: "We are aware of no case prior to 1789 going the detainees' way, and we are convinced that the writ in 1789 would not have been available to aliens held at an overseas military base leased from a foreign government."[91]

Notwithstanding the obvious logic of these prior cases, the Supreme Court in *Boumediene*,[92] *supra*, adopts a factor analysis approach which allows them to ignore precedent and the history of the writ's application at common law and hold that aliens held abroad at Guantanamo are subject to habeas jurisdiction.[93]

FUTURE IMPLICATIONS IN LIGHT OF THE *BOUMEDIENE* AND *RASUL* DECISIONS

With the 2008 Supreme Court decision in *Boumediene, supra*, the limitations inherent in the Detainee Treatment Act of 2005[94] and the Military Commissions Act of 2006,[95] (beyond Section 7 which is declared unconstitutional) are magnified and more difficult to overcome. While the extension of habeas corpus in *Boumediene* only addresses detention of enemy combatants at the U. S. Naval Base at Guantanamo, the requirements inherent in the Global War on Terror will likely warrant expansion of habeas corpus limitations through broader congressional mandates and further amendment of 22 U.S.C. 2241 (habeas statute). It is clear, for example, that challenges to the detention of enemy combatants in Iraq held by the U.S. government will be the next step in the detainee litigation process.

Now that the provisions of the Detainee Treatment Act and the Military Commissions Act have been largely emasculated vis-à-vis the detainees held at Guantanamo as a result of *Boumediene* [96] , at least with respect to the right to detention hearings, these legislative enactments may no longer provide the road map to proscribe habeas jurisdiction for enemy combatants held elsewhere in the current conflict. For those enemy combatants held in U.S. custody in Iraq and/or Afghanistan, it is hard to believe that U.S. courts, now that the distinction of foreign confinement is removed, will not have to face the hard question of whether the insurgency in either or both nations currently constitutes a "rebellion or invasion" against the United States. If it is not deemed to meet that standard, without legislation applicable to the specific incarceration facilities in Baghdad or Kabul, for example, *Rasul* would appear to dictate that these petitioners would have access to any of the U.S. District Courts.

The lack of any restriction on enemy combatants in terms of the forum in which they can challenge their foreign confinement stands in stark contrast to the jurisdictional limits for domestic "confinees," including U.S. citizens, who are limited to the District Court in the jurisdiction of their confinement.[97] Not only does the Court's interpretation of 22 U.S.C 2241 in *Rasul*[98] appear to grant foreign detainees access to any of the ninety-four federal district courts, as the key to jurisdiction is now the custodian and not the detainee, but it invites forum shopping in the most liberal fora.

A more fundamental problem arises from the impact of bringing the cumbersome machinery of our domestic courts into military affairs.[99] The obvious potentially harmful effect of the recent decisions upon the nation's conduct of war is reflected in the judicial adventurism of *Rasul, Hamdi*, and *Boumediene, supra*, where heretofore authorized actions in furtherance of the war effort are now subject to blatant judicial direction. This new approach by the courts, unless halted, threatens the historic division among the three branches of government, and will frustrate our military leaders' traditional reliance upon clearly stated prior law.

Chapter Nine

Torture and the Interrogation of Detainees

Following the September 11, 2001, attack on the United States by al Qaeda, the United States captured a number of "high value" detainees who were believed to have knowledge of imminent terrorist threats against the United States and its allies.[1] CIA operatives, who understood that the use of torture is unlawful under both international and domestic law, and above all, is abhorrent to American values, interrogated the high value detainees. The United States rejects torture as a means to garner information, a fact reflected in our domestic criminal law, but also by the country's signature on the United Nations Convention Against Torture.[2]

FRAMING THE DEBATE

In consideration of the legal restrictions above, the Central Intelligence Agency (CIA), with Justice Department approval through its Office of Legal Counsel (OLC),[3] used a series of enhanced techniques in interrogating high value al Qaeda detainees. One technique, water-boarding, was used on three detainees by CIA interrogators (more than thirty kills by U.S. drones have taken out suspected al Qaeda targets).[4] These techniques, even when combined, were determined by the Bush OLC not to violate the applicable provisions against the use of torture within 18 U.S.C. Sections 2340–2340A.[5] The Administration of President Barack Obama does not hold this view.[6]

Following the harsh interrogation of high value detainees, the Department of Justice OLC prepared a memorandum, dated May 30, 2005, that described highly valuable information obtained by the CIA using these methods.[7] For the proposition that these methods saved American lives, the memorandum reported some of the CIA information obtained from Khalid Shaykh Muhammad (KSM) and Abu Zubaydah:

> You have informed us that the interrogation of KSM—once enhanced techniques were employed—led to the discovery of a KSM plot, the "Second Wave," "to use East Asian operatives to crash a hijacked airliner into" a building in Los Angeles. You have informed us that information obtained from KSM also led to the capture of Riduan bin Isomuddin, better known as Hambali, and the discovery of the Guraba Cell, a 17-member Jemaah Islamiyah cell tasked with executing the "Second Wave." More specifically, we understand that KSM admitted that he had tasked Majid Khan with delivering a large sum of money to an al Qaeda associate. Khan subsequently identified the associate (Zubair), who was then captured. Zubair, in turn, provided information that led to the arrest of Hambali. The information acquired from these captures allowed CIA interrogators to pose more specific questions to KSM, which led the CIA to Hambali's brother, al-Hadi. Using information obtained from multiple sources, al-Hadi was captured, and he subsequently identified the Guraba cell. With the aid of this additional information, interrogations of Hambali confirmed much of what was learned from KSM.
>
> Interrogations of Zubaydah—again, once enhanced techniques were employed—furnished detailed information regarding al Qaeda's "organizational structure, key operatives, and modus operandi" and identified KSM as the mastermind of the September 11 attacks. You have informed us that Zubaydah also "provided significant information on two operatives, [including] Jose Padilla[,] who planned to build and detonate a 'dirty bomb' in the Washington DC area." Zubaydah and KSM have also supplied important information about al-Zarqawi and his network.
>
> More generally, the CIA has informed us that, since March 2002, the intelligence derived from CIA detainees has resulted in more than 6,000 intelligence reports and, in 2004, accounted for approximately half of CTC's reporting on al Qaeda. You have informed us that the substantial majority of this intelligence has come from detainees subjected to enhanced interrogation techniques. In addition, the CIA advises us that the program has been virtually indispensable to the task of deriving actionable intelligence from other forms of collection.[8]

The above concludes that the interrogation of KSM led to the discovery of the planned "Second Wave" attacks on the United States and the connection to Hambali. However, as noted by President George W. Bush in a presidential statement on February 9, 2006, the plot and even the connection to Hambali had been thwarted before KSM had even been captured:

> Since September the 11th, the United States and our coalition partners have disrupted a number of serious al Qaeda terrorist plots—including plots to attack targets inside the United States. Let me give you an example. In the

weeks after September the 11th, while Americans were still recovering from an unprecedented strike on our homeland, al Qaeda was already busy planning its next attack. We now know that in October 2001, Khalid Shaykh Muhammad—the mastermind of the September the 11th attacks—had already set in motion a plan to have terrorist operatives hijack an airplane using shoe bombs to breach the cockpit door, and fly the plane into the tallest building on the West Coast. We believe the intended target was Liberty [sic] Tower in Los Angeles, California.

Rather than use Arab hijackers as he had on September the 11th, Khalid Shaykh Muhammad sought out young men from Southeast Asia—whom he believed would not arouse as much suspicion. To help carry out this plan, he tapped a terrorist named Hambali, one of the leaders of an al Qaeda affiliated group in Southeast Asia called "J-I." JI terrorists were responsible for a series of deadly attacks in Southeast Asia, and members of the group had trained with al Qaeda. Hambali recruited several key operatives who had been training in Afghanistan. Once the operatives were recruited, they met with Osama bin Laden, and then began preparations for the West Coast attack.

Their plot was derailed in early 2002 when a Southeast Asian nation arrested a key al Qaeda operative. Subsequent debriefings and other intelligence operations made clear the intended target, and how al Qaeda hoped to execute it. This critical intelligence helped other allies capture the ringleaders and other known operatives who had been recruited for this plot. The West Coast plot had been thwarted. Our efforts did not end there. In the summer of 2003, our partners in Southeast Asia conducted another successful manhunt that led to the capture of the terrorist Hambali.

As the West Coast plot shows, in the war on terror we face a relentless and determined enemy that operates in many nations—so protecting our citizens requires unprecedented cooperation from many nations as well. It took the combined efforts of several countries to break up this plot. By working together, we took dangerous terrorists off the streets; by working together we stopped a catastrophic attack on our homeland.[9]

KSM was captured on March 1, 2003, and, as President Bush noted in praising the antiterrorism efforts of coalition partners, the "Second Wave" attacks were broken up in early 2002, almost a year before. In addition, Hambali was tied to that effort in 2002, again before KSM was captured.

The information that Abu Zubaydah purportedly divulged under interrogation, including water-boarding interrogation, has been questioned as well.[10] Ali Soufan, a former FBI agent who participated in the initial questioning of Abu Zubaydah, has directly refuted some of the claims made in the May 30, 2005 declassified OLC Memorandum.[11] For example, Soufan has said that Abu Zubaydah was already providing intelligence before torture techniques were employed:

One of the most striking parts of the memos is the false premises on which they are based. The first, dated August 2002, grants authorization to use harsh interrogation techniques on a high-ranking terrorist, Abu Zubaydah, on the grounds that previous methods hadn't been working. The next three memos cite the successes of those methods as a justification for their continued use. It is inaccurate, however, to say that Abu Zubaydah had been uncooperative. Along with another FBI agent, and with several CIA officers present, I questioned him from March to June 2002, before the harsh techniques were introduced later in August. Under traditional interrogation methods, he provided us with important actionable intelligence.

We discovered, for example, that Khalid Shaikh Mohammed was the mastermind of the 9/11 attacks. Abu Zubaydah also told us about Jose Padilla, the so-called dirty bomber. This experience fit what I had found throughout my counter-terrorism career: traditional interrogation techniques are successful in identifying operatives, uncovering plots and saving lives.

There was no actionable intelligence gained from using enhanced interrogation techniques on Abu Zubaydah that wasn't, or couldn't have been, gained from regular tactics. In addition, I saw that using these alternative methods on other terrorists backfired on more than a few occasions—all of which are still classified. The short sightedness behind the use of these techniques ignored the unreliability of the methods, the nature of the threat, the mentality and modus operandi of the terrorists, and due process.

Defenders of these techniques have claimed that they got Abu Zubaydah to give up information leading to the capture of Ramzi bin al-Shibh, a top aide to Khalid Shaikh Mohammed, and Mr. Padilla. This is false. The information that led to Mr. Shibh's capture came primarily from a different terrorist operative who was interviewed using traditional methods. As for Mr. Padilla, the dates just don't add up: the harsh techniques were approved in the memo of August 2002, Mr. Padilla had been arrested that May. [12]

These remarks demonstrate, that despite claimed intelligence "takes," the use of enhanced interrogation techniques is certainly not without its detractors. [13] Constant criticism of the methodology by those opposed to the war policies of President Bush prior to and during the 2008 presidential campaign led to a commitment by President Obama to review all aspects of the detention program and to shut down the U.S. facility at Guantanamo Bay by January 2010. [14]

In addition, military interrogators and FBI agents have questioned the usefulness and reliability of enhanced interrogations:

Without more transparency, the value of the CIA's interrogation and detention program is impossible to evaluate. Setting aside the moral, ethical, and legal issues, even supporters, such as John Brennan, acknowledge that much of the information that coercion produces is unreliable. As he put it, "All these methods produced useful information, but there was also a lot that was bogus." When pressed, one former top agency official estimated that "ninety per cent of the information was unreliable." Cables carrying Mohammed's interrogation transcripts back to Washington reportedly were prefaced with the warning that "the detainee has been known to withhold information or deliberately mislead." Mohammed, like virtually all the top Al Qaeda prisoners held by the CIA, has claimed that, while under coercion, he lied to please his captors.[15]

And Jack Cloonan of the FBI noted, "[t]he proponents of torture say, 'Look at the body of information that has been obtained by these methods.' But if KSM and Abu Zubaydah did give up stuff, we would have heard the details. . . . What we got was pabulum."[16]

This chapter describes the specific enhanced techniques used in the interrogation program. The legal parameters of the Torture Convention are then dissected, as are the implementing provisions within Title 18 of the United States Code. Next, the law applicable to lesser forms of enhanced interrogation are addressed. Finally, the policy concerns that have been raised in regard to the use of enhanced techniques are addressed with respect to solutions for future conflicts.

The United States interrogation program at Guantanamo Bay consisted of three separate categories of enhanced interrogation methodologies: conditioning techniques, corrective techniques, and coercive techniques.[17]

CONDITIONING TECHNIQUES

The conditioning techniques included nudity, dietary manipulation, and sleep deprivation.[18] They were described in the May 30, 2005, OLC Memorandum as placing the detainee in a "baseline" state, in order to "demonstrate to the detainee that he has no control over basic human needs."[19]

Nudity was imposed to create psychological unease. It had the benefit of allowing interrogators to provide the detainee nearly instant reward for his cooperation by returning his clothing.[20] The OLC Memorandum describing this technique made clear that no sexual abuse or threats of sexual abuse were involved.[21]

The *dietary manipulation* program involved the substitution of a bland liquid meal in lieu of the detainees' normal dietary regime. Dietary manipulation magnified the effectiveness of other techniques—especially sleep deprivation.[22] The program required that the detainee receive at least one thousand calories each day, and each detainee on the program be monitored to ensure they not lose more than 10 percent of their starting weight.[23] The detainees' water intake was not restricted in any way.[24]

Sleep deprivation was employed to weaken a detainee's resistance through an extended period of sleeplessness. Although the program authorized up to 180 hours of sleeplessness, the May 30, 2005, OLC Memorandum reported that only three detainees were subjected to more than ninety-six hours of sleep deprivation.[25] Sleep deprivation, according to the literature, while not physically painful in itself, may have the effect of reducing tolerance to some forms of pain in some subjects.[26] In one significant study, researchers found that sleep deprivation caused a significant decrease in heat pain thresholds and some decrease in cold pain thresholds after one night without sleep.[27] In another, sleep deprivation was found to cause a statistically significant drop of between 8 and 9 percent in tolerance thresholds for mechanical or pressure pain after forty hours.[28] As described in the OLC Memorandum on Techniques, a detainee undergoing sleep deprivation was shackled in a standing position with his hands in front of his body, which would prevent him from falling asleep but allow him to move around within a two- to three-foot diameter.[29]

CORRECTIVE TECHNIQUES

Corrective techniques were used "to correct, startle, or to achieve another enabling objective with the detainee."[30] As described, these techniques "condition[ed] a detainee to pay attention to the interrogator's questions and . . . dislodge[d] expectations that the detainee [would] not be touched."[31] The enhanced techniques in this category included: insulting (facial) slaps; abdominal slaps; facial holds; and "attention grasps."[32]

The facial or insult slap was used to induce shock, surprise, or humiliation, but not to inflict physical pain of a severe and lasting nature.[33] With this technique, the interrogator slapped the individual's face with fingers slightly spread.[34] Medical and psychological personnel are physically present or otherwise observing whenever this technique is applied.[35]

The *abdominal slap* involved striking the abdomen of the detainee with the back of the interrogator's hand.[36] Standing in front of the detainee and approximately eighteen inches away, with fingers extended and held tightly together, the interrogator slapped the detainee's abdomen above the navel and below the sternum.[37] The interrogator could not use a fist.[38] The abdominal slap was not intended to inflict injury or cause any significant pain. As with the facial slap, medical personnel were present or observing whenever this technique was employed.[39]

The *facial hold* was used to hold the face immobile during interrogation. One open palm was placed on either side of the detainee's face.[40] The fingertips were kept well away from the individual's eyes.[41]

The *attention grasp* consisted of grabbing the individual with both hands, one hand on each side of the collar opening, in a controlled and quick motion.[42] In the same motion as the grasp, the individual was drawn toward the interrogator.[43]

COERCIVE TECHNIQUES

Coercive techniques, according to the May 30, 2005, OLC Memorandum, "place[d] the detainee in more physical and psychological stress" than the other techniques and were "considered to be more effective tools in persuading a resident [detainee] to participate with CIA interrogators."[44] The coercive techniques reportedly were not used simultaneously, and include walling, water dousing, stress positions, wall standing, cramped confinement, and waterboarding.[45]

The *walling* technique involved placing the detainee against a flexible false wall with a normal appearance.[46] The detainee was then pulled forward by the interrogator and slammed against the flexible false wall, creating a loud sound and shocking the detainee without causing significant pain.[47] The CIA regarded walling as "one of the most effective interrogation techniques."[48] It was designed to wear down and shock the detainee while altering his expectations about the treatment he would receive.[49]

Water dousing involved pouring cold water on the detainee either from a container or from a hose without a nozzle.[50] This technique is intended to weaken the detainee's resistance and persuade him to cooperate with interrogators. In employing this technique, the following applies: for water temperature of 41 degrees Fahrenheit, total duration of exposure may not exceed twenty minutes without drying and re-warming; for water temperature of 50 degrees Fahrenheit, total duration of exposure may not exceed forty minutes without drying and re-warming; for water temperature of 59 degrees Fahrenheit, total duration of exposure may not exceed sixty minutes without drying and re-warming.[51]

Stress positions are designed to produce the physical discomfort associated with temporary muscle fatigue.[52] The three principal stress positions force detainees to (1) sit on the floor with legs extended straight out and arms raised above their head, (2) kneel on the floor while leaning back at a forty-five degree angle, or (3) lean against a wall, generally about three feet away from the detainee's feet, with only the head touching the wall and with wrists handcuffed in front of him or behind the back.[53]

Wall standing, according to the CIA, is used only to induce temporary muscle fatigue.[54] The detainee stands about four to five feet from a wall, with his feet spread approximately shoulder width. His arms are stretched out in front, with only his fingers resting on the wall to support his body weight.[55] The detainee is not permitted to move or reposition his hands or feet.[56]

Cramped confinement involves placing the detainee in a confined space that restricts the individual's movement. The confined space is usually dark, and the duration of confinement varies based upon the size of the container.[57] In a larger space, the detainee can stand up or sit down; the smaller space is only large enough for the detainee to sit down.[58] Confinement in the larger space may last no more than eight hours at a time and for no more than eighteen hours in a day; for the smaller space, confinement may last no more than two hours.[59] Limits on the duration of cramped confinement are based on considerations of the detainee's size and weight as well as his response to the technique.[60]

Waterboarding is a technique in which the detainee lays on a gurney horizontally inclined at an angle of ten to fifteen degrees, his head toward the lower end of the gurney.[61] A cloth is placed over the detainee's face, and cold water is poured on the cloth from a height of approximately six to eighteen inches. The wet cloth creates a barrier through which it is difficult, and in some cases impossible, to breathe.[62] A single application of water may not last for more than forty seconds, with the duration of an application measured from the moment the water is first poured onto the cloth until the moment the cloth is removed from the detainee's face. The effects include a sensation of drowning, even if he is aware he is not physically drowning.[63] While the process is not physically painful, it usually causes fear and panic.[64] CIA interrogators used this technique on only three detainees, and did not use it after March 2003.[65]

There were further conditions placed on the use of the waterboarding technique; the waterboard may be authorized for, at most, one thirty-day period, during which the technique can actually be applied no more than five days. Further, there can be no more than two sessions in any twenty-four-hour period.[66] However, the CIA Inspector General's report found that the CIA waterboarded Khalid Shaykh Mohammed 183 times in March 2003 and Abu Zubaydah 83 times in August 2002.[67] Those figures far surpass the CIA's own internal guidelines for the use of waterboarding, and raises the question of whether a technique, authorized under strict guidelines to avoid being deemed torture, could be considered torture if those guidelines are excessively exceeded.[68]

THE PROHIBITION AGAINST TORTURE IN INTERNATIONAL LAW

The Convention Against Torture, negotiated during the Reagan Administration, was considered and consented to by the Senate in the first Bush Administration.[69] The Convention prohibits "torture," which is defined as:

any act by which severe pain or suffering, whether physical or mental, is intentionally inflicted on a person for such purposes as obtaining from him or a third person information or a confession, punishing him for an act he or a third person has committed or is suspected of having committed, or intimidating or coercing him or a third person, or for any reason based on discrimination of any kind, when such pain or suffering is inflicted by or at the instigation of or with the consent or acquiescence of a public official or other person acting in an official capacity. [70]

The Convention distinguishes between torture, as defined above, and "other acts of cruel, inhuman or degrading treatment or punishment which do not amount to torture as defined in article 1." [71] While state parties are called upon in Article 16 of the Convention to prevent these other acts as well, there is no legal requirement imposed on state parties, as in the case for torture, that they enact criminal penalties for enforcement of prohibitions against the cruel and inhuman treatment that is lesser than torture. This dual-level approach is consistent with the 1975 nonbinding UN Resolution which describes torture as "an aggravated and deliberate form of cruel, inhuman or degrading treatment or punishment." [72]

When the Convention was submitted to the Senate for consideration, the administration under President George H. W. Bush included the following understanding to clarify the difference between torture and other lesser acts in Article 16 described above:

The United States understands that, in order to constitute torture, an act must be specifically intended to inflict severe physical or mental pain or suffering and that mental pain or suffering refers to prolonged mental harm caused by or resulting from (1) the intentional infliction or threatened infliction of severe physical pain or suffering; (2) the administration or application, or threatened administration or application, of mind altering substances or other procedures calculated to disrupt profoundly the senses or the personality; (3) the threat of imminent death; or (4) the threat that another person will imminently be subjected to death, severe physical pain or suffering, or the administration or application of mind-altering substances or other procedures calculated to disrupt profoundly the senses or personality. [73]

In submitting the Convention to the Senate for ratification, the administration also included a reservation to article 16, addressing other lesser acts of inhumane treatment, as follows:

[T]he United States considers itself bound by the obligation under Article 16 . . . only insofar as the term 'cruel, inhuman or degrading treatment or punishment' means the cruel, unusual, and inhumane treatment or punishment prohibited by the Fifth, Eighth, and/or Fourteenth Amendments to the Constitution of the United States. [74]

In accepting this reservation, the Senate clearly intended to limit United States obligations under Article 16 to those existing obligations already imposed by those Amendments to the Constitution.[75] Those amendments have never been construed by U.S. Federal Courts to extend protections to aliens outside the United States.[76]

INTERPRETATION BY OTHER NATIONS

Other organizations and states that are parties to the Convention Against Torture have likewise drawn similar distinctions between torture and the lesser category of cruel, inhuman, or degrading treatment or punishment. The European Court of Human Rights, for example, reviewed interrogation techniques analogous to the enhanced interrogation techniques used at Guantanamo. In *Ireland v. United Kingdom*,[77] the methods at issue were:

a. *wall standing*: forcing the detainees to remain for periods of some hours in a "stress position," described by those who underwent it as being "spreadeagled against the wall, with their fingers put high above the head against the wall, the legs spread apart and the feet back, causing them to stand on their toes with the weight of the body mainly on the fingers";

b. *hooding*: putting a black or navy coloured bag over the detainees' heads and, at least initially, keeping it there all the time except during interrogation;

c. *subjection to noise*: pending their interrogations, holding the detainees in a room where there was a continuous loud and hissing noise;

d. *deprivation of sleep*: pending their interrogations, depriving the detainees of sleep.

e. *deprivation of food and drink*: subjecting the detainees to a reduced diet during their stay at the centre and pending interrogations.[78]

In reviewing these techniques, applied in combination and for hours at a time, the Court concluded they were inhumane and degrading, but did not amount to torture.[79] The Court treated the five categories of enhanced interrogation as a single program.[80] In reaching its judgment, the Court determined:

> Although the five techniques, as applied in combination, undoubtedly amounted to inhuman and degrading treatment, although their object was the extraction of confessions, the naming of others and/or information and although they were used systematically, they did not occasion suffering of the particular intensity and cruelty implied by the word torture.[81]

A similar result occurred in the Israeli Supreme Court in *Public Committee Against Torture in Israel v. Israel (Public Committee)*.[82] In this case, the Supreme Court heard a challenge to the General Security Service's use of five enhanced interrogation techniques. These were described as:

1. Shaking: the forceful shaking of the suspect's upper torso, back and forth, repeatedly, in a manner which causes the neck and head to dangle and vacillate rapidly.
2. The Shabach: a combination of methods wherein the detainee is seated on a small and low chair, whose seat is tilted forward, towards the ground. One hand is tied behind the suspect, and placed inside the gap between the chair's seat and back support. His second hand is tied behind the chair, against its back support. The suspect's head is covered by an opaque sack, falling down to his shoulders. Powerfully loud music is played in the room.
3. The Frog Crouch: consists of consecutive, periodic crouches on the tips of one's toes, each lasting for five minute intervals.
4. Excessive Tightening of Handcuffs: simply refers to the use of handcuffs too small for the suspect's wrists.
5. Sleep Deprivation: occurs when the Shabach was used during intense nonstop interrogations.[83]

In each instance, the Supreme Court of Israel found that these acts reflected cruel and inhumane treatment, but carefully avoided describing any of these acts as having the severity of pain or suffering indicative of torture.[84]

THE GENEVA CONVENTIONS OF 1949

Because the al Qaeda members captured in Afghanistan and elsewhere do not qualify as prisoners of war (they don't carry arms openly, wear identifying insignia, adhere to the law of armed conflict, or reflect a recognizable command structure), the general provisions of the Third 1949 Geneva Convention do not apply.[85] Article 3, common to each of the four Geneva Conventions, however, does apply, at least since 2006 with respect to U.S. personnel.[86] It is important to note that Common Article 3 addresses both torture as well as other lesser forms of treatment identified as "[o]utrages upon personal dignity, in particular, *humiliating and degrading treatment*" in subsection 1(c).[87]

Until 2006 with the decision in *Hamdan v. Rumsfeld*[88] (long after the harshest interrogation of the detainees had ceased in March 2003), there was great debate concerning whether the struggle to suppress al Qaeda was an "armed conflict not of an international character."[89] Because nearly seventy-five states were involved in the struggle, many international lawyers were not convinced that Article 3 could be held to apply in Afghanistan, a party to the Geneva Conventions, which was struggling against the Taliban, an organization with roots in both Pakistan and Afghanistan, and with funding largely emanating from Pakistan, also a state party to the Conventions.

Nor, as Professor Robert Turner pointed out, could it be easily argued that the conflict against al Qaeda was clearly "occurring in the territories of one of the High Contracting Parties," as attacks by al Qaeda had occurred in several: the United States, in Dar es Salaam, Tanzania, in Nairobi, Kenya, and in the territorial waters of Yemen, not to mention Saudi Arabia, where the Khobar Towers had been bombed.[90] Of equal concern was the legislative history of Common Article 3. White House attorneys and the Department of Justice in the George W. Bush Administration argued that Common Article 3 is intended only to apply "to internal conflicts between a State and an insurgent group,"[91] and the conflict with al Qaeda clearly takes place in several nations. Thus, they argued, it is an international conflict and not an "armed conflict not of an international character" that would be covered by Common Article 3.[92]

The legislative history, or *travaux,* of Common Article 3 suggests that the Bush Administration position had merit. Pictet's *Commentary* on the 1949 Geneva Conventions repeatedly references Common Article 3 as addressing "civil wars," "insurrections," and armed conflicts "of an internal character."[93] In discussing the Article, Pictet refers to "cases where armed strife breaks out in a country," "civil disturbances," and conflicts involving "internal enemies."[94] The late British scholar Col. G.I.A.D. Draper introduced his discussion of Common Article 3 by asserting: "This is the sole article in each of the four Conventions that deals exclusively with so-called 'internal armed conflicts.'"[95] Other scholars make similar points.[96]

Despite these concerns, the Supreme Court in *Hamdan v. Rumsfeld* found that Common Article 3 did apply to the conflict with al Qaeda.[97] The Court overturned the 2005 decision of the Court of Appeals for the District of Columbia, which had ruled that Common Article 3 was inapplicable to Hamdan because the conflict with al Qaeda is international in scope and thus not a "conflict not of an international character."[98] In reversing the court, Justice Stevens found that "Common Article 3 . . . affords some minimal protection, falling short of full protection under the Conventions, to individuals associated with neither a signatory nor even a non-signatory 'Power' who are involved in a conflict 'in the territory of a signatory.'"[99] However, as noted by Professor Robert Turner, that was "based upon an interpretation of the 1949 Conventions, and, under *Whitney v. Robertson,* [124 U.S. 190 (1888)], the Court will be bound by an inconsistent statute of more recent date."[100]

DOMESTIC LAW: THE LAW ADDRESSING TORTURE

The Convention Against Torture required all signatories "to ensure that all acts of torture are offenses under its criminal law."[101] Sections 2340-2340A of Title 18 were included in the Senate version of the 1994 Foreign Affairs Authorization Act.[102] The House took no parallel action, but the House and Senate Conferees accepted without change the Senate version.[103] It is clear from the limited legislative history that Congress intended that Section 2340's definition of torture track directly with the definition set forth in the Convention.[104] The Senate report said as much: "The definition of torture emanates directly from Article 1 of the Convention."[105]

Section 2340A makes it a criminal offense for any person "outside the United States [to] commit[ ] or attempt[ ] to commit torture."[106] The act of torture is defined in Section 2340 as "an act committed by a person acting under the color of law specifically intended to inflict severe physical or mental pain or suffering—other than pain or suffering incidental to lawful sanctions—upon another person within his custody or physical control."[107]

Therefore, the offense of torture can be established only if the prosecutor can show: (1) the torture occurred outside the United States; (2) the defendant acted under color of law; (3) the victim was within the defendant's custody or physical control; (4) the defendant specifically intended to cause severe physical or mental pain and suffering; and (5) that the act inflicted severe physical or mental pain or suffering.[108] Further, those involved in the infliction of severe pain or suffering through *planning* or *approval*, although not direct participants, can be prosecuted as conspirators to commit torture.[109]

There have been no criminal prosecutions under Section 2340A. The sections were passed into law with no debate over the definition of torture and were clearly intended solely to fulfill the United States' obligation under the Convention Against Torture. Despite the lack of prosecutions, federal courts have defined conduct that would constitute torture in civil suits brought under the Torture Victims Protection Act (TVPA).[110] This act provides a tort remedy for victims of torture.[111] More importantly, the cases interpreting the TVPA offer insights into what acts U.S. federal courts will conclude constitute torture under the criminal statutes. As with Section 2340, the TVPA's definition of torture was intended to follow closely the definition found in the Convention.[112]

The cases brought under the TVPA reference seven distinct forms of severe abuse that would constitute torture: (1) severe beatings using weapons such as truncheons and clubs; (2) threats of imminent death, to include mock executions; (3) threats of removing body parts and or extremities; (4) burning, especially burning with cigarettes; (5) electric shocks to genital areas, or threats to do so; (6) rape or sexual assault, to include injury to sexual organs, or threats of the same; and (7) forcing the detainee to watch the extreme physical or mental torture of others.[113] The severity of these examples of treatment found in civil proceedings suggests that similar severity would have to be found to warrant conviction under the criminal provisions in 18 U.S.C. Sections 2340–2340A.

THE LAW ADDRESSING HUMILIATING AND DEGRADING TREATMENT

Quite apart from the issue of whether torture occurred in the use of the harshest techniques in the interrogation of high value detainees, it is clear from the program described above that even the lesser conditioning and corrective techniques used in the CIA's detainee interrogation program implicated the prohibition against *humiliating and degrading treatment* within Common Article 3.

The reason this is important is that the War Crimes Act of 1996[114] includes within its definition of "war crimes" any conduct "which constitutes a grave breach of Common Article 3."[115] At a minimum, the corrective and coercive measures used in the CIA interrogations at Guantanamo would qualify as humiliating and degrading treatment. This would trigger application of the War Crimes Act unless an exception under carefully circumscribed conditions for cases of imminent harm or extreme emergency is legislatively carved. Such an exception may be warranted.

PERSPECTIVE

The question of what constitutes improper interrogation, and the role of Congress and the courts in that determination, continues to be a vexing problem. As the Supreme Court recognized in 2004, the president's constitutional authority to deploy military and intelligence capabilities to protect the interests of the United States in time of armed conflict necessarily includes authority to effect the capture, detention, *interrogation*, and, where appropriate, trial of enemy forces, as well as their transfer to other nations.[116] President Clinton's Justice Department further recognized in 1996 that Congress "may not unduly constrain or inhibit the president's authority to make and to implement the decisions that he deems necessary or advisable for the successful conduct of military operations in the field."[117]

Concurrently, Article I, Section 8 of the Constitution grants significant war powers to Congress. Its power to "define and punish . . . offenses against the laws of nations"[118] provides a basis for Congress to establish a statutory framework, such as that set forth in the Military Commissions Act (MCA) of 2006 for trying and punishing unlawful enemy combatants for violations of the law of war and other hostile acts in support of terrorism.[119] This view was confirmed by former President Bush's support for enactment of the MCA following the Supreme Court's decision in *Hamdan v. Rumsfeld*.[120] Furthermore, the power "[t]o make rules for the government and regulation of the land and naval forces" gives Congress the recognized authority to establish standards for the detention, interrogation, and transfer to foreign nations.[121] This is precisely what the Congress did in passing the Detainee Treatment Act of 2005 that addresses the treatment of alien detainees held in the custody of the Department of Defense.[122]

While the Executive and the Congress share responsibility for detainee matters, the detention of unlawful combatants rests solely with the Executive. Early in the present conflict, Congress passed Senate Joint Resolution (SJR) 23,[123] which recognizes that "the President has authority under the Constitution to take action to deter and prevent acts of international terrorism against the United States."[124] Effective interrogation of those with knowledge of terrorist planning is directly related to preventing future terrorist acts.[125]

These views were distilled most succinctly by then–Congressman (later Judge) Abe Mikva in 1971 when addressing the effect on the president's power of the repeal of the 1950 Emergency Detention Act. Representative Mikva stated:

> After all, if the President's war powers are inherent, he must have the right to exercise them without regard to congressional action. Arguably, any statute which impeded his ability to preserve and protect the republic from imminent harm could be suspended from operation. It is a contradiction in terms to talk of Congress' limiting or undercutting an inherent power given by the Constitution or some higher authority.[126]

Relating this to the harsh interrogation used by intelligence agency professionals[127] against Khalid Shaykh Mohammed, some intelligence was secured that is purported to have saved American lives.[128]

While the harsh interrogation measures delineated above probably do not meet the standard of torture, if the precedents for tort recovery from tortuous acts previously addressed have any meaning, we are left searching for guidance on what constitutes the line between lawful and unlawful interrogation in light of the Common Article 3 prohibitions against humiliating and degrading treatment.[129] This is of special concern in circumstances involving "imminent harm" or "extreme necessity."

The answer may come from the commander-in-chief himself. When President Obama was campaigning for office, he was sharply critical of then-President Bush's acceptance of practices involving enemy operatives and detainees in foreign locations deemed necessary to secure information and keep the nation free from subsequent attack. These practices included warrantless wiretaps, enhanced interrogation, and detention without trial (as provided at that time by *Eisentrager*).[130] Upon his election, however, President Obama has moderated these statements and opined recently on ABC's *This Week* that, "we shouldn't be making judgments based upon the basis of incomplete information or campaign rhetoric."[131] As cautious a leader as President Obama apparently is, he will likely be reluctant to throw away the entirety of the intelligence architecture that has kept the United States safe for the past eight years.

In late 2005, the Senate passed an amendment sponsored by Senator John McCain to the Defense Authorization Bill that now regulates the interrogation of detainees held by U.S. military forces.[132] The amendment severely restricts harsh interrogation practices and prohibits "cruel, inhuman or degrading" treatment of detainees.[133] Senator McCain has subsequently indicated he does not rule out harsh treatment in an emergency such as a hostage rescue or an imminent attack.[134]

To obtain the best possible balance between the obligations of both national security and human rights, three fundamental steps should now be considered to more carefully define this process. The first, as suggested by Charles Krauthammer,[135] John McCain, and others, would prohibit military personnel from ever engaging in the harsh techniques addressed by the McCain Amendment and would require that, when they are authorized under limited and discrete circumstances, their application be restricted to nonmilitary interrogation professionals. The second is that the rationale be carefully circumscribed to situations of imminent danger to the United States, as suggested by Senator McCain.[136] The third, given voice by President Obama himself in August 2009, would require prior NSC approval for the parameters of interrogation of high value targets, and these could only be conducted by FBI personnel, and not CIA operatives as occurred prior to April 2003.[137] This careful balancing of interests, with the new procedures in place, will make the process of drawing a line between the unlawful and the legally justified defensible, would satisfy our need to carefully interrogate high value targets and obtain valuable information, and would ensure the support of both the U.S. domestic population and that of our allies.

Chapter Ten

Federal Court or Military Commission

The Dilemma

The November 2009 decision announced by Attorney General Eric Holder (since rescinded) to try Khalid Sheikh Mohammed (KSM) and four other alleged terrorists[1] in federal court in New York has raised a number of important and timely questions concerning the nature of law of war violations and the challenges raised to their successful prosecution in federal court. Following the September 11, 2001, attack on the United States by al Qaeda, the United States captured and/or apprehended a number of "high value" detainees who were believed to have committed or conspired to commit terrorist acts against the United States, its military forces, or its citizens. These acts also constituted violations of federal criminal law under Title 18, United States Code.

Where prosecution in federal court is contemplated, however, the Fourth, Fifth and Sixth Amendments addressing the right to privacy, the right to due process in criminal investigations, and the right of confrontation, respectively, often collide with the need to ensure the nation's security. The Fourth Amendment, authored by James Madison, for example, requires specificity on the part of federal agents in obtaining judicial authorization to physically invade the privacy of individuals. In that regard, the Fourth Amendment was designed to preclude overreaching in investigations of criminal enterprises. The forefathers simply did not contemplate the investigation and prosecution of terrorist threats to the nation.

The refinement of Fifth Amendment standards in the context of national security has had a similarly uneven development. Statements obtained from detainees such as KSM through harsh interrogation as a result of perceived extreme necessity have led to the development of other evidence that could

89

be the subject of successful constitutional challenge. The Congress recognized the obvious conflict between normal federal prosecutions and the special requirements in prosecuting national security violations by al Qaeda and, accordingly, passed the Military Commissions Act of 2006.[2]

This chapter addresses, first, the actions taken by the Congress to address the dichotomy between national security cases and normal federal prosecutions; second, the standards developed by the Legislative branch to ensure the successful prosecution of national security violations in military commissions; and third, the constitutional concerns that are likely to arise in the five federal prosecutions in New York, to include: the detainees' right to counsel and to a speedy trial, the problem of coerced statements and their fruit, and limitations upon the admissibility of hearsay and classified evidence in criminal cases.

NATIONAL SECURITY VERSUS PROTECTION OF PERSONAL LIBERTY

There will always be tension between the requirements of national security and the protection of personal liberties found in the first ten amendments to the Constitution. While these amendments were never intended to provide for the nation's security, their application, especially when Fourth and Fifth Amendment values are implicated, has differed in times of national crisis when compared to times of relative peace. This is clearly reflected in the probable cause requirements in normal criminal investigations when compared to national security investigations. In solely criminal investigations, the probable cause requirement is "a fair probability that contraband or evidence of a crime will be found in a particular place."[3] Conversely, the probable cause standard in national security investigations is an external threat to the security of the nation.[4]

In the days immediately following the 9/11 attacks, the Bush Administration issued the military order of November 13, 2001, which established military commissions to address detention and trial of noncitizens held in the war against terrorism.[5] It was contemplated that these unlawful combatants would be tried by military commission outside the United States.[6] In *Rasul v. Bush*,[7] however, the Supreme Court in 2004 found that U.S. federal courts do have jurisdiction to hear the *habeas corpus* petitions of these detainees.

Following the submission of numerous petitions for habeas corpus in the Federal District Court for the District of Columbia, the Congress in 2005 revoked federal district court jurisdiction over these petitions through enactment of the Detainee Treatment Act (DTA).[8] The DTA provided that the Court of Appeals for the District of Columbia would hear all appeals from final decisions of military commissions. In 2006, the Supreme Court decided

Hamdan v. Rumsfeld,[9] reversing a DC Circuit Court decision upholding military commissions. *Hamdan* provided that although the Congress had approved military commissions, their procedures must be as similar as possible to court-martial proceedings.[10] *Hamdan* held that it was immaterial whether or not the Geneva Conventions of 1949, and specifically Common Article 3, provided rights enforceable on behalf of detainees in federal district court. It found that by incorporating the laws of war into the Uniform Code of Military Justice in Article 21, Congress brought the Geneva Conventions within the body of law to be applied in courts martial and military commissions.[11]

Shortly after his election, President Barack Obama ordered the detention facility at Guantanamo closed no later than January 22, 2010.[12] Under the Executive Order, the Attorney General, in coordination with other administration officials,[13] was required to assess the status of each detainee and determine whether the individual detainees should remain in U.S. custody, be transferred to a third country, or be prosecuted for criminal offenses.[14] When this review was completed, the Attorney General and Secretary of Defense jointly announced on November 13, 2009, that ten detainees, all of whom had been previously charged before military commissions, would be tried.[15] Five, previously identified herein, would be tried in the U.S. District Court for the Southern District of New York and the remaining five would be tried by military commission.[16]

EXECUTIVE AUTHORITY TO ESTABLISH MILITARY COMMISSIONS

The President's authority to convene military commissions to try criminal violations by those involved in armed conflict flows from his commander-in-chief powers under the Constitution.[17] Under a statute in Title 10 of the U.S. Code,[18] the president may convene such bodies to try offenses against the laws of war. Unlike the court-martial process established by the Uniform Code of Military Justice[19] to maintain discipline and order among U.S. forces, the military commission is directed at enemy combatants as a means of deterring and punishing violations of the law of armed conflict.[20] When President Bush first signed a military order[21] establishing commissions to try terrorism suspects in 2001, the process had not been used since World War II.[22] As courts established under the president's executive authority, as opposed to the judiciary under Article III, military commissions are not subject to the same constitutional requirements applied in federal (Article III) courts.[23]

The Supreme Court in *Hamdan v. Rumsfeld* further determined that although Common Article 3 of the Geneva Conventions of 1949 "tolerates a great degree of flexibility in trying individuals captured during armed conflict,"[24] and was "crafted to accommodate a wide variety of legal systems,"[25] the procedures established in Military Commission Order Number 1[26] to effectuate the president's military order of November 13, 2001, did not meet even this low threshold.[27]

To effect the mandate in *Hamdan*, Congress then enacted the Military Commissions Act of 2006 (MCA),[28] which authorized military commissions, and established procedural rules that are modeled after, but differ in several significant ways from, the Uniform Code of Military Justice (UCMJ). The MCA established a new chapter 47a in Title 10, U.S. Code, and declared that the new chapter is "based upon the procedures for trial by general courts-martial under [the UCMJ]."[29] It then exempted the new military commissions from UCMJ requirements under Article 10 (speedy trial), Article 31 (self-incrimination warnings), and Article 32 (right to a formal pretrial investigation).[30]

These legislative efforts were successfully challenged, at least in part, in 2008 in *Boumediene v. Bush,* which held that *habeas corpus* extends to noncitizens detained at Guantanamo and that these noncitizens could seek habeas review of their status.[31] *Boumediene* struck Section 7 of the MCA as it relates to the right of detainees in Guantanamo to challenge their detention in federal court. The extent to which Fourth, Fifth and Sixth Amendment protections extend to these noncitizens has not yet been determined, however.[32] Many believed these issues would be addressed in *Kiyemba v. Obama,*[33] which was scheduled to be heard by the Supreme Court in the spring of 2010. The Supreme Court vacated and remanded the case, however, and the issues remain unresolved.

CONGRESS'S ROLE IN THE MILITARY COMMISSION PROCESS

Article I, Section 8 of the Constitution grants significant war powers to Congress. Its power to "define and punish . . . offenses against the laws of nations"[34] provides a basis for Congress to establish a statutory framework, such as that set forth in the Military Commissions Act (MCA) of 2006[35] for trying and punishing unlawful enemy combatants for violations of the law of war and other hostile acts in support of terrorism. This view was confirmed by former President Bush's support for enactment of the MCA following the Supreme Court's decision in *Hamdan v. Rumsfeld.*[36] Furthermore, the power "[t]o make rules for the government and regulation of the land and naval forces"[37] gives Congress the recognized authority to establish standards for the detention, interrogation, and transfer to foreign nations. This is precisely what the Congress did in passing the Detainee Treatment Act of 2005,[38] which addresses the treatment of alien detainees held in the custody of the Department of Defense.

While the Executive branch and the Congress share responsibility for detainee matters, the detention and prosecution of unlawful combatants rests solely with the Executive. Early in the Iraqi conflict, Congress passed Senate Joint Resolution (SJR) 23,[39] which recognized that "the President had authority under the Constitution to take action to deter and prevent acts of international terrorism against the United States."[40] Additionally, the resolution specifically authorized

> the President . . . to use all necessary and appropriate force against those nations, organizations, or persons he determines planned, authorized, committed, or aided the terrorist acts that occurred on September 11, 2001, or harbored such organizations or persons, *in order to prevent any future acts of international terrorism against the United States* by such nations, organizations or persons.[41]

Thus, Congress in SJR 23 has specifically endorsed not only the use of appropriate military force, but also the included authority to detain and try enemy combatants to prevent them from conducting further hostilities against this nation.

Under the provisions of the Military Commissions Act of 2006, as amended in 2009,[42] the Secretary of Defense has established regulations for the conduct of commission proceedings. The jurisdiction of any military commission established is limited to time of war. Only offenses recognized under the law of war or designated by statute may be tried by military commissions. The Military Commissions Act (MCA) further provides that only aliens may be tried.[43]

PROCEDURES BEFORE MILITARY COMMISSIONS IN COMPARISON WITH FEDERAL DISTRICT COURT

The five detainees currently awaiting military commission proceedings in Guantanamo[44] will face proceedings that differ greatly from those in Federal District Court. For example, the requirement in the Fifth Amendment that no prosecution for a capital or otherwise infamous crime proceed unless on presentment or indictment of a Grand Jury has been specifically excepted for military commission proceedings.[45] Similarly, the requirements concerning trial by jury in the Sixth Amendment have been found to be inapplicable to trials before military commissions.[46] Due process requirements also differ. Fifth Amendment due process protections in military commissions and courts are subject to Congress's "plenary control over rights, duties, and responsibilities in the framework of the Military Establishment, including regulations, procedures and remedies related to military discipline."[47] In *Weiss v. United States* (quoted in the previous sentence), the Supreme Court upheld a narrowed interpretation of Fifth Amendment due process in the context of military criminal proceedings.[48]

The military commissions authorized by the MCA, in fact, afford the detainees fewer procedural protections overall than would be available to defendants in either a military court martial or in federal court.[49] A careful review of procedural and substantive rights in a military commission versus a federal district court may prove helpful.

ASSISTANCE OF COUNSEL

The right to assistance of counsel in any criminal proceeding is considered the most basic of constitutional rights under U.S. law. The Sixth Amendment to the Constitution makes clear that every criminal defendant has the right "to have the Assistance of counsel for his defense."[50] The Supreme Court has ruled that it is not just the assistance of counsel, but the *effective* assistance of counsel that is required.[51] In federal criminal courts, the right is effected through Rule 44 of the Federal Rules of Criminal Procedure.[52] Under this rule, a defendant who is unable to afford counsel will have one appointed to represent him at every stage of the proceedings, unless he waives that right.[53]

The rule concerning the right to counsel before military commissions is similar.[54] Rule 506 of the Rules for Military Commissions provides a detainee charged with criminal offenses with a detailed military defense counsel at no cost to him. The detainee may also request a specific military defense counsel, and if reasonably available, that counsel will be provided.[55] The detained unlawful combatant may also retain a civilian counsel, but at no cost to the government. Specific requirements are imposed with respect to U.S. citizenship and a security clearance for any nonmilitary counsel, in light of the sensitivity of the charges in this forum.[56] As in the case of a federal court proceeding, the defendant before a military commission may waive his right to attorney representation and represent himself.[57]

RIGHT AGAINST SELF-INCRIMINATION

The Fifth Amendment to the Constitution makes clear that "[n]o person. . . shall be compelled in any criminal case to be a witness against himself."[58] The Supreme Court has clearly articulated the self-incrimination clause rationale for excluding coerced statements in federal courts.[59] The Supreme Court has also recognized a Fourteenth Amendment due process rationale for excluding statements in federal courts where they are the product of coercive interrogation methods.[60] As a general rule, federal courts do not admit statements of a defendant in criminal proceedings unless the law enforcement or other federal official taking the statement has issued *Miranda* warnings before the statements were made.[61]

There were two exceptions to the *Miranda* rule possibly germane to the federal court proceedings in New York, had they taken place. The first was the public safety exception addressed in *New York v. Quarles*.[62] In *Quarles*, however, the time sensitive nature of the question "Where is the gun?" was key.[63] In certain of the detainee cases, it was not relevant. The second possible *Miranda* exception applicable to certain detainees relates to foreign interrogations and the fact that courts have not found that *Miranda* applies to questioning by foreign officials overseas,[64] unless they are working jointly with U.S. officials or the interrogation would "shock the conscience."[65]

The Congress has taken a very different view of *Miranda* for detainees held outside the United States and tried by military commission. In the 2009 Amendments to the 2006 MCA,[66] Congress barred enemy combatants in military custody held outside the United States from being read *Miranda* warnings, absent a court order.[67] Though *Miranda* does not apply, detainees tried by military commission do have a statutory right against self-incrimination. Under the 2009 amendments to the MCA, all detainee statements obtained through torture, or "cruel, inhuman or degrading treatment," are inadmissible in military commission proceedings, regardless of when taken.[68] Similarly, a detainee before a military commission may not be required to testify against himself.[69] The 2009 amendments to the MCA do provide an opportunity to consider incriminating statements of detainees where the commission is satisfied the statements are *trustworthy*. Specifically, the 2009 amendments to the MCA provide that for statements to be admissible, the military commission must determine that:

1. the totality of the circumstances renders the statement reliable and possessing sufficient probative value; and
2. (A) the statement was made incident to lawful conduct during military operations at the point of capture or during closely related combat engagement, and the interests of justice would best be served by admission of the statement into evidence, or (B) the statement was voluntarily given.[70]

EVIDENTIARY ISSUES

A critical prosecution issue in either federal court or before a military commission will be the rules applied with respect to hearsay evidence. Hearsay is a prior out-of-court statement offered at trial by another person or in written form to prove the truth of the matter asserted. This is especially significant in the context of a terrorist trial where crucial witnesses detained by foreign

governments may be unavailable to come to the United States to testify, or
the U.S. or a foreign government may be unwilling to make intelligence
operatives available for the proceeding. Both federal courts and military
commissions have established procedural rules governing the admission of
evidence. The Federal Rules of Evidence guide the federal courts while the
Military Commission Rules of Evidence provide guidance to military commissions. Procedural rules may limit the introduction of hearsay unless it can
be characterized under one of the exceptions provided in law that ensure its
reliability and trustworthiness.

Under the Federal Rules of Evidence, hearsay, unless an exception can be
asserted, is generally inadmissible.[71] Exceptions to the hearsay rule are provided where the context in which the statement was made or the nature of the
content of the statement gives it greater inherent trustworthiness than other-
out-of-court statements. Exceptions include statements of a self-incriminat-
ing nature, records of a regularly conducted activity, excited utterances made
in response to a startling event, or certain statements by a person who is
deceased and thus unavailable.[72] A further exception permits the introduction
of evidence, over hearsay objection, when the statement has an "equivalent
circumstantial guarantee of trustworthiness."[73] An example of the statements
federal courts have recognized under this exception, and that would have
been critical to proceedings in New York (had they occurred), include those
contained within the files of foreign intelligence authorities.[74]

Also excepted from hearsay challenge in federal court are statements
made by co-conspirators in furtherance of the conspiracy. These statements
are not technically considered hearsay. While the conspiracy must be proved
before this rule can be applied, the same statements may be used to prove the
existence of the conspiracy, but only if the out-of-court statements do not
constitute the only evidence of the existence of the conspiracy.[75]

The evidentiary rules under the Military Commission Rules of Evidence,
as amended in 2009, are far more flexible, and even permissive. Under Commission Rules, hearsay is not excluded if (1) it would be admitted under rules
of evidence applicable in a trial by general courts-martial or (2) the propo-
nent of the evidence makes known to the adverse party thirty days in advance
the intention to offer the evidence, as well as the circumstances under which
it was taken.[76] These particulars should include the time, place, and conditions under which the statement was taken.[77] The evidence would only be
excluded if the totality of the circumstances under which it was taken show
the statement to be unreliable.[78]

RIGHT TO A SPEEDY TRIAL IN CRIMINAL PROSECUTIONS

The right to a speedy trial is guaranteed to all defendants in criminal prosecutions by the Sixth Amendment to the Constitution.[79] The right applies to prosecutions in both federal and state courts, as the Supreme Court has found the right to be one of the "fundamental" constitutional rights the Fourteenth Amendment incorporated to the states.[80] As noted in *Barker v. Wingo*,[81] the various justifications for the right to a speedy trial include not only a concern regarding lengthy incarceration but also the interest of the American people in resolving criminal allegations in a timely and effective manner.[82] Furthermore, the *Barker* court found "there is a societal interest in providing a speedy trial which exists separate from, and at times in opposition to, the rights of the accused."[83]

The right to speedy trial is codified for federal courts in the Federal Speedy Trial Act of 1974.[84] Under this Act, the Government is required to bring an indictment against a person within thirty days of his arrest, and the trial must commence within seventy days of indictment.[85] Nevertheless, the Supreme Court has qualified the right by stating that "not every constitutional provision applies to governmental activity even where the United States has sovereign power" and that "aliens receive constitutional protections when they have come within the territory of the United States and developed substantial connections with the country."[86] Moreover, the Speedy Trial Act provides several specific exceptions to the timelines provided above. Relevant exceptions likely applicable to detainees include the "ends of justice" exception and the "unusual or complex" rationale for delaying trial.[87] Under either exception, a trial judge would be permitted to delay proceedings when he or she determines that a delay serves the "ends of justice" that outweigh the interests of the public and the accused in a speedy trial, or permit a delay when the facts at issue are "unusual or complex."[88]

Under the 2009 amendments to the MCA, there are no statutory or procedural requirements addressing speedy trial in the case of enemy combatant detainees. Nevertheless, we can expect that detainees tried by military commission will raise the argument that their Fifth Amendment right to due process has been violated by "caus[ing] substantial prejudice to [the detainees'] right to a fair trial," as a result of the delay in prosecution of their cases.[89]

RIGHT OF DETAINEES TO CONFRONT CLASSIFIED INFORMATION

One of the dilemmas facing prosecutors when trying persons associated with al Qaeda is the risk of disclosing classified information that could be useful to terrorist elements. Because of the Sixth Amendment requirement that "the accused shall enjoy the right . . . to be confronted with the witnesses against him,"[90] the risk of disclosure of classified information critical to successful prosecution presents a very real concern. This dilemma was a leading factor in the enactment of the Classified Information Procedures Act (CIPA), which provides procedures to preclude the disclosure of classified information during criminal litigation, but nevertheless provides the accused with sufficient information to craft a defense.[91]

The Federal Rules of Criminal Procedure and CIPA both authorize federal judges to prevent the disclosure of classified information to the defendant, in cases where nondisclosure would not prejudice his rights.[92] Under these procedures, the judge may authorize the prosecution to provide substitute statements, or an unclassified summary, provided this alternative gives the defendant the real opportunity to challenge the prosecution's evidence. In that regard, the redaction may exclude sources and methods of intelligence gathering that do not go to the substance of what the evidence states but rather simply do not identify the operatives or methods used. In all cases, however, the substitute must provide sufficient context such that the defendant has a real opportunity to discount or discredit the authenticity of the information being presented.

The protection of classified information and its disclosure in military commissions is addressed in the 2009 amendments to the Military Commissions Act.[93] As amended, the MCA procedures are nearly identical to the practice under CIPA in federal courts. Under the 2009 procedures, the presiding military judge must allow the introduction of otherwise admissible evidence "while protecting from disclosure the sources, methods, or activities" through which the evidence was obtained.[94] The military judge may also order an *in camera* hearing to determine how the evidence shall be handled.[95] The accused may be excluded from such hearings as long as his attorney, who must have an appropriate security clearance, is permitted to argue the release of the information on behalf of his client.[96] Under these procedures, the accused will have the opportunity to review all evidence actually submitted into the record and considered by the commission members.

The planned prosecution of detainees in federal district court in New York and before military commissions, whether in Guantanamo or in the United States, will pose significant challenges to U.S. civilian and military prosecutors. The greater difficulties, however, would likely have been faced by U.S. attorneys in New York had that decision been made. The federal court system and its Federal Rules of Criminal Procedure were not structured to try law-of-war violators who have been held without indictment and without access to the federal court system for a significant period of time.

Three specific areas would likely have caused significant litigation on appeal should conviction have occurred in the district court. The first involves the right against self-incrimination under the Fifth Amendment and the likely debate in the courtroom concerning whether statements taken by U.S. officials using certain interrogation techniques were voluntary. In the commission setting, the debate will center not on whether they are voluntary, but on the lesser standard of whether they are reliable and trustworthy.

A second major area of concern for the district court proceedings relates to the right of confrontation under the Sixth Amendment and the difficulty in ensuring the attendance of witnesses from abroad when not under the control of the U.S. government. In light of the more stringent rules regarding the admission of hearsay in federal court compared to the commission setting, procedural rules may limit the introduction of certain evidence in federal court unless it can be established as reliable under one of the exceptions to the hearsay rule.

The right to speedy trial may also prove troublesome for federal prosecutions. While there are exceptions provided, the right to speedy trial requires the government to bring an indictment against a person within thirty days of his arrest, and the trial must commence within seventy days of indictment.[97] In no instance are these requirements met in any of the cases under consideration for prosecution. Even under the new amendments to the MCA, we can expect that detainees tried by military commission will raise the argument that their Fifth Amendment right to due process has been violated by the significant delay in prosecution.

These cases reflect the fact that careful consideration must be given when an administration makes a choice of forum in national security cases. An administration decision made without appreciating Congress's obvious recognition in the MCA of the need to tailor procedures to accommodate the nature of evidence available in these cases may cause prosecution hazards that could have been avoided.

Chapter Eleven

The International Criminal Court and the Trial of Terror-Related Crimes

Since the attacks on September 11, 2001, many have argued that the United States' national security policy requires a more integrated approach with its strategic partners, including in the area of judicial cooperation. It is important to remember that at any given time, U.S. forces are located in close to one hundred nations around the world assisting in peacekeeping and humanitarian operations. They urge this would not only ensure success in managing the War on Terror but also ensure that the United States' principles and our national interests are not in conflict. They argue that the United States' current stance with respect to the International Criminal Court (ICC) could have the strategic consequence of fostering the decline of America's image and influence in the world community.

Just as in 1937,[1] when discussions focused on similar development of an international tribunal, the concern early in the twenty-first century relates to guaranteed constitutional rights of American citizens and military personnel, and whether those rights can be recognized under international law, in this case the Rome Statute, *independent* of U.S. domestic law and constitutional guarantees. Despite these differences, the U.S. Government shares the commitment of parties to the Rome Statute to bring to justice those who perpetrate genocide, war crimes, and crimes against humanity. While the United States and other nations may have honest differences on how accountability is best achieved, the United States has always worked closely with other states to ensure that perpetrators of these atrocities are held accountable for their actions.

This chapter focuses not only on the legal requirements and policy reasons for a separate approach, but also the United States' respect for the right of other nations to become parties to the Rome Statute.

THE ROME STATUTE

When the representatives of more than 130 nations gathered in Rome in 1998 for negotiations to create a permanent International Criminal Court, the U.S. representatives arrived with the firm belief that those who perpetrate genocide, crimes against humanity, and war crimes must be held accountable. In fact, the United States has traditionally been a world leader in promoting the rule of law and ensuring the effective prosecution of these offenses. Following World War II, it was U.S. leadership that responded to the worst tyranny on record and supported, through funding and personnel, the tribunals at Nuremburg and in Japan. More recently, it was U.S. support which ensured the success of the International Criminal Tribunals in the former Yugoslavia and Rwanda.

Without question, it has been the United States which has been in the forefront of promoting human rights, ensuring international justice, and demanding accountability of the world's worst criminal offenders. But as worthy as the precepts underlying the Rome negotiations were, the statute that emerged establishing the ICC, which began functioning on July 1, 2002, did not effectively advance these worthy goals with respect to the constitutional protections guaranteed American service members and citizens.

Now in effect for more than nine years, the United States' posture on the ICC has not precluded the effectiveness of U.S. relations with other national states in any meaningful way. The U.S. continues to believe that without significant changes in the ICC and the Rome Statute, it can never become a full partner in its operation. The problems identified by U.S. negotiators from 1998 onward are well known and much publicized, but are nevertheless worth reciting here.

The U.S. concerns with the Rome Statute fall into three main categories. The first is that subjecting American service members to trial before the International Criminal Court for offenses within the judicial authority of the United States would violate the exclusive rights of U.S. citizens. [2] The second concern is that ratification of the Rome Statute would constitute a partial surrender of American sovereignty for those U.S. forces serving in a UN–monitored military conflict. The third concern, addressed in the next section, relates to the corrosive impact the ICC, as presently structured, could have on the effectiveness of other UN institutions.

The first category relates to the fact that the ICC's prosecutors and judges are not bound by the Constitution, are not appointed by the president as are all federal prosecutors and judges and all military officers, are not confirmed with the advice and consent of the Senate, and are not required to guarantee for defendants the application of protections within the first ten Amendments to the Constitution. In fact, U.S. citizens brought before the ICC would only generally enjoy the rights held so dear within the United States.

For example, under U.S. law, a military prosecutor must bring a defendant to trial within ninety days or release him.[3] Under the Rome Statute, ICC prosecutors must only ensure defendants "the right to be tried without undue delay." Under the International Criminal Tribunal for the Former Yugoslavia (ICTFY), which contains the same speedy trial language in its charter, and serves as the model for the ICC, criminal defendants can often wait more than a year in confinement prior to trial. In fact, ICTFY prosecutors have argued at The Hague that a far longer period of confinement, up to five years, would not violate the defendant's fundamental rights.

Equally significant, the right of confrontation, guaranteed by the Sixth Amendment to the Constitution, is largely diluted under the ICC's practice. The ICTFY practice, upon which the ICC is based, allows virtually unlimited hearsay evidence and anonymous witnesses to testify in trials, large portions of which have been conducted in secret. Such practices do vengeance to the presumption of innocence.

In a similar way, the ICC Statute permits a judgment of acquittal to be appealed to an appellate body. This directly conflicts with the Constitution's protection against double jeopardy, but again, parallels the ICTFY statute. In the Yugoslav Tribunal to date, the prosecutors have appealed every judgment of acquittal.

Likewise of great concern is the failure of the ICC to afford the right to a jury trial, guaranteed to U.S. citizens in both the Sixth Amendment and in Article III, Section 2 of the Constitution. While some would argue that this right is more than offset by the wisdom represented by three experienced jurists, this procedure permits the ICC to perform all functions of the judicial process (investigator, prosecutor, court and jury), an approach fundamentally at odds with the legal tradition within the United States.

Those supportive of ratifying the Rome Statute argue that because the ICC, if the United States were to accede, would not be a court of the United States, the provisions of the Bill of Rights and Article III, Section 2 would not apply. They further argue that in extradition treaties with myriad nations, the United States provides reciprocal rights to foreign governments, with different legal systems, to try Americans for crimes committed abroad. The difference is, the ICC Statute would permit the ICC to try Americans who have never left the United States, for actions taken within U.S. borders, without providing these Constitutional protections.

While there has been no case precisely on point, in *United States v. Balsys*,[4] a 1998 case, the Supreme Court stated that where a prosecution by a foreign court is, at least in part, undertaken on behalf of the United States, and where "the United States and its allies had enacted substantially similar criminal codes aimed at prosecuting offenses of international character" then an argument can be made that the first ten amendments to the Constitution would apply "simply because that prosecution [would not be] fairly characterized as distinctly 'foreign.' The point would be that the prosecution was acting as much on behalf of the United States as of the prosecuting nation." This is arguably the case with the International Criminal Court.

Proponents of ratification have also urged that it is highly unlikely that the ICC's jurisdiction would ever be directed to U.S. service members or citizens, and thus the import of the U.S. Constitutional arguments should be minimized. Unfortunately, it is hard to imagine that the divisions among nations should the ICC's jurisdiction be applied in a conflict in which the United States is involved would be any different than the experience in Bosnia from 1991–95, where Russia and China objected to the United States' actions. Under their pressure and with the support of international human rights activists, ICTFY investigators in The Hague targeted NATO's actions based upon the civilian deaths resulting from the air bombardment. This occurred despite the precise targeting involved and the fact that the United States' actions were designed to preclude a humanitarian disaster.

It is also asserted by proponents of ratification that the principle of "complimentarity" will ensure that only the United States can prosecute U.S. citizens. This principle, addressed in Article 17 of the Rome Statute, prohibits the ICC from exercising jurisdiction if the appropriate national authorities investigate and prosecute the matter.

Unfortunately, the reasons this purported check on ICC power are illusory are threefold. First, it is the ICC, not the participant nation, that decides how this provision shall be interpreted and applied. This is similarly true of all provisions within the Statute. Second, Article 17 provides the ICC an exception to a ratifying state's exercise of jurisdiction in any case in which it (the ICC) determines the national proceedings were not conducted "independently or impartially." In a governmental system like the United States where the president is both the chief executive with coordinate law enforcement authority and commander-in-chief of all military forces, it is not hard to imagine the claims by unfriendly member states, however absurd, of lack of independence and partiality in a U.S. decision that there is no basis to prosecute.

Finally, by placing within the ICC the sole jurisdiction of ultimately determining whether, for example, national leaders committed criminal violations by ordering certain military actions, the sovereign will of the citizens of the United States are both circumscribed and diminished. While sovereign nations have the authority to try noncitizens who have committed crimes against their citizens or on their territory, the United States has never recognized the right of an international organization to do so absent consent or a UN Security Council mandate. This court, however, claims the power to detain and try American citizens, even though democratically elected representatives have not agreed to be bound by the Statute.

With ratification, the ultimate accountability of national leaders to the citizenry would literally be transferred, at least with respect to matters before the ICC, to that body. Fundamentally, this transfer of sovereignty would be to an institution with values and interests greatly divergent from our own. When one considers that the ICC member states include Syria, Iran, Yemen, and Nigeria, all accused of directing extra-judicial killings abroad, ratification of the Rome Statute could constitute a significant surrender of American sovereignty.

THE ICC ERODES THE AUTHORITY OF OTHER UNITED NATIONS' INSTITUTIONS

Under the United Nations' Charter, the Security Council has primary responsibility for maintaining international peace and security. But the Rome Statute removes this existing system of checks and balances, and places enormous unchecked power and authority in the hands of the ICC prosecutors and judges. The Rome Statute has created a self-initiating prosecutor, answerable to no state or institution other than the Court itself.

During the negotiations in Rome, the United States representatives urged that placing this kind of unchecked power in the hands of prosecutors would lead both to controversy and politicized prosecutions.[5] As an alternative, the United States urged that the Security Council should maintain its responsibility to check any possible excesses of the ICC prosecutor. This request was denied.

Equally significant, the Statute creates a yet to be defined crime of "aggression," and authorizes the court to decide when and if it has occurred, while permitting its prosecutors to investigate and prosecute this undefined crime. This provision was approved over U.S. objection despite the fact that the UN Charter empowers only the Security Council to decide when a state has committed an act of aggression.

From a U.S. perspective, the inherent right of self-defense, memorialized in Article 51 of the Charter, could also be adversely diminished by the current court structure absent the checks and balances of Security Council oversight. With the ICC prosecutors and judges presuming to sit in judgment of actions of nonmember states, the ICC could have a chilling effect on the willingness of states to project power in defense of their moral and security interests. As observed in Kosovo, Afghanistan, and Iraq,[6] the principled projection of force by the world's democracies is critical to protecting human rights, to stopping genocide, or changing regimes. By placing U.S. officials, and the men and women in uniform, at risk of politicized prosecutions, the ICC could complicate U.S. military cooperation with many friends and allies[7] who now have a treaty obligation to hand over U.S. nationals to the court, even over U.S. objection, unless an Article 98 agreement, discussed below, is in place.

THE U.S. EFFORTS TO ADDRESS AND COUNTER THE ICC'S FLAWS

Despite voting against the Rome Statute (Treaty) in 1998, for the reasons outlined above, the United States remained committed and engaged, and continued to work to shape the court and to seek the necessary safeguards that would permit ratification. U.S. officials from State and Defense urged, without success, required changes to ensure effective oversight and to prevent politicization. Despite this frustration, U.S. experts participated in the Preparatory Conferences (Prep Cons) and took a leadership role in drafting the elements of offenses and the procedures necessary for the court's operation.

In December 2000, over the objections of many,[8] President Clinton signed the Rome Treaty on the International Criminal Court. The president nevertheless made clear that the United States was not abandoning its concerns about the treaty. He stated:

> In particular, we are concerned that when the Court comes into existence, it will not only exercise authority over personnel of states that have ratified the Treaty, but also claim jurisdiction over personnel of states that have not. With signature, however, we will be in a position to influence the evolution of the court. Without signature, we will not.[9]

Unfortunately, the United States was not able to further influence the evolution of the Court. On April 11, 2002, the ICC was ratified by a sufficient number of countries (60) to bring it into force on July 1, 2002. On May 6, 2002, President George W. Bush directed the following diplomatic note be sent to the Secretary-General of the United Nations, Kofi Annan:

> Dear Mr. Secretary-General:
>
> This is to inform you, in connection with the Rome Statute of the International Criminal Court adopted on July 17, 1998, that the United States does not intend to become a party to the treaty. Accordingly, the United States has no legal obligations arising from its signature on December 31, 2000. The United States requests that its intention not to become a party, as expressed in this letter, be reflected in the depository's status lists relating to this treaty.
>
> Sincerely,
> John R. Bolton,
> Under Secretary of State for Arms Control and International Security[10]

The dilemma posed for the United Nations in 2002 was the need for the continued leadership of the United States in the peace enforcement operations in Bosnia, a presence the United States was prepared to abandon unless its forces were protected from the unfettered jurisdiction of the ICC. The United States represents the only nation that can combine those elements of power required to sustain such large-scale operations: Overhead intelligence gathering; lift; logistic support; communications; planning; operational coordination; and close air support. In a compromise to prevent U.S. withdrawal, the Security Council, in July 2002, granted U.S. troops conducting peace enforcement operations in Bosnia a renewable one-year immunity from the jurisdiction of the ICC.

On August 3, 2002, President Bush signed into law the American Service-Members Protection Act (ASPA).[11] This law, the final version of which was proposed by Chairman Hyde, is designed to protect American servicemembers from the reach of the ICC. It provides for the withdrawal of U.S. military assistance from countries ratifying the ICC treaty, and restricts U.S. participation in UN peacekeeping and peace enforcement operations unless the United States obtains immunity from prosecution before the ICC. These provisions can be, and have been, waived by the president on "national interest" grounds. In addition, the law allows the United States to assist international efforts to bring to justice those accused of war crimes, crimes against humanity, or genocide.[12] More importantly, the provisions precluding assistance to those nations which have ratified the ICC Treaty do not apply if the ratifying nation has negotiated an Article 98 Agreement (described below) with the United States. As of mid-2012, 104 nations have concluded agreements with 97 of those currently in force.

At the same time, the United States initiated negotiations to secure Article 98[13] Agreements with all nations for whom it provided foreign assistance as a condition for that assistance to continue. These bilateral agreements likewise provide assurance that U.S. forces will not be subjected to ICC jurisdiction when the United States is operating with forces from these nations in UN peacekeeping or peace enforcement operations.[14] These agreements have largely permitted the United States to continue its support for United Nations operations and to continue its unique role and responsibility in helping to preserve international peace and security.

REFLECTIONS ON THE ICC

The ICC represents a step forward in the evolution of a justice process addressing more than national interests and national prerogatives. But a great deal more remains to be done before the United States should ratify the Rome Statute. Court jurisdiction over U.S. personnel should be permitted only after U.S. ratification of the Treaty. The United States should continue to press for changes to the court's statute authorizing a trial by one's peers, a limit on the evidence allowed to direct evidence and not hearsay, the strict adherence to a non–double jeopardy standard, and a willingness to consider an oversight mechanism in the Security Council to preclude politicized prosecutions (as occurred in Bosnia when NATO leaders were charged in the ICTFY).

Despite its limitations, the United States has optimized the benefits of the ICC among other participants in UN peacekeeping and peace enforcement operations through the careful management of foreign assistance as directed in the ASPA legislation. Through negotiation of Article 98 Agreements with all those states desiring to continue such aid and/or the continued participation of the United States in UN–sponsored operations, the United States has ensured its soldiers and sailors serving abroad will enjoy the same legal protections as those serving in garrison at Fort Bragg or Camp Lejeune.

There is no question that a properly constituted and structured International Criminal Court would make a profound contribution in deterring egregious human rights abuses worldwide. Unfortunately, the current structure represented by the ICC is in direct conflict with certain of the constitutional protections guaranteed to military personnel and civilians serving at the behest of the United States on foreign soil or directing activities on foreign territory from the United States. Considering the fact that the United States contributes more than 60 percent of all peace enforcement forces for UN operations, this is significant. While U.S. interests are not served by ratification at this time, the nation remains committed to promoting the rule of law and assisting in the successful prosecution of violators of humanitarian law.

Chapter Twelve

High Seas Terror and the Elimination of Piracy

On December 16, 2008, the UN Security Council unanimously passed Resolution 1851 authorizing states to mount land-based operations in Somalia against pirate strongholds.[1] This reflects the deep concern of all United Nations members with respect to the unacceptable level of violence at sea perpetrated by Somali pirates. As noted by then–Secretary Condoleezza Rice in her statement in support of the Resolution prior to the Council's vote,

> [B]ecause there has been no existing mechanism for states to coordinate their actions, the result has been less than the sum of its parts. The United States envisioned a contact group serving as a mechanism to share intelligence, coordinate activities and reach out to partners; and that it could work quickly on that initiative. Also limiting was the impunity; piracy currently paid, and pirates paid little for their criminality.[2]

The effort to combat piracy, not only off the coast of Somalia, but in other areas of the Indian Ocean, the Gulf of Aden, the Gulf of Oman, the Arabian Sea, and the Red Sea, has been the subject of great U.S. concern for years, although accentuated in the first two decades of the twenty-first century. In November 2008, the Saudi supertanker Sirius Star, with $100 million worth of crude aboard, was seized by Somali pirates and held for more than two months until January 9, 2009, when a $3 million ransom was paid.[3] Somali pirates held a Ukrainian cargo ship, the MV Faina, seized in late September 2008 with thirty-three tanks and other weaponry aboard, for a similar period until ransom was paid.[4] These incidents are not unique. In 2008 alone, there were more than one hundred reported pirate attacks in the busy shipping lanes off eastern and southern Somalia.[5] Similar numbers have been reported since.

THE LEGAL DIMENSION FOR COMBATING PIRACY

There is no question that the increase in acts of piracy emanating from Somali territory is a reflection of the near state of anarchy plaguing that nation. Nevertheless, nearly all member states, in passing Security Council Resolution 1851, underscored that actions to combat this dangerous phenomenon must conform to international law standards, including the Law of the Sea Convention.[6]

The standards for addressing the international crime of piracy and the available enforcement mechanisms are not in dispute. Piracy, at its core, encompasses "illegal acts of violence, detention, or depredation committed for private ends by the crew or passengers of a private ship or aircraft in or over international waters against another ship or aircraft or persons or property on board. (Depredation is the act of plundering, robbing or pillaging.)"[7] The 1982 Law of the Sea Convention would add "any act of voluntary participation in the operation of a ship or of an aircraft with knowledge of facts making it a pirate ship or aircraft," and "any acts of inciting or intentionally facilitating [such acts]."[8]

In international law, piracy is a crime that can be committed only on or over international waters, including the high seas, exclusive economic zones, in international airspace and in other places beyond the territorial jurisdiction of any nation.[9] The same acts committed within the internal waters, territorial sea, or national airspace of a country are within that nation's domestic jurisdiction.[10]

The U.S. law addressing the international crime of piracy emanates from the U.S. Constitution, which provides: "The Congress shall have Power . . . to define and punish piracies and felonies committed on the high seas, and offenses against the Law of Nations."[11] Congressional exercise of this power is set out in Titles 18 and 33 of the United States Code.[12] The U.S. law makes criminal the international offense in Section 1651 of Title 18, where it states: "Whoever, on the high seas, commits the crime of piracy as defined by the law of nations, and is afterward brought into or found in the United States, shall be imprisoned for life."[13]

U.S. statutes further authorize the president to deploy "public armed vessels" to protect U.S. merchant ships from piracy and to instruct the commanders of such vessels to seize any pirate ship that has attempted or committed an act of depredation or piracy against any foreign or U.S. flag vessel in international waters.[14] These sections also authorize issuance of instructions to naval commanders to send into any U.S. port any vessel which is armed or the crew of which is armed, and which shall have "attempted or committed any piratical aggression, search, restraint, depredation, or seizure, upon any vessel," U.S. or foreign flag, or upon U.S. citizens; and to retake any U.S. or foreign vessel or U.S. citizens unlawfully captured on the high seas.[15]

While U.S. law makes criminal those acts proscribed by international law as piracy, other provisions of U.S. municipal law describe related conduct. For example, federal statutes make criminal arming or serving on privateers,[16] assault by a seaman on a captain so as to prevent him from defending his ship or cargo,[17] unlawfully departing with a vessel within the admiralty jurisdiction,[18] corruption of seamen to unlawfully depart with a ship,[19] receipt of pirate property,[20] and robbery ashore in the course of a pirate cruise.[21]

Under provisions of the High Seas Convention[22] and the Law of the Sea Convention,[23] a pirate vessel or aircraft encountered in or over international waters may be seized and detained only by a nation's warships, military aircraft, or other ships or aircraft clearly marked and identifiable as being on government service.[24] U.S. warships seizing pirate vessels or aircraft are guided by U.S. Navy Regulations and the fleet commanders basic operational orders.[25] Under this guidance, U.S. authorities may also arrange with another nation to accept and try the pirates and dispose of the pirate vessel or aircraft, since every nation has jurisdiction under international law over acts of piracy.[26]

THE UNITED NATIONS' EFFORT TO STEM SOMALI PIRACY

The United Nations Security Council has been concerned with the disintegration of Somali government control over its territory since the late 1980s. It has addressed piracy arising from that state in Council resolutions since 1992.[27] By 2008, the Security Council got serious about addressing the piracy issue *directly* and not just in the context of the crisis inland in Somalia. In May 2008, in Resolution 1814, for example, it called upon member states "to take action to protect shipping involved with . . . United Nations authorized activities."[28] This was followed by Resolution 1816 in June 2008, which called upon all nations "to combat piracy and armed robbery at sea off the coast of Somalia."[29]

On October 7, 2008, in Resolution 1838, the Security Council ratcheted up its direction to states with maritime interests. What made this resolution significant was its specific call for "States interested in the security of maritime activities to take part actively in the fight . . . , in particular by deploying naval vessels and military aircraft."[30] This resolution further advised all states to issue guidance to their flag shipping on appropriate precautionary measures to protect themselves from attack or actions to take if under attack or threatened with attack when sailing in waters off the coast of Somalia.[31] On December 2, 2008, after Somali pirates seized the Saudi super-tanker Sirius Star, the Security Council, in an unprecedented provision in Resolution 1846 under Chapter VII of the Charter (authorizing all necessary means), determined that for a period of twelve months, warships of member nations were permitted to enter Somali territorial waters for the purpose of repressing acts of piracy consistent with such action permitted on the high seas.[32]

The December 2, 2008, Resolution, when paired with the December 16, 2008, UN Security Council Resolution (1851), weaves a tight pattern around piracy activities in the waters of the Indian Ocean and Gulf of Aden off the coast of Somalia. In Resolution 1851, moreover, the Security Council went one step beyond authorizing member nations to enter territorial waters, when it extended that right to the Somali landmass for the purpose of suppressing piracy. The Resolution provides that states and regional organizations can "undertake all necessary measures 'appropriate in Somalia,' to interdict those using Somali territory to plan, facilitate or undertake such acts."[33]

Having dealt with the jurisdictional issues related to operations, the Council next addressed the criminal jurisdiction concerns affecting all nations who happened to take individuals engaged in piracy into custody. In Resolution 1851, states and regional organizations were asked to conclude special agreements with countries willing to take custody of pirates and who were willing to embark law enforcement officials[34] from the latter countries to facilitate the investigation and prosecution of persons detained.[35] Following passage of Resolution 1851 on December 16, 2008, U.S. and allied leaders who are represented in the Combined Maritime Force agreed to enhance the entire ongoing counterpiracy effort in the USCENTCOM (U.S. Central Command) area of responsibility.

CONGRESSIONAL SUPPORT FOR ANTI-PIRACY INITIATIVES

On February 4, 2009, the House Transportation and Infrastructure Committee in the House held a lengthy hearing on *International Piracy On the High Seas* in their Subcommittee on the Coast Guard and Maritime Transportation. The hearing, the first held by the Subcommittee on this subject, was precipitated by a Congressional Research Service (CRS) report dated December 3, 2008, that focused attention on economic and humanitarian threats posed by pirates to the global seafaring community and the smooth flow of international trade.[36] The specific focus of that CRS report was that, given the marked increase of pirate attacks, the cost of transporting cargo in international waters could rise dramatically because of the sharp increase in ocean marine insurance for ships transiting the Gulf of Aden. The CRS report found that commercial shippers could require a special war risk insurance premium costing an additional tens of thousands of dollars per day, and that these additional costs could adversely impact international trade during the current global economic downturn. [37]

The Subcommittee hearing on February 4 provided a comprehensive examination of piracy, to include its prevalence, its current and potential impact on shipping, and the nature and effectiveness of the international efforts being implemented to combat this threat. The hearing established that the international community has mounted a multifaceted response in the Gulf of Aden–Indian Ocean Region, and that the United States is taking an active role in this effort through its leadership in Task Force 151. However, as Subcommittee Chair Elijah Cummings stated in his opening remarks, "given the size of the ocean area that international forces must patrol and their limited manpower, international naval powers are unlikely to be able to protect every ship passing the Horn of Africa from pirates."[38]

The hearing identified recent actions by the U.S. government to respond to this threat, including the national strategy document, *Countering Piracy off the Horn of Africa: Partnership and Action Plan*[39] (hereinafter National Strategy), issued by the National Security Council with the president's approval in December 2008. The National Strategy recognizes that lasting solutions to the piracy problem require significant improvements in governance, rule of law, security and economic development in Somalia. [40] The Strategy is realistic, however, in recognizing that, in light of the current threat there are steps that can be taken in the near term to deter, counter, and reduce the risk of attacks by Somali pirates. The Strategy calls for preventative and precautionary measures that include: (1) establishing a senior level contact group of nations that have the political will, operational capability, and resources to combat piracy off the Horn of Africa; (2) strengthening and encouraging the use of the Maritime Security Patrol Area (MSPA) in the Gulf of Aden; (3) updating Ship's Security Assessment and security plans to harden commercial shipping against pirate attacks; and (4) establishing strategic communications plans to emphasize the destructive effects of piracy on trade, human and maritime security, and to encourage the rule of law. [41]

The second prong of the National Strategy addressed at the Hearing on February 4, 2009 looks to interrupt and terminate acts of piracy through effective antipiracy operations. These operations are designed to interdict vessels used by pirates, and where possible to intervene in acts of piracy. The National Strategy also calls for identifying, disrupting and eliminating pirate bases in Somalia, and, to the extent possible, impacting pirate revenue. [42]

The final prong of the National Strategy addressed at the February 4, 2009, hearing on *International Piracy on the High Seas* relates to the requirement to hold pirates accountable for their crimes. All participants agreed during the hearing with the statement in the National Strategy that piracy is flourishing because it is highly profitable and nearly consequence free.[43] For this reason, developing the capacity to capture and successfully prosecute these criminals is critical to combating piracy. To that end, the National Strategy supports the development of agreements and arrangements with states in Africa and around the world that will allow pirates to be captured, detained, and prosecuted.[44]

THE OPERATIONAL RESPONSE BY THE MULTI-NATIONAL COMBINED MARITIME FORCE

The Combined Maritime Force (CMF), comprised of ships and assets from more than twenty nations and commanded by a U.S. flag officer from US-NAVCENT (U.S. Naval Forces, Central Command), has its headquarters in Manama, Bahrain. On January 8, 2009, the CMF formally established Combined Task Force (CTF) 151 for counterpiracy operations.[45] Previously, in August 2008, the CMF created the Maritime Security Patrol Area in the Gulf of Aden to support international efforts to combat piracy. At that time, the only organization within the multinational Combined Maritime Force tasked with counterpiracy operations was Combined Task Force (CTF) 150, which had been established at the onset of Operation Enduring Freedom in Afghanistan.[46]

The mission of CTF 150, however, was focused on the deterrence of all destabilizing activities at sea in the region, with a focus on drug smuggling and weapons trafficking. Piracy, although destabilizing, was not a major focus. Moreover, several of the navies of the twenty nations whose assets participated did not have the authority to conduct counterpiracy missions. It was for this reason that CTF 151, with its sole focus on piracy, was established. This would allow CTF 150 assets and the nations supporting this mission to remain focused on drugs and weapons trafficking, while at the same time providing tailored training and operations for the counterpiracy requirement in CTF 151.[47]

The unclassified Execute Order (EXORD) for Combined Task Force (CTF) 151 was published by the Commander, Combined Maritime Force on December 30, 2008.[48] The mission of CTF 151 is clear:

> 3. (U) CTF 151 is to conduct counter piracy operations in
> the CMF battlespace under a mission-based mandate to actively
> deter, disrupt and suppress piracy in order to protect global
> maritime commerce, enhance maritime security and secure freedom
> of navigation for the benefit of all nations.

The EXORD for CTF 151 mirrors the prior authorizations described above provided in UN Security Council Resolutions. It provides that ships of nations cooperating in the counterpiracy operations may board and search vessels where there are reasonable grounds for suspecting the vessel is engaged in piracy; may seize and dispose of these vessels, arms, and equipment used in the commission of piratical acts; and may detain those suspected of engaging in piracy with a view to prosecution by competent law enforcement authorities.[49] While the EXORD authorizes entry into the Somali territorial seas by participating warships,[50] it nowhere provides CTF personnel the authority to enter the land territory of Somalia as provided in UN Security Council Resolution 1851 on December 16, 2008.

Despite this limitation, CTF 151 has deployed highly trained U.S. Navy Visit, Board, Search, and Seizure (VBSS) Teams as well as the Coast Guard's elite Law Enforcement Detachment (LEDET) 405 aboard the command ship USS San Antonio.[51] The role of LEDET 405 is to supplement and train the VBSS Teams in various Maritime Interdiction Operations mission areas, including maritime law, boarding policies and procedures, evidence collection and preparation, and tactical procedures.[52]

THE WAY FORWARD

The rapid escalation of armed attacks off the Horn of Africa in the Gulf of Aden and the Indian Ocean has prompted an unprecedented counterpiracy response within the National Security Council, the U.S. Congress, and the United Nations and within the multinational Combined Maritime Force operating out of Manama, Bahrain. The December 2008 national strategy document *Countering Piracy off the Horn of Africa: Partnership and Action Plan,* issued by the National Security Council, while recognizing that lasting solutions to the piracy problem require significant improvements in governance, rule of law, security, and economic development in Somalia, is realistic in recognizing that there are steps that can be taken in the near term to deter, counter, and reduce the risk of attacks by Somali pirates.

The United Nations has similarly begun to seriously examine the dangerous conditions in the Gulf of Aden and the Indian Ocean off Somalia's coast. In December 2008, the Security Council unanimously passed two sweeping resolutions that authorized the warships of the multinational Combined Maritime Force to enter both the territorial waters of Somalia and the land territory of that state when necessary to destroy pirate strongholds. These actions and this authority are unprecedented and reflect the United Nations' deep commitment to deal effectively with this threat to international peace and security.

The establishment of Combined Task Force 151 in January 2009 reflected the United States' and allied nations commitment to provide a choke hold around the actions of pirates in the waters of the Indian Ocean and Gulf of Aden off the coast of Somalia. In the Navy's commitment of its VBSS Teams and the Coast Guard's assignment of its LEDET Unit, moreover, the U.S. military has committed the resources.

There is no question that piracy will continue in the highly vulnerable shipping lanes of the Gulf of Aden as long as the rewards outweigh the risk. With the establishment of CTF 151, that equation may be changing.

Chapter Thirteen

Outsourcing Defense Support Operations in the War on Terror

The current military operations in Afghanistan, and Iraq previously, are unique in the *extent* to which the Department of Defense (DoD) has contracted defense services to private U.S., host nation, and third country firms. Beginning with the First Gulf War in 1990–1991, however, DoD has increasingly relied on contractors to meet many of its logistical and operational support needs during combat operations, peacekeeping missions, and humanitarian assistance missions. These have included Operations Desert Shield and Desert Storm,[1] peacekeeping operations in the Balkans (e.g., Bosnia and Kosovo),[2] and Operations Enduring Freedom and Iraqi Freedom in Afghanistan and Iraq, respectively.[3] Significant factors that have contributed to this increase in outsourcing include an increased number of missions and operations, a reduction in the size of the U.S. military after the breakup of the former Soviet Union, and the increased sophistication of U.S. weapons systems used in these operations.

The DoD contracts awarded in these operations fall into three broad categories: Theater support; external support; and systems support. In the Regional Combatant Command in Iraq, for example, U.S. Central Command or one of its service component commands was responsible for negotiating and overseeing theater support contracts, which were normally for recurring services, to include equipment repair, security, minor construction, and intelligence services. External support contracts, awarded and managed by commands external to the combatant commands involved in the operations, such as the Defense Logistics Agency and the Army Corps of Engineers, were negotiated and awarded for supplies and services, respectively, to forces at their forward deployed location. An example of service contracts included Brown and Roots's contract to run the mess halls for the army in Iraq. The third genre of privatized outsourcing, systems support contracts, provide technical and logistics support to maintain weapons and other systems. These contracts are awarded by commands responsible for either building or procuring the system in the United States.

The concerns raised with this process over the years have centered on contract management and oversight. Despite the fact that the Defense Department has continually updated its written guidance to Defense officials charged with oversight of contractor performance,[4] it (DoD) has faced continuing problems related to a lack of visibility over the totality of contractor support at deployed locations; a lack of adequate contract oversight personnel; the failure to collect and share institutional knowledge on the use of contractors at deployed locations; and limited or no training of military personnel in the use of contractors as part of their pre-deployment training or professional military education.[5]

What this review of DoD contractor support reinforces is that where strong oversight and management is provided, contractor-provided services are dispensed in an economical and efficient manner. When the customer (e.g., military unit) commits itself to consistently reviewing the contractor's work for contract compliance, savings are realized, delays in completing critical contract task orders are minimized, and contractor's cost control incentives are preserved.

PRIVATIZATION IN CONTRACTING: THE IRAQI MODEL

The heightened awareness of issues related to privatization in the Global War on Terror (GWOT) was fueled in 2007 by the civilian deaths attributed by Iraqis to improper discipline by the Blackwater security firm. And this had not been the first incident where the oversight and management of outsourced requirements in Iraq had been questioned. In addressing contracting fraud before the Senate Judiciary Committee in March of 2007, the Acting DoD Inspector General stated:

> The presence of the Defense Criminal Investigative Service (DCIS) in the region has led to 83 investigations. Our investigations have focused on matters such as bribery, theft, gratuities, bid rigging, product substitution, and conflicts of interest. These alleged crimes expose U.S. and coalition forces to substandard equipment and services, or shortages that aggravate an already harsh and harmful environment. Currently DCIS is conducting 56 investigations involving war profiteering, contract fraud, and contract corruption in Iraq. . . . The criminal activities being investigated involve members of the U.S. Armed Forces, U.S. contractor personnel, as well as foreign personnel. For example, in January 2004, an investigation was initiated on information from the Defense Contract Audit Agency concerning allegations of kickbacks and gratuities that were solicited and/or received by Kellogg, Brown & Root (KBR)

employees. KBR has also been alleged to have been overcharging for food and fuel.[6]

The army's Logistics Civil Augmentation Program (LOGCAP) contract was by far the largest logistics support contract used by DoD in support of U.S. forces in Iraq. Like most other support contracts in Iraq and Afghanistan, the LOGCAP contract was a cost-plus award fee contract. Cost-plus contracts allow the contractor to be reimbursed for reasonable, allowable, and allocable costs incurred to the extent prescribed in the contract. A cost-plus award fee contract provides financial incentives on the basis of performance. These contracts allow the government to evaluate a contractor's performance according to specified criteria and to grant an award amount within designated parameters. Award fees can serve as a valuable tool to help control program risk and encourage excellence in contract performance. To reap the advantages that cost-plus award fee contracts offer, the government must implement an effective award fee process.

Recurring contractor problems under the LOGCAP contract such as poor cost reporting, difficulties with producing and meeting schedules, and weaknesses in purchasing system controls made this contract difficult to administer. An element of these concerns may be the sheer size of the contract, as LOGCAP was providing life and logistics support for more than 165,000 soldiers and civilians under difficult circumstances in Iraq. A significant aspect of the problems faced in Iraq was the lack of clarification (called "definitizing") of task orders, that is, a timely reaching of agreement with the contractor on the determination of contract terms, specifications, and cost. Delays in clarifying task orders make cost-control incentives under these award fee contracts less effective. Equally significant, the army held few if any award fee boards in Iraq, although they were required every six months under the contract, because the customer military units did not evaluate and document the contractor's performance.[7]

In response to these GAO concerns raised in its 2004 review, the army issued the first DoD–wide instruction on the use of contractors to support deployed forces in October 2005, which addressed many of the concerns raised above.[8] A subsequent December 2006 review of the implementation of this instruction, however, found that: (1) DoD continued to lack the capability to provide military commanders with information on the totality of contractor support available to their deployed forces in Iraq; (2) too few contract oversight personnel precluded DoD from obtaining reasonable assurance that contractors were meeting contract requirements at every location where work was being performed; (3) DoD had made few efforts to leverage its institutional knowledge and experiences using contractors to support deployed forces, despite facing many of the same difficulties managing contractors in Iraq that it faced in prior military operations; (4) lessons learned on the use of contractor support at deployed locations were not routinely gathered and shared; and (5) improvements had not been made to include more information on the use of contractors in pre-deployment training.[9]

In follow-up oversight reporting in January 2008, while acknowledging some improvement, GAO found that, based on the Iraqi experience, several challenges will need to be addressed by DoD to improve the oversight and management of contractors supporting deployed forces in future operations and to ensure those forces receive the support they require in an effective and efficient manner. Those challenges, in their view, included a number of broader issues, to include that: (1) contractors in the future are fully incorporated as part of the total force; (2) the proper balance of contractors and military personnel in future contingencies and operations must be determined; (3) DoD must resolve how it will integrate its effort with other government agencies in future operations; and (4) DoD must address and incorporate the use and role of contractors in its plans to expand and transform the army and Marine Corps.[10]

It has been in the area of security contracting, however, that DoD has faced its most difficult challenges. In the section that follows, privatized Defense security contracting is reviewed as well as DoD General Counsel actions to ensure contractor personnel comply with not only international law requirements, but also provisions of the Uniform Code of Military Justice (UCMJ).

DEFENSE SECURITY CONTRACTING: ENFORCING ACCOUNTABILITY

Following the end of major combat actions in Iraq at the end of April 2003, coalition forces began employing civilian contractors in a number of ways to contribute to post-conflict security throughout Iraq. During this phase of initial support for the new transition government of Iraq, the U.S. determined that there was no legal prohibition against using contractors where the risk of direct confrontation with a *uniformed enemy* was not probable, and thus their use would not rise to the level of "taking a direct part in hostilities."[11] During this transition phase, the United States determined it would be a step backward to prohibit contractor security services from being used to provide security against terrorists or other criminal elements, and that these functions were appropriate for civilian contractors.[12] This was especially important in a time of constrained force structures and exacerbated troop rotation concerns within the army and Marine Corps.

The United States viewed the security operations not only in Iraq but also in Afghanistan to be against remnants of the former regime, local criminal elements, and indigenous and foreign terrorists, thus not controlled by rules applicable when a uniformed armed force of a sovereign nation was engaged. Since the security operations being conducted did not constitute major combat operations, and coalition forces were supporting democratically elected governments there, these operations were considered more analogous to stability operations or operations in support of foreign internal defense. The DoD Deputy General Counsel (International Affairs) has defined the situation in these countries as follows:

> Currently, operations both in Iraq and Afghanistan are in the transition, or stability operations, phase of an international armed conflict. (In Iraq, operations may also be characterized as post-occupation.) Application of the law of war in the fact situations presented by current operations should not be viewed as the same as during a period of major combat operations of an international armed conflict. Resolution of the inquiry rests on this and other relevant facts and requires a careful mission analysis to determine whether the particular task, in the circumstances in which it is likely to be performed, is highly likely to place the contractors in direct contact or confrontation with hostile forces. [13]

The "stability" operations described above are those operations where there is no longer a risk of direct contact with or confrontation with hostile forces. While private security contractors are not precluded from participating during combatant operations, their role must be carefully tailored to preclude their use as combatants. In stability operations of the kind currently being undertaken in Afghanistan, and Iraq previously, where the possibility of traditional military force-on-force confrontation no longer exists, they, the private security firms, are permitted to participate in a broad range of security activities in support of the coalition forces and the government.

The stability operations described above are controlled by the provisions of the October 2005 DoD Instruction signed by the Under Secretary of Defense for Acquisition, Technology, and Logistics. [14] That directive requires that when using contractors for security services, the purpose must be to perform other than uniquely military functions. A specific paragraph of the Instruction provides that whether a particular use of contract security services is permissible is dependent on the facts. [15] As stated in the DoD Deputy General Counsel's Memorandum, the private security companies in Afghanistan, and Iraq previously, "are being employed for security missions that would normally be performed by the host government." [16] This use is entirely consistent with the mandates within the two applicable Security Council Resolutions calling on the Coalition to assist the host nation directly in the maintenance of stability and security. [17]

There are distinct limits on how these private security firms can be used, however, even in stability operations of the kind described. As noted in the 2006 DoD General Counsel Memorandum, the private firms should not be employed where the likelihood of direct participation in hostilities is high. The Memorandum further indicated that it would be improper to assign the private security company personnel to quick-reaction-force missions, local patrolling, or military convoy security operations where the likelihood of hostile contact is high.[18] Activities that are authorized under these security contracts were described by the Deputy General Counsel as follows:

> Commanders may employ such contractor personnel at military compounds only for individual self-defense, defense of others in the vicinity, and defense of critical military property and supplies. Such use must be consistent with the terms of their contracts.[19]

USE OF DEADLY FORCE BY CONTRACTOR PERSONNEL

As important as determination of the missions these private security companies (PSCs) can be assigned are the circumstances under which the personnel of these PSCs can respond to hostile acts or intent with deadly force. Unlike military personnel who are guided by rules of engagement (ROE) which derive from the Law of Armed Conflict, contractor personnel are civilians who are not subject to the military or legal norms reflected in the Geneva Conventions of 1929 and 1949 or the Hague Conventions of 1899 and 1907, in that they are not combatants under the law of war.[20] The Rules on the Use of Force (RUF) for contractor personnel are those set forth in the contracts themselves and in directives issued by each combatant commander.

Clear guidance for contractor personnel and provisions on their conduct that were to be incorporated in contracts signed by private security companies were clearly enunciated for all Central Command contractors and contractor personnel in a December 2005 message by USCENTCOM. As stated in this unclassified message, "[c]ontract security personnel always retain their ability to exercise self-defense against hostile acts or demonstrated hostile intent, but are not authorized to take a direct part in offensive operations."[21] The message further stated: "Notwithstanding any Iraqi regulations relating to private security company use of deadly force solely to protect property of any type, DoD contract security can be specifically authorized to protect designated mission essential and U.S. national security equipment/property with force, including deadly force."[22]

All guidance changed in Baghdad following the Blackwater incident on September 6, 2007. In that incident, Blackwater employees fired on Iraqi civilians that contract security personnel claimed had committed a premeditated attack on their convoy. The Iraqi citizens involved, and subsequently the Iraqi government, alleged but never established that Blackwater security employees wantonly fired on unarmed civilians. The Deputy Secretary of Defense, in a September 25, 2007, memorandum, held all combatant commanders responsible in their areas of responsibility for oversight and management of DoD contractors and for discipline of DoD contractor personnel when appropriate.[23]

This Memorandum, directed to the secretaries of the military departments, combatant commanders, directors of defense agencies, and directors of DoD field activities, required a complete review of the management of DoD contractors.[24] A key element of this memorandum was the emphasis that DoD contractor personnel, regardless of nationality, accompanying U.S. armed forces, are currently subject to UCMJ jurisdiction.[25] The Memorandum further stated:

> Commanders have UCMJ authority to disarm, apprehend, and detain DoD contractors suspected of having committed a felony offense in violation of the Rules on the Use of Force (RUF), or outside the scope of their authorized mission, and to conduct the basic UCMJ pretrial process and trial procedures currently applicable to the courts-martial of military service members. Commanders also have available to them contract and administrative remedies, and other remedies, including discipline and possible criminal prosecution.[26]

Just as significant as the Deputy Secretary's memorandum in detailing the authority enjoyed by the combatant commanders, the Military Extraterritorial Jurisdiction Act (MEJA) of 2000[27] provides federal jurisdiction over felony offenses committed outside the United States by contractor personnel of any federal agency or provisional authority whose employment relates to supporting the DoD mission. Implementing guidance under this act is provided through DoD instruction[28] and military department regulations. This DoD Instruction requires Defense Department coordination with the Department of Justice for the return to the United States of contractor personnel subject to MEJA for prosecution.

Further, under the Deputy Secretary's memorandum described above, combatant commanders and all other addressees are required to ensure that: (1) all required clauses are included in DoD contracts when contract performance requires contractors and contractor personnel to accompany U.S. forces; (2) contractor personnel who are suspected of committing a felony are prevented from leaving the country until approved by the senior commander in country; (3) RUF are reviewed periodically and changed accordingly to ensure the risk of innocent civilian casualties is minimized; and (4) combatant commanders are directed to require contractors to provide copies of their standard operating procedures and guidance to their employees on escalation of the use of force, the use of deadly force, and the rules for interaction with host country nationals.[29] Compliance with these dictates since 2007, just as in all other areas where oversight and management of defense outsourcing has been enhanced, has greatly improved relations with local civilian leadership and citizens in areas in which U.S. forces are operating.[30]

Statistics alone don't begin to show the degree to which privatization has penetrated the assignment of requirements within the Department of Defense in Operations Iraqi Freedom and Enduring Freedom. Many tasks and services once reserved exclusively for government employees are being handled by civilian contractor employees. For example, private contractors provide security, perform equipment repair, do minor construction, and provide intelligence services. At forward deployed locations, they are providing laundry and food services, as well as systems support, and technical and logistics support to maintain weapons and other systems.

Contractors currently write reports analyzing intelligence data that are passed up the line to on-scene commanders, as well as supply and maintain software programs that integrate data used to track terrorist suspects and determine what targets to eliminate in critical areas of Iraq and Afghanistan. Contractors also provide sophisticated tools to help individual agencies communicate with each other, and they supply security elements to protect critical networks from outside tampering. These functions encompass vital support to our military forces engaged in combat operations in Iraq and Afghanistan to include security for convoys, sites, personnel, and the like.

The numbers employed under government contracts in Afghanistan, and Iraq previously, for functions once carried out by the U.S. military can only be estimated. As GAO noted, it was reported that as of March 2006, there were a total of 181 private security companies with just over 48,000 employees working in Iraq.[31] Private security contractors constitute a small but significant portion of the many thousands of individuals employed under U.S. government contracts to perform the spectrum of functions once carried out by U.S. military personnel. According to a July 2007 news report, some 182,000 were employed under U.S. government contracts in Iraq alone at that time.[32]

This emphasis on contracting out has led to allegations of fraud and other misconduct, to include kickbacks, bid rigging, embezzlement, and fraudulent overbilling. While IG and Defense and Service Criminal Investigative Service investigations have uncovered much of this misconduct, the cost has been high. Equally significant, contracts for security services have engendered more visible concerns where host nation civilians have been killed by security personnel.

This has led to a re-emphasis on oversight and management on the part of the Congress, the various Departments and the combatant commands. The DoD has been highly visible in this effort to correct deficiencies in the contracting process. Through top-down guidance, as in the 2007 Deputy Secretary's memorandum, and through carefully drafted DoD instructions, this Department has responded to these concerns with an effort to ensure that contracts clearly and accurately specify the terms and conditions under which the contractor is to perform, describe the specific support relationship between the contractor and the Department, and contain standardized clauses to ensure adequate visibility of contractor personnel. More significantly, additional resources have been committed to ensuring effective oversight and management of the contracts' terms.

With respect to contracts for security services, DoD has instituted precise requirements for the use of force by contractor personnel and the training required to develop accountability and maintain weapons proficiency, and has developed clear requirements for the continuing review of security contractors' standard operating procedures. The extension of U.S. jurisdiction for criminal misconduct on the part of contractor personnel will likewise ensure accountability for all personnel supporting the force in theater.

The proliferation of contractor support personnel in Operation Enduring Freedom and Iraqi Freedom previously is unlike anything the United States has been tasked with coordinating since the occupation following the Second World War. The efforts undertaken, largely by DoD, since the clear evidence of the level of overreaching on the part of contractor personnel became evident in early 2005, will provide an effective road map for future operations of this scale.

Chapter Fourteen

Stabilization Operations

Addressing Post-Conflict Unrest In Iraq and Afghanistan

Civilian agencies, and private civilian contractors who execute their policies, currently play a major role in stabilization and reconstruction operations in Iraq and Afghanistan alongside their military counterparts. The NATO, State Department (USAID), Department of Defense (DoD) and nongovernmental organizations' (NGO) initiatives currently working in Afghanistan (and previously in Iraq) involve thousands of military personnel and civilian contractors supporting hundreds of projects designed to ensure these two nations not only survive but grow in self-sufficiency.

The road map for the coordination of these initiatives must establish a sequencing of actions for progress across a range of operations. The activities involved must be designed to lead to the desired endstate for the assisted nations. These activities include, by necessity and design, the plans and direction for actions the nations themselves should embark upon. The planning process involves a security component, as well as both economic and governance initiatives. Postconflict reconstruction and growth involves both an initiation phase and an implementation phase. Key to successful execution of the implementation phase is the effort to build the indigenous military and police forces to provide for the nation's own security. The execution phase is dominated by those activities and agencies that ensure the basic needs of the people are met and that prepare the people in Iraq and Afghanistan to provide those needs for themselves. The governance piece is the most complex and encompasses the necessary activities to establish government institutions and an environment free from the threat of renewed conflict. This framework offers tremendous advantages in that the functions can be assigned to international agencies and nongovernmental organizations to facilitate the distribution of responsibilities along each of the three distinct lanes of operation.

THE REALITIES OF THE POST-CONFLICT ENVIRONMENT

The environment immediately following the initial combatant operations in Iraq and Afghanistan provided important lessons concerning security, governance, and reconstruction realities. The immediate and primary concern after the cessation of open hostilities was security, as it must be in every conflict. In the immediate aftermath of combatant operations, local security forces are likely to be unable, unavailable, or unwilling to address civilian lawlessness and violence. For this reason, U.S. and coalition forces must have clear orders and an effective plan to provide law enforcement in the major population centers immediately after hostilities cease. This did not occur in Baghdad, and because it did not, street crime, looting, and general lawlessness were rampant. In the end, this failure greatly slowed the stabilization process.

An important element of the need for immediate security is the concomitant requirement of a plan to retrain and to equip local police and security forces. This plan must be given the highest priority and be properly staffed and funded. Initially in Baghdad, this task fell to five members of the Justice Department and became a task impossible. In Afghanistan as well, both effective training and an appropriate pay scale to ensure sustainability of a security force were not properly focused at first. In both countries, the institutions (Interior Ministry and Justice Ministry) that stood behind the local police were initially lacking or inadequate. Law and order, the desired endstate when an effective security force is in place, can only succeed if the other elements of public safety are present and properly functioning, to include a judicial system with courts and prisons.

The recognition that security, stabilization, and reconstruction are interdependent and must have integrated strategies is critical. When security was assured in areas of both nations, the opportunity to undertake ambitious reconstruction goals was possible, but far less so when the security footprint was smaller and more tenuous. It is extremely important to examine the Provincial Reconstruction Team (PRT) model currently being used in Afghanistan as an effective approach for linking security and reconstruction.

Just as these elements are interdependent, their success largely depends on a funding stream that allows for a rapid dispersal of aid to local leaders and contractors, who are vital to success. Local government officials and community leaders must be identified and relied upon for advice as to the local contractors with the ability to get things done and who are reliable and honest. Advance planning before and during the combat phase must include the prepositioning of resources, both financial and physical, so that local communities and their leaders can be given a catalytic boost when local governance is reestablished. The experience in Iraq has shown that the coordination of resources is key to successful implementation, and that failure to coordinate between agencies often results in overlapping and duplicative effort, which can hinder progress on this important front. For example, in Baghdad and outlying communities after the cessation of hostilities, the coalition forces leadership, USAID (through its contractor Research Triangle Institute) and the Coalition Provisional Authority (CPA) all were engaged in attempting to reestablish local governance without effective coordination or planning. This led to identification of, and support for, different community leaders by organizations that should have been unified in their approach.

Similarly, the postconflict efforts in these two nations demonstrated that while reestablishing governance cannot occur overnight, it requires an understanding of local history and culture to be successful. While reestablishing functioning institutions is important, it is equally, if not more, important to gain the trust of the local populace in this effort. The local leaders must believe coalition forces are attempting to find local solutions for them rather than just imposing a Western system on their country. This is especially true in a country like Afghanistan with a history of oppressive governance and a tendency to be skeptical of imposed solutions. The local leaders must also be convinced that the commitment to their succeeding is long-term and not merely the imposition of a Western-style system that they will be uncomfortable with and unable to maintain into the future.

Just as establishing trust among the populace is critical, maintaining that trust is directly tied to the United States' ability, and that of the coalition in both countries, to deliver on our promises. Early in the postconflict stabilization of Iraq, the CPA promised dramatic and timely improvements to the Iraqi economy. When the coalition was unable to suppress the insurgency for a lengthy period resulting in critical delays in economic development, frustration mounted among the people and the fledgling Iraqi government. The key lesson was that coalition leaders must match authority and capacity in postconflict settings, while carefully managing the expectations of the local populace. More importantly, sound planning must ensure that right-sized missions are undertaken so that achievable goals can be met. As important as the matching of authority with capacity is the need to demonstrate the ability to implement projects quickly. The Commanders Emergency Response Fund (CERF) assisted in providing this capacity in Iraq at the local level, and is doing so in Afghanistan as well.

Finally, both Iraq and Afghanistan have shown that the speed with which we introduce private enterprise and promote economic development is fundamental to the success of the stabilization effort. The one–crop narcotic economy in Kabul poses special challenges to stabilization efforts because unless alternative livelihoods are provided, and quickly, the narcotic economy will likely take the whole process down. Fortunately, the Afghan people are motivated and dedicated, and the United States' extension of credit and assistance in the development of real alternatives, combined with effective training, will be key to success in Kabul.

BUILDING THE INSTITUTIONS AND LAWS OF A POSTCONFLICT DEMOCRACY

Rebuilding the foundations of a civil society and establishing effective governance is always the most difficult and time-consuming element of the transition process. A transfer of power from the intervening power to a newly established government, usually through both a security agreement as well as a strategic framework agreement (as in Iraq), is accompanied by the development and adoption of laws and regulations, training in their application and enforcement, investments in appropriate infrastructure, and the transfer to civilian control from the coalition leadership. This transfer to indigenous political institutions, to include functioning legislative bodies and accountable executives, requires both time and the willingness of local leaders to take ownership.

The most significant challenges faced by the fledgling governments include development of economic capacity, civilian control of security structures, and administering the rule of law. Building a viable economic base involves the creation of markets, the chartering of a banking system, and the development of a fair and accepted system of taxation. As the people in Iraq and Afghanistan transition from a society based upon imposed order to one based on openness and competition, they must also develop regulations to address clashing economic interests, legal systems to adjudicate disputes, and a political process with sufficient authority to check excessive executive behavior.

The most often cited failures in nation building include the failure to develop necessary local capacity, legitimacy, and effectiveness to sustain the rule of law and maintain order. Key to this challenge is effective civilian control of security structures, to include civilian police, civilian control of the military, and competent and respected defense and interior ministries. Similarly, administering the rule of law fairly and impartially is critical to the new government being perceived as having legitimacy, and key to this legitimacy is respect for the judiciary, the court system, the penal system, and the constitution under which they operate. Creating local capacity takes time, often far more time than donor countries and their citizens are willing to give the process. For this reason, timely development of effective local leadership and control is critical to a positive transition from stabilization to other stages of postconflict development.

FUTURE CONSIDERATIONS

For the United States to better assist in fostering the development of internal capacity in newly re-minted states like Iraq and Afghanistan, it must develop a *permanent* civilian capability that both complements our military effort and contributes to the leveraging of multilateral efforts. The United States began that effort six years ago when it established the Office of Stabilization and Reconstruction (S/CRS). With the signing of National Security Presidential Directive (NSPD) 44 a year later in 2005, and the issuance of DoD Directive 3000.05 that same year, an organization was created to lead interagency civilian efforts and coordination between these agencies and the military to help countries emerging from conflict build a sustainable government.

The purpose of S/CRS vis-a-vis civilian agencies is much like the Joint Chiefs of Staff (JCS) role with respect to the combatant commands. That charge is to lead the design of a common U.S. stabilization strategy in a given theater for civilian agencies, and between those agencies and the military. Like the JCS, which ensures that all forces function interoperably within a theatre, its task is to ensure all civilian capabilities are used effectively to achieve a common goal.

Other core elements are also critical to establishing a viable stabilization organization. The first is the capability to quickly deploy a competent field team to survey requirements and spearhead civilian program strategies on the ground. It should include a mix of economic, security, communications, construction, and political specialists. Presently, these teams are established by assignment on an ad hoc basis from various State Department posts, rather than serving in primary assignments where their expertise is constantly reinforced through continuous training. A permanent corps established under the aegis of S/CRS would ensure that the civilian side of the government has skills that more fully complement the military's capacity.

Provincial Reconstruction Teams (PRTs) in Afghanistan reflect a successful application of these principles in that these teams include a mix of military and civilian personnel and can be tailored to reflect the level of threat in the area being worked. The capacity to deploy trained and capable civilians in military-led PRTs increases their effectiveness and permits stabilization and reconstruction efforts to begin under the military umbrella. The PRT can help build the host nation's legitimacy and effectiveness in providing security to its citizens and delivering essential government services. The focus of these combined military and civil efforts is to diminish the means and motivations for conflict, while developing local institutions so they can take the lead role in national governance.

The PRT can bridge the gap between conflict and stability and assist in areas that have not been pacified sufficiently to remove security forces. The military can operate effectively but lacks the development skills to enhance economic viability and deliver essential public services. The PRT solves this problem and, when stability objectives are fulfilled, can be dismantled in favor of traditional development programs.

The State and Defense Departments have begun to take steps to better coordinate stability and reconstruction activities, but key challenges remain. Without an interagency planning framework that better defines roles and responsibilities, as contemplated by NSPD 44, unity of effort may remain difficult to achieve and DoD–centric planning will likely continue. More importantly, unless the State Department develops and implements a credible plan to build a permanent civilian stabilization organization, rather than the current ad hoc approach, DoD will continue to be heavily relied upon to provide the needed expertise for transition operations.

Chapter Fifteen

Environmental Terrorism

From Oil Fires to Fouling Gulf Waters

The Iraqi invasion of Kuwait in August 1990 and the resulting environmental carnage caused by the burning of oil wells and the fouling of Gulf waters in early 1991 have heightened international concern for the adverse environmental effects of armed conflict. The questions that arise relate to the sufficiency of the existing legal regime intended to protect the environment, and to parallel concerns that more extensive strictures could restrict legitimate defensive military operations under the law of armed conflict. This chapter examines these issues, and concludes that the current framework of relevant international law, when understood and applied, protects both the environment and the broader interests represented in the law of armed conflict.

THE DEBATE

The Charter of the United Nations both prohibits the unlawful use of force by states and guarantees the right of self-defense against such unlawful coercion. Articles 2(4) and 51 of the Charter, together with the Hague and Geneva Conventions limiting methods and means of conducting warfare and protecting combatants, noncombatants, and their environment, create a comprehensive legal fabric designed to limit the destructiveness of international armed conflict. Inherent within the law of armed conflict is the understanding that even the most sophisticated and precise weapons systems will exact a price upon the environment.

Environmentalists contend that that price is too high, and demand that any system destructive of the environment be banned. Those responding during

133

the First Gulf War and subsequently explain that only through a military capability such as reflected in the coalition responses in 1991 in Kuwait, in 2001 in Afghanistan, and in 2003 in Iraq can the environment, in the long term, best be preserved. Those responding further remind the environmentalists that had existing environmental provisions within the law of armed conflict been adhered to by the Iraqis in 1991, the destruction of Kuwaiti resources would have been minimal.

DEVELOPMENT OF RESTRICTIONS ON THE USE OF THE ENVIRONMENT

Restrictions on the use of the environment have a long history in both national initiatives and international agreement and custom. The practice and acceptance by states of certain restrictions and limitations on the use of the environment have been observed both with regard to means and methods of warfare and to protection of victims. These two strands have come to be known as the Hague and Geneva law, respectively.

In the United States, for example, the army's Lieber Code of 1863 restricted means and methods of warfare for Union forces during the Civil War so as to protect property whose destruction was not necessary to the war effort.[1] The 1868 Declaration of St. Petersburg, equally significant, proclaimed that the only legitimate objective of states during war is to weaken the military forces of the enemy.[2] In the years following, largely as a result of the massive destruction and loss of life occasioned by the American Civil War, the Crimean War, and the Wars of German Unification, an international consensus to limit wars' destructiveness developed and found expression in the Hague Conventions of 1899 and 1907.

The theme of the peace conferences at The Hague centered on agreement among participants that the right of belligerents in an armed conflict to choose methods or means of warfare is not without limit, and that wanton destruction, superfluous injury, and unnecessary suffering should be eliminated by regulation from warfare. The Regulations Annexed to Hague Convention IV of 1907 Respecting the Laws and Customs of War on Land remain the centerpiece of the two conferences.[3] It is important to note that during the Nuremberg Trials following World War II, the International Tribunal found the Annexed Regulations to be "declaratory of the laws and customs of war," and thus applicable to all nations whether parties to Hague Convention IV or not.[4]

The Regulations annexed to Hague Convention IV have application to the environmental depredation which occurred in the first Gulf conflict and similar situations thereafter. Article 22 provides that "the right of belligerents to adopt means of injuring the enemy is not unlimited." Article 23(g) specifies that it is especially forbidden "to destroy or seize the enemy's property, unless such destruction or seizure be imperatively demanded by the necessities of war." Article 46 adds that "private property cannot be confiscated" by an occupying force, and Article 47 that "pillage is formally forbidden." To further clarify the restrictions upon occupying powers such as Iraq during the conflict with Kuwait, Article 55 states that "the occupying State shall be regarded only as administrator . . . of . . . real estate, forests and agricultural estates belonging to the hostile State, and situated in the occupied country. It must safeguard the capital of these properties, and administer them in accordance with the rules of usufruct."[5] Had these strictures been observed by Iraq in 1991, there would have been no significant violation of the Kuwaiti environment.

The Geneva Conventions of 1949 merely build upon the requirements and prohibitions of the 1907 Conference at The Hague. Article 50 of Geneva Convention I (Wounded and Sick in the Field), for example, provides that it shall be a grave breach to commit extensive destruction and appropriation of property that is not justified by necessity and is carried out unlawfully and wantonly. Article 51 of Geneva Convention II (Wounded and Sick at Sea) merely restates this rule. The fourth Geneva Convention (Geneva Civilians Convention), while restating in Article 147 the general protections for the environment seen in the Hague Rules, also places significant requirements upon the occupying power. Article 53 provides the "any destruction by the Occupying Power of real or personal property belonging individually or collectively to private persons, or to the State, or to other public authorities, or to social or cooperative organizations, is prohibited, except where such destruction is rendered absolutely necessary by military operations." It can certainly be argued that Kuwait's territorial seas, bays, beaches, and oilfields were subjected to wanton unlawful destruction unjustified by military necessity.

The importance of the Geneva Conventions of 1949 to preservation of the environment extends far beyond the provisions of the articles themselves. An enforcement regime represented in articles common to each of the four Conventions requires that grave breaches by each of the contracting parties be identified and addressed.[6] Moreover, another article common to each requires penal sanctions.[7] That article, the cornerstone of the enforcement system, obligates each contracting party to: enact implementing legislation; search for persons alleged to have committed breaches of the Conventions; and bring such persons before its own courts or, if it prefers, hand them over for trial to another state party concerned. Article 146 of Geneva Convention IV further provides that the accused persons shall benefit from proper trial and defense no less favorable than the safeguards provided by Article 105 (and those following) of the 1949 Geneva Convention Relative to the Treatment of Prisoners of War. When these provisions addressing violations by individuals are considered in conjunction with the requirement in Article 3 of Hague Convention IV (that violating states are liable to pay compensation to the injured states), a very comprehensive scheme, and one appropriate for addressing the events in the First Gulf War, is apparent.[8]

PROSCRIPTION OF ENVIRONMENTAL MODIFICATION

Although the United States renounced the use of climate modification techniques in July 1972, it was not until the entry into force of the 1977 Convention on the Prohibition of Military or Any Other Hostile Use of Environmental Modification Techniques (ENMOD Convention) that the use of this weapon was legally proscribed.[9] In brief, this Convention commits each party not to engage in military or any other hostile use of environmental modification techniques that cause widespread, long-lasting, or severe destruction, damage or injury to another state that is party.[10] A formal "understanding" among all the participants defines the phrase "widespread, long-lasting or severe." "Widespread" is defined as "encompassing an area on the scale of several hundred square kilometers"; "long-lasting" is defined as "lasting for a period of months, or approximately a season"; and "severe" is defined as "involving serious or significant disruption or harm to human life, natural or economic resources or other assets."[11]

Kuwait is (and was in 1990) a party of long-standing to this Convention. Iraq is one of seventeen nations that that are signatories but (having failed to ratify) never became parties. While under Article 18 of the Vienna Convention on Treaties a signatory is obligated not to "defeat the object and purpose" of the agreement, the ENMOD Convention itself addresses relations specifically between full, ratifying parties; its enforcement mechanisms, accordingly, could not have been brought to bear on Iraq. In light of Security Council Resolution 674 (1990), which made Iraq "liable for any loss, damage or injury arising in regard to Kuwait and third States, and their nationals and corporations, as a result of the invasion and illegal occupation of Kuwait by Iraq," a complaint under the ENMOD Convention was not necessary.

1977 GENEVA PROTOCOL I

Protocol I Additional to the 1949 Geneva Conventions was negotiated to protect not only the population of countries at war but also the environment as such. Two articles in the Protocol combine to prohibit the use of methods and means of warfare that that are intended or "may be expected" to cause widespread, long-term, and severe damage to the environment: Articles 35(3) and 55(1) attempt to prevent intended or reasonably predictable excessive environmental damage. Battlefield damage incidental to warfare is not proscribed by these provisions, however. [12]

Neither the United States nor Iraq is a party to the Protocol. During negotiations in Geneva, the United States made clear its understanding that nuclear weapons were not to be included within the scope of Protocol I. During the ratification debate, however, it became clear that many nations took the more expansive view that Articles 35(3) and 55(1) would indeed place limitations upon nuclear weapons. Should the provisions be held to apply to nuclear arms in the future, the careful balance fashioned with the other nuclear powers in existing agreements affecting those weapons would be adversely impacted. [13] It can be persuasively argued, however, that the prohibitions included within Protocol I merely replicate the regime established to protect the environment in Geneva Convention IV of 1949.

THE INTERNATIONAL RESPONSE TO THE GULF CARNAGE

On March 1, 1991, Japan's parliamentary Minister for the Environment proposed that the Governing Council of the United Nations Environmental Program adopt a declaration urging that the kind of environmental destruction observed in the Gulf should never again occur as an act of war. That same day, French representatives to the Governing Council proposed two initiatives: prohibiting the targeting of ecological areas, and protecting world heritage monuments in time of war.

At Nairobi, Kenya, on May 20,1991, the sixteenth session of the Governing Council of the United Nations Environmental Program was convened. The Japanese and French proposals were raised, as were Canadian and Greenpeace concerns. The latter two announced their intention to host international conferences of legal experts to explore ways to strengthen international law to protect the environment more effectively.

A one-day conference in London on June 3, 1991, sponsored by Greenpeace, the London School of Economics, and Britain's Center for Defense Studies considered a possible "Fifth" Geneva Convention on the Protection of the Environment in Time of Armed Conflict. Greenpeace urged the 120 participants, including twenty-four representatives from government and environmental groups, to create a new convention which would state that the environment may not be used as a weapon, that weapons aimed at the environment must be banned, and that indirect damage to the environment must be forbidden.

This was followed by a July 1991 meeting of legal experts in Ottawa, Canada, that reviewed the use of the environmental weapon in the Gulf context and examined existing international law regulating such use. U.S. participants at the Ottawa meeting carefully underscored the merits of the existing regulatory regime, which is based on the principles of necessity and proportionality under the law of armed conflict. The U.S. concern regarding more restrictive environmental provisions is that they could be implemented only at the expense of otherwise lawful military operations—such as attacking targets which require fuel-air explosives for their destruction.

CONCLUSIONS FROM THE FIRST GULF WAR

Because the environment was ravaged during the First Gulf conflict, some considered the relevant legal regime inadequate. In point of fact, the international agreements and customary international law to which Iraq was legally bound would have precluded the carnage had it complied with their terms. Conversely, had a more restrictive environmental regime been applied that prohibited the prudent use of modern weapons systems (systems which have some inherent incidental and collateral environmental impact), the effective coalition response to Iraqi aggression may not have been possible. [14]

Chapter Sixteen

Defense of Critical Infrastructure Systems from Terrorists

Computer Network Defense (CND)

In May 2007, coordinated cyber attacks originating in Moscow shut down the entire nation of Estonia. Nor has the United States been immune. In 1997, in an exercise emphasizing infrastructure security, the National Security Agency exposed the United States vulnerability to the disruption of computer operations at our major military commands at the hands of a hostile state or an organization with hostile intent.[1] A year earlier, U.S. authorities had detected the introduction of a program, called a "sniffer," into computers at NASA's Goddard Space Flight Center, permitting the perpetrator to download a large volume of complex telemetry information transmitted from satellites. The Deputy Attorney General reported that the "sniffer" had remained in place for a significant period of time.[2]

Of equal concern, an FBI report in 1999 detailed Chinese efforts to attack U.S. government information systems, including the White House network.[3] These actual and projected interstate intrusions into government computer networks once thought secure raise important questions concerning what, if any, rights in self-defense are triggered by such attacks, and more importantly, how would the right of self-defense, if attack impacts a vital national security interest, be translated into effective rules of engagement, and more specifically, legally defensible targeting decisions.

The world of information operations represents an environment created by the confluence of cooperative networks of computers, information systems, and telecommunication infrastructures. The concern we address relates to the threat posed to these systems when operations are unlawfully disrupted, denied, or degraded, or when secure information that is stored in computers or computer networks is destroyed, compromised, or altered in such a way that it has a destructive effect on the national security interests of a nation. Computer espionage, computer network attacks, as well as the subversion of political, economic and/or nonmilitary information bearing on a nation's capabilities and vulnerabilities may well constitute an unlawful use of force warranting a military response under traditional international law principles.

The threshold issues that emerge are (1) which peacetime interstate activities within the telecommunications highway constitute a threat or use of force, (2) when does such a threat constitute an attack under international law such that the right of self-defense exists, and (3) what is an appropriate response. To answer these questions, we must understand the military applications of information technology. This requires an understanding of the Internet. The Internet was originally a network of computers linked by communications infrastructure and managed by the Department of Defense (DoD) in the 1970s. The process through which the internal computer networks of universities and private research facilities were merged was through the development of hypertext, created in 1989 as the primary platform of the Internet. Hypertext translates diverse computer protocols into standard format.

The hypertext process, while extremely beneficial to both the military and civilian sectors, has created vulnerabilities. The World Wide Web, the full implementation of the Internet, which is at once the heart of the Defense Reform Initiative and key to the reengineering and streamlining of our business practices, can provide our adversaries with a potent instrument to obtain, correlate, evaluate, and *adversely affect* an unprecedented volume of aggregated information critical to proper management of DoD and U.S. infrastructure capabilities.

This chapter addresses these attacks on U.S. infrastructure. Even though international law could not have anticipated these specific information-warfare concerns when the Hague Conventions of 1899 and 1907—addressing means and methods of warfare—were negotiated, the drafters of those conventions did anticipate technological change. The "Martins Clause," included within both Hague II and Hague IV of the 1899 Conventions, provides that even in cases not covered by specific agreements, civilians and combatants remain under the protection and authority of principles of international law derived from established custom, principles of humanity, and from the dictates of public conscience, and that they are not left to the arbitrary judgment of military commanders.[4] This provision was considered necessary to prevent future unnecessary and/or disproportionate destruction from weapons systems not yet developed. The drafters had just witnessed unimaginable carnage in the Crimean War and the American Civil War resulting from advanced rifling techniques and other innovations, and were cognizant that warfare was rapidly changing. As Greenberg et al., so accurately state, as a result of the Martins Clause, "attacks will be judged largely by their effects, rather than by their methods."[5]

THE LEGAL AND OPERATIONAL PARAMETERS FOR RESPONSE

Because the real-time relationship between threat and threat recognition is often compressed in the techno-violence arena, legal recourse and strategy development are often severely limited. This is especially true of the nonmilitary initiatives that may be considered in response to cyber attack, although always the option of choice where available. Traditional means of conflict resolution, authorized by law and customary practice, are often precluded because attacks on computer systems are, by nature, covert in execution, unacknowledged by the state or group sponsor, and practiced with silent effectiveness.

It must be noted, however, that noncoercive efforts to counter attacks on computer systems and telecommunications networks are also important. Diplomatic action, alone or in concert with allies or international organizations with conceivable successful impact upon a state or group considering such a cyber initiative, should be considered and employed wherever possible. In 1998, for example, the UN General Assembly passed Resolution 53/70,[6] an initiative of the Russian Federation, that called upon member states "to promote at multilateral levels the consideration of existing and potential threats in the field of information security."[7] The United States supported this resolution with the following pertinent comments:

> The General Assembly's adoption of the resolution in plenary session will launch the international community on a complex enterprise encompassing many interrelated factors which delegates . . . do not ordinarily address. For example, the topic includes technical aspects that relate to global communications—as well as non-technical issues associated with economic cooperation and trade, intellectual property rights, law enforcement, anti-terrorist cooperation , and other issues that are considered in the Second and Sixth Committees. Further the actions and programs of governments are by no means the only appropriate focus, for the initiative also involves important concerns of individuals, associations, enterprises, and other organizations that are active in the private sector.[8]

Despite such international initiatives focusing on multilateral cooperation, the opportunity to look to outside assistance in protecting secure transmissions and critical systems in circumstances where our national security is threatened is likely illusory. That authority will most likely remain exclusively within the National Command Authorities.

The rules of necessity and proportionality in the information warfare scenario are given operational significance through rules of engagement (ROE). ROE are directives that a government may establish to define the circumstances and limitations under which its forces will initiate and continue responsive actions to eliminate the threat posed by an attack through technical or other means on critical communications/information infrastructure. In the United States' context, this ensures that National Command Authorities' guidance for handling crisis responses to techno-violence and other threats is provided, through the Joint Chiefs of Staff (JCS), to subordinate headquarters and deployed U.S. forces both during armed conflict and in crisis periods short of war.

ROE reflect domestic law requirements and U.S. commitments to international law. They are impacted by political, as well as operational considerations. For the U.S. commander concerned with responding to a threat to his communications and command and control infrastructure, ROE represent limitations or upper bounds on how to utilize defensive and/or responsive systems and forces, without diminishing the authority to effectively protect his own critical infrastructure from attack.

Evolution of United States Rules of Engagement

Techno-violence against a critical U.S. computer system, whether information, communications, or command and control related, represents hostile activity which may trigger the applicable ROE. U.S. ROE provide the on-scene commander with the flexibility to respond to hostile intent as well as hostile acts and unconventional threats with minimum necessary force and to limit the scope and intensity of the threat. The strategy underlying the U.S. ROE seeks to terminate violence quickly and decisively, and on terms favorable to the United States. In October 1994, Secretary of Defense Aspen approved the Standing Rules of Engagement for U.S. Forces (SROE), which significantly broadened the scope of our national ROE.[9] As established in the SROE, U.S. policy, should deterrence fail, provides flexibility to respond to crises with options that are proportional to the provocation, designed to limit the scope and intensity of the conflict, discourage escalation, and achieve political and military objectives. The inherent right of self-defense establishes the policy framework for the SROE. These SROE are intended to provide general guidelines on self-defense and are applicable worldwide to all echelons of command, provide guidance governing the use of force consistent with mission accomplishment, and are to be used in operations other than war (to include response to terror violence), during transition from peacetime to armed conflict or war, and during armed conflict in the absence of superseding guidance.

The expanded national guidance represented in the 1994 SROE has greatly assisted in providing both clarity and flexibility of action for theater commanders. The approval by the Secretary of Defense has ensured consistency in the way all military commanders, wherever assigned, address unconventional threats such as those posed to advanced command and control infrastructure systems when these systems or computer networks are destroyed, compromised, or altered in such a way that it has a destructive effect on the national security interests of the nation.

Application of the Law of Targeting to Infrastructure Protection

The SROE, as they relate to information warfare, are implemented through the Law of Targeting, a subset of the Law of Armed Conflict. The Law of Targeting is based upon three fundamental principles. These are: (1) The right of states to adopt means of injuring the enemy is not unlimited; (2) the launching of attacks against the civilian population as such is prohibited; and (3) distinctions must be made between combatants and noncombatants, to the effect that noncombatants are spared to the extent possible. [10]

Because the Law of Armed Conflict is an eminently practical law which takes into account military efficiency, these basic principles are also consistent with the response authorized for nonviolent but equally destructive forms of coercive activity, such as sabotage of critical defense computer systems. Moreover, targeting theory is premised upon practical considerations that serve the purpose of defining the objects of legitimate and proportional response to each variant of aggression, whether it be an armed attack on U.S. facilities or an equally debilitating computer-assisted attack, and of providing functional targeting criteria to the responsible official, whether military or civilian.

The key, then, to an effective response to the threat posed by states or groups engaging in attacks against critical infrastructure must be the commitment to address the attacks within the scope of the Law of Armed Conflict. Recent U.S. administrations have appropriately treated cyber aggression as a variant of terrorist activity.

For the U.S., the issue remains, however, should the Critical Infrastructure Plan fail, as it did on September 11, 2001, what legal remedy could be applied under the Law of Armed Conflict. If a response is justified, as it was in Afghanistan, what targets in a perpetrator country are proportional to the threat posed by destruction or compromise of critical infrastructure. Again, our experience in addressing terrorism must be reviewed. The reason this is necessary is that the flexibility of the Law of Armed Conflict in addressing unconventional threats provides far more salient options than domestic law or intelligence law in cases where the very fiber of our national security is placed at risk.

For example, an unlawful entry into and/or compromise of a critical national security system by an individual or individuals can be viewed as criminal activity under the jurisdiction of Federal and state law enforcement officials. The same intrusion by the same individual or individuals could be viewed as lawful espionage or intelligence gathering practiced by all states. If, however, that intrusion and the debilitating effect it has on national security can appropriately be characterized as an attack on vital national interests, the range of options is greatly enhanced. [11]

This is important because the state or group attempting to compromise national security through the calculated sabotage of critical infrastructure *is attacking the nation*, not with bombs or bullets, but with the intent of destroying equally critical elements of national well-being and sovereignty. The loss of a power grid or a telecommunications network through computer-generated viruses for an extended period of time would have the capacity of placing more citizens at risk than a significant military threat.

The United States was jolted into an awareness of the changing character of aggression when its embassy in Tehran was seized on November 4, 1979, by Iranian militants who enjoyed the support of Ayatollah Khomeini's revolutionary government. [12] In August 1998, U.S. embassies in Nairobi and Dar es Salaam were the subject of unconventional warfare attacks, resulting in the significant loss of life in Nairobi. In the September 11, 2001, attacks, a U.S. response was only possible because of the linkage established between bin Laden's organization and the assault on U.S. personnel and property. [13] The thrust of the U.S. strategy, outlined in PDD 62 and reflected in Operation Enduring Freedom in Afghanistan, is to reclaim the initiative lost when the United States pursued a reactive policy toward unconventional threats and attacks, as represented by its inaction in response to the attacks on its embassies in Beirut, Nairobi, and Dar es Salaam, and on the *USS Cole.*

An examination of authorized responses (and the selection of appropriate targets) to techno-violence and other unconventional threats requires an understanding that these strategies do not follow any of the traditional military patterns. In fact, a fundamental characteristic of attacks on critical infrastructure and other prohibited targets is their violation of established norms of international law. The only norm for cyber terrorism and other terrorist attacks is effectiveness. While traditional international law requires discrimination among those affected by an attack and proportion in its intensity, the nature of information warfare and cyber terrorism is such that success is measured by the extent and duration of destructiveness to the systems targeted, with no concern for those affected.

For this reason, there must be an assured, effective reaction that imposes unacceptable costs on the perpetrators and those who make possible their activities. For domestic intruders, the criminal law may suffice. For those operating outside the targeted country, the reaction must counter the cyber terrorist's strategy within the parameters of international law and, in the U.S., policy directives such as PDD 62.

In this regard, a case for response in national self-defense is not persuasive either on the political or legal level unless a reasonable basis of necessity is perceived and carefully structured. Those to whom a justification is addressed (that is, other governments or the public) will consider whether it is well founded; they will not support the use of force as a purely discretionary act. An important dimension of this question then is: When is the use of force necessary to enforce adherence to the norm of information security? As Professor Lauterpacht has pointed out, every state judges "for itself, in the first instance, whether a case of necessity in self-defense has arisen" but that "it is obvious that the question of legality of action taken in self-preservation is suitable for determination and must ultimately be determined by a judicial authority or political body."[14] The United States has long taken the position that each nation is free to defend itself and is the "judge of what constitutes the right of self-defense and the necessity . . . of same."[15]

The decision to respond with force against techno-violence must always focus on the underlying political purpose of the state or group attempting to degrade or destroy an element of critical infrastructure, whether that element be commercial, communications, intelligence, or defense related. That purpose is unquestionably the degradation of critical systems leaving a country unable to defend itself militarily or protect itself from serious political or financial overreaching on the part of adversaries.

To counter this threat, the nation-state must fully implement the proactive policies represented in these Directives. This will require the fullest use of all the weapons in its arsenal. These should include not only those defensive and protective measures which reduce U.S. systems vulnerability, but also new legal tools and agreements on international sanctions, as well as the collaboration of other concerned governments. While the use of military power should be a last resort and when lesser means are not available, there will be instances where the use of force is the only alternative to eliminate the threat to critical civil or military infrastructure.

The thrust of this new, comprehensive strategy must be an effective, coordinated policy to address the threat posed by those willing to target our critical infrastructure and the commitment to hold those accountable responsible under the Law of Armed Conflict. For the United States, full implementation of the two PDDs should lead to increased planning for protective and defensive measures to address this challenge to national security, and where deterrence fails, to respond in a manner which eliminates the threat; rather than, as prior to September 11, 2001, treating each incident after the fact as a singular crisis provoked by international criminals. By treating cyber terrorists and others attempting to destroy critical infrastructure as participants in international coercion where clear linkage can be tied to a state actor, the right of self-defense against their sponsor is triggered, and responding coercion (political, economic, or military) may be the only proportional response to the threat.

THE WAY FORWARD

On June 23, 2009, then–Defense Secretary Robert Gates directed the Commander of U.S. Strategic Command (USSTRATCOM) to establish the United States Cyber Command (USCYBERCOM).[16] The command was fully activated on May 21, 2010, at Fort Meade. Maryland, and reached "fully operational" status in October 2010.[17] The command assumes responsibility for several existing organizations. The Joint Task Force for Global Network Operations (JTF-GNO) and the Joint Functional Component Command for Network Warfare (JFCC-NW) were dissolved in October 2010. The Defense Information Systems Agency, where JTF-GNO now operates, provides technical assistance for network and information assurance to CYBERCOM, and has moved its headquarters to Fort Meade.[18]

The mission of USCYBERCOM is to plan, coordinate, integrate, synchronize, and direct operations in defense of specified Department of Defense (DoD) information networks. It will prepare to and—when directed—conduct full-spectrum military cyberspace operations in order to enable actions in all domains, ensure US/Allied freedom of action in cyberspace, and deny the same to adversaries.[19] USCYBERCOM centralizes command of cyberspace operations, strengthens DoD cyberspace capabilities, and integrates and bolsters DoD's cyber expertise. Consequently, USCYBERCOM improves DoD's capability to ensure resilient, reliable information and communication networks and counter cyberspace threats. USCYBERCOM's efforts also support the armed services' ability to confidently conduct high-tempo, effective operations as well as protect command-and-control systems supporting weapons system platforms from disruptions, intrusions, and attacks.[20]

The creation of the U.S. Cyber Command appears to have motivated other countries to take parallel measures to address similar threats. In December 2009, South Korea announced the creation of a Cyber Warfare Command. This was reportedly in response to North Korea's establishment of a cyber warfare unit.[21] The British have also begun preparing a cyber force.[22] In addition, the recent shift in military interest in cyber warfare has motivated the creation by the U.S. Air Force of the first U.S. Cyber Warfare Intelligence Center.[23] These actions on the part of the United States and its allies reflect both the great fear of not being proactive and the threat posed to systems by cyber warfare.

Chapter Seventeen

The Legality of Attack on Foreign Infrastructure Posing A Threat

Computer Network Attack (CNA)

When the FY 2000 version of the Unified Command Plan (UCP) was signed on September 29, 1999, it marked a new era in operational planning for information warfare, to include the possible targeting of an adversary's computer networks where necessary to protect vital U.S. or Allied interests. The UCP provides planning guidance and requirements for the operational commands within the Department of Defense (DoD). In the FY 2000 version, responsibility for maintaining and managing the Joint Information Operations Center (JIOC) located in San Antonio, Texas, was transferred to the U.S. Space Command at Petersen Air Force Base, Colorado.[1] In 2006, the JIOC changed its name to the Joint Information Operations Warfare Command. On May 15, 2009, the JIOWC was re-designated as the Joint Information Operations Warfare Center (JIOWC).

The JIOWC, before 1999 known as the Joint Command and Control Warfare Center, provides "full-spectrum" information warfare and information operations support to U.S. operational commanders worldwide. That is, the JIOWC provides support in planning, coordination, and execution of all DoD information warfare and information operations missions, as well as assistance in the development of related doctrine, tactics and procedures.

What made the transfer of the then–JIOC significant was the enhancement of its missions. In August 1999, the mission of the JIOC was broadened from command and control to include operations support. The enhanced operations support now required of the JIOWC includes psychological operations, security, electronic warfare, targeting of command and control facilities, military deception, computer network defense, *computer network attack* (CNA), civil affairs, and public affairs.[2]

For the first time in the UCP, computer network attack was specifically identified in the planning requirements for unified commanders.[3] This was significant because, by implication, the planning requirements recognized the legality of targeting critical foreign computer infrastructure when U.S. or allied vital national interests are threatened.

DEFINING THE CNA DEBATE

For the United States, the renewed emphasis on considering critical computer infrastructure as a legitimate target category arises from recent incidents where its critical infrastructure has been threatened by government-sponsored intrusions or by individual hackers using sophisticated software. From these incidents, we have recognized that electronic or physical elimination of this threat may be necessary to protect the U.S. defense capability or ensure the continued effective operation of other critical infrastructure.

Several incidents beyond those described previously in chapter 16 are significant. In February 1998, two California teenagers were able to breach computer systems at eleven Air Force and Navy bases, causing a series of "denial of service" cyber attacks and forcing defense officials to reassess the security of their networks.[4] The investigation of these incidents, code-named Solar Sunrise, however, pales in comparison with "Moonlight Maze," the code name for the investigation of an early 1999 electronic assault involving hackers based in Russia. In these attacks, intruders accessed sensitive DoD science and technology information.[5] Computer tracing determined that Moonlight Maze attacks originated from the Russian Academy of Science, a government organization that interacts closely with the military.[6] Until the April 2007 coordinated cyber attacks that shut down the entire nation of Estonia, the full destructive potential of cyber terror was not fully appreciated by the international community. This raises the possibility of an asymmetrical attack sponsored by a nation-state.

These incidents raise important issues for defense planning. How can these threats be discovered and eliminated? What is the interplay between the role of investigating agency and that of operational planner? It is clear that while the targeting of these threats may require a military component, the gathering of indicators of an imminent threat requires a far broader participation. It is for this reason that the United States established the National Infrastructure Protection Center (NIPC) in February 1998.[7]

The NIPC's mission is to serve as the government's focal point for threat assessment, warning, investigation, and response to threats or attacks against critical infrastructures. These critical infrastructures include defense communication networks, telecommunications systems, energy grids, banking and finance organizations, water systems, government operations apparatus, and emergency service organizations.[8]

The NIPC is organized with both an "indications and warning" arm and an operational arm. The Analysis and Warning Section (AWS) provides analytical support during computer intrusion investigations and long-term analysis of vulnerability and threat trends. The Computer Investigations and Operations Section (CIOS) is the operational arm of the NIPC. This section manages computer intrusion investigations conducted by FBI field offices throughout the country, provides subject matter experts, equipment, and technical support to investigators in federal, state, and local government agencies involved in critical infrastructure protection and provides an emergency response capability to help resolve a cyber incident.[9]

Neither the JIOC at USSPACECOM nor the NIPC, however, possess the capability to eliminate a hostile cyber threat. Only the operational assets assigned to the various unified commands within the Department of Defense possess that unique capability, and they may only be employed when the strict parameters of the law of armed conflict are satisfied.

LEGAL CONSTRAINTS ON ATTACKS ON CRITICAL INFRASTRUCTURE

The legal regime available to authorize responding attacks in lawful self-defense on critical enemy infrastructure includes the UN Charter system and customary international law. The basic provision restricting the threat or use of force in international relations is Article 2, Paragraph 4, of the UN Charter, addressed extensively in previous chapters. That provision states: "All Members shall refrain in their international relations from the threat or use of force against the territorial integrity or political independence of any state, or in any manner inconsistent with the Purposes of the United Nations.[10]

The underlying purpose of Article 2, Paragraph 4, to regulate aggressive behavior between states, is identical to that of its precursor in the Covenant of the League of Nations. Article 12 of the Covenant stated that the League members were obliged not to "resort to war." This language, however, left unnoticed actions which, although hostile, could not be considered acts of war. Thus in drafting Article 2, Paragraph 4, the term "war" was replaced by "threat or use of force," to include applications of force of a lesser intensity. This distinction may be all important, for example, when a nation's commercial infrastructure is attacked, and actions in lawful self-defense are contemplated which include targeting critical infrastructure of the adversary, an element of which may have been used in the initial attack.

When the UN Charter was drafted in 1945, the right of self-defense was the only included exception to the prohibition of the use of force. This right was codified in Article 51 of the Charter. The use of the word "inherent" in the text of Article 51 suggests that self-defense is broader than the immediate Charter parameters. During the drafting of the Kellogg-Briand Treaty, for example, the United States expressed its view as follows:

> There is nothing in the American draft of an anti-war treaty which restricts or impairs in any way the right of self-defense. That right is inherent in every sovereign state and is implicit in every treaty. Every nation is free at all times and regardless of treaty provisions to defend its territory from attack or invasion and it alone is competent to decide whether circumstances require recourse to war in self-defense. [11]

Because self-defense is an inherent right, its contours have been shaped by custom and are subject to customary interpretation. Although the drafters of Article 51 may not have anticipated its use in protecting states through defensive actions using technological means, international law has long recognized the need for flexible application.

When a vital U.S. national interest such as one of the critical infrastructure systems is threatened or attacked by electronic or other computer-driven means, the system responsible for the threat may constitute a legally appropriate target for destruction or neutralization by military assets, and destruction may be both necessary and proportionate under the law of armed conflict to eliminate the threat perceived. [12] While military objectives, including computer networks supporting military requirements, are properly included within target sets, civilians and civilian objects are not. [13] Civilian objects consist of all civilian property and activities *other than those used to support or sustain the capability for armed aggression on the part of the attacker.* [14] Thus, activities normally considered civilian in character, when conducted in support of a nation's aggression, where implemented to shield an aggressor's identification, or where employed to preclude effective and lawful response to unlawful attack, would, under these circumstances, become the lawful objects of attack. The point has been made succinctly by the DoD General Counsel in a May 1999 treatise on information operations wherein she states:

> the international community were persuaded that a particular computer attack or a pattern of such attacks should be considered to be an "armed attack," or the equivalent to an "armed attack," it would seem to follow that the victim nation would be entitled to respond in self-defense either by computer network attack or by traditional military means in order to disable the equipment and personnel that were used to mount the offending attack. [15]

Stated another way, a civilian computer system, used either to conduct an attack or shield an aggressor's attack from discovery, becomes a valid and lawful target, when aggression against critical infrastructure equating to an armed attack has occurred.[16]

From this examination, we see that computer networks are not *per se* illegal targets under traditional international law criteria. We must apply the standard law of armed conflict analysis in every instance to determine whether critical computer infrastructure of an attacking state or other nonstate aggressor constitutes a valid target under the circumstances of each case. In that review, as in all reviews of target lists, we must determine whether the specific computer network or other critical infrastructure system under consideration, by its nature, location, capability, purpose, or use, makes an effective contribution to the military capability of the offending state and whether its destruction, capture, or neutralization offers the United States or its allies a definite military advantage.

The fact that a computer system or other critical infrastructure is a valid target does not mean that it should be attacked, however. In weighing the political and strategic implications, refraining from a response in kind, although legally justified, may provide greater benefit, that is, a shift in world sentiment, a movement of certain nations in terms of their allegiances, the opportunity for international bodies such as the UN to become engaged, and an opportunity to open previously closed political channels.

A final concern related to responding attacks on computer-based critical infrastructure, under traditional international law principles, relates to the issue of collateral damage. While collateral damage does not have a different definition in a CNA context, we may have to take additional steps to show that reasonable precautions were taken to avoid unnecessary destruction. This is because of the more predictable effects of conventional weapons and delivery systems and the maxim that a weapon must be targetable and not so indiscriminate that it unnecessarily endangers the civilian population of the offending state. Lawrence G. Downs Jr. explains a related and even more important consideration for the state using digital data warfare in lawful self-defense. In his essay, "Digital Data Warfare: Using Malicious Computer Code as A Weapon," he states:

> When the US Army contracted a study to determine the feasibility of developing DDW–type [digital data warfare–type] viruses for military use, [footnote omitted] many people had misgivings that were summed up by Gary Chapman, program director of Computer Professionals for Professional Responsibility. "Unleashing this kind of thing is dangerous," he said. "Should the virus escape, the United States heads the list of vulnerable countries. Our computers are by far the most networked [footnote omitted]."[17]

From this it is clear that any weapon developed to provide CNA capability must be both predictable and capable of being armed and disarmed, if it is not to unduly threaten innocent civilians in the target state *or the user state.* Downs is correct when he suggests that weaponeers

> should, in general, co-develop a detection and immunization program for all viruses they intend to use. In this way, a DDW attack gone wrong cannot inadvertently do harm to the attacker. In short, users and developers of DDW need to be aware of risks and the absolute requirement for predictability when developing DDW code. [18]

THE IMPACT OF INTERNATIONAL AGREEMENTS AND DOMESTIC COMMUNICATIONS LAW ON CAN

Another consideration of military planners developing a cyber-defense capability must be those international agreements regulating the use of space through which data used for CNA must travel. Those agreements include four principal multilateral conventions to which the United States is party. These four treaties are: (1) the 1967 Treaty on Principles Governing the Activities of States in the Exploration and use of Outer Space, including the Moon and Other Celestial Bodies (Outer Space Treaty); [19] (2) the 1968 Agreement on the Rescue Astronauts, Return of Astronauts, and Return of Objects Launched in Space (Rescue and Return Agreement); [20] (3) the 1972 Convention on International Liability for Damages Caused by Space Objects (Liability Convention); [21] and (4) the 1975 Convention on Registration of Objects Launched into Outer Space (Space Objects Registration Treaty). [22] The four conventions collectively reiterate principles which are so widely accepted that they are viewed as reflective of customary international law, even as between nonparties. These general principles include the premise that (a) access to outer space is free and open to all nations; [23] (b) each user of outer space must show due regard for the rights of others; [24] (c) states that launch space objects are liable for any damage they may do in space, in the air, and on land; [25] and (d) space activities are subject to general principles of international law. [26]

The DoD General Counsel concluded in her 1999 assessment of international legal issues related to information operations, however, that the non-interference principle recited in these and other conventions addressing the right to use outer space does not apply during armed conflict. She stated:

> There appears to be a strong argument that the principle of non-interference established by these agreements is inconsistent with a state of hostilities, at least where the systems concerned are of such high military value that there is a strong military imperative for the adversary to be free to interfere with them, even to the extent of destroying the satellites in the system. As indicated in the

discussion of treaty law in the introduction to this paper, the outcome of this debate may depend on the circumstances in which it first arises in practice. Nevertheless, it seems most likely that these agreements will be considered to be suspended between the belligerents for the duration of any armed conflict, at least to the extent necessary for the conduct of the conflict.[27]

Underlying this statement by the DoD General Counsel is the obvious principle that the right of self-defense is in no way abrogated by other international commitments entered into by a nation.

One significant convention with apparent applicability to U.S. interdiction of foreign communications infrastructure is the International Telecommunications Convention (ITC) of 1982. In Article 35, the convention prohibits interference by member states with the communications of other member states. The convention has an exception for military transmissions in Article 38, however, which arguably would authorize information operations conducted by military forces.[28] In fact, the Office of Legal Counsel in the U.S. Department of Justice ruled in July 1994 with respect to planned broadcasts into Haiti concerning boat operations that the ITC did not prohibit these broadcasts.[29]

An unlikely convention that must be considered when discussing cyber operations is the 1907 Hague Convention on Neutrality on Land,[30] which could impact satellite relay operations. This convention does not apply to systems that generate information, but does apply to relay facilities and requires that those of other states not be disrupted. While Articles 8 and 9 contemplate only telegraph and telephone cable links, they would arguably apply to satellite links as well. Since most computer-based systems, and certainly all that control critical infrastructure, generate information as well as relay that information, the prohibition against disruption would likely not apply.

Another potential concern is raised by international consortia that lease satellite nodes for commercial communications. These organizations include INTELSAT, INMARSAT, ARABSAT, EUTELSAT, and EUMETSAT. The contract signed by each user, which is nearly identical in the case of each provider, states that the system must be used exclusively for peaceful purposes.[31] While the United States has leased one or more nodes from at least one of these providers in the past, it retains separate satellite capabilities should it need to defend itself through digital data warfare.

Finally, domestic communications law must also be considered. The United States Congress passed 47 USC 502[32] to implement the ITC requirement that member states enact legislation to prohibit interference with the communications of other members. During Haiti operations in 1993, just as it would again in July 1994, the Office of Legal Counsel to the Department of Justice issued a written opinion to the effect that section 502 does not apply to military actions of the United States executing the instructions of the President.[33] Thus, domestic law will not preclude the appropriate use of CNA by the United States where it is engaged in an armed conflict or where necessity and proportionality dictate in periods short of war.

ANALYTICAL REVIEW

From this examination, it is clear that the method of computer network attack first authorized under the FY 2000 Unified Command Plan and which continues today, whether it be digital data, kinetic, or electronic, does not change the legal analysis. Computer networks critical to the functioning of enemy infrastructure systems can be, under proper circumstances, valid military targets under traditional international law principles and use of CNA does not violate applicable international conventions. This follows because military and dual-use infrastructure are legitimate targets at all times during armed conflict as long as they meet the two-pronged test that they make an effective contribution to the adversary's military effort and that their destruction would offer a definite military advantage.

The analysis under the law of armed conflict that must be followed to determine whether a military advantage is to be expected requires examination of the nature, location, purpose, or use of the offending network and whether it is used to threaten U.S. or allied interests. Similarly, these same computer networks may constitute a lawful target in self-defense prior to armed conflict if their neutralization or elimination is a necessary and proportional response to an attack sustained. A corollary to this rule is that simply because a particular target is valid in a military sense does not mean it must be attacked. A nation must always analyze any potential target in light of the political, tactical, and strategic implications that apply.

In the target analysis required for CNA, just as for more traditional target sets, reasonable precautions must be taken to discriminate military targets from civilian networks. This will be most difficult with regard to those dual-use systems such as commercial telephone exchanges that can serve both a civilian and military purpose. It is here that the political implications described above must be carefully weighed. However, from our analysis, it is clear that networks serving commercial infrastructure, government agencies, and banking and financial institutions can constitute legitimate targets if those infrastructures contribute to the enemy's war-sustaining capability such that their destruction would constitute a definite military advantage. Conversely, attacks on computer networks serving infrastructure that is designed solely to support the civilian population, such as civilian food distribution systems and civilian water supply systems, would be prohibited.

International-communications law likewise contains no direct or specific prohibition against the conduct of CNA or other information operations by military forces during armed conflict or in response to aggression, emphasizing the superior position enjoyed by the law of self-defense in the hierarchy of a nation's sovereign rights. Moreover, the practice of nations as established in World War II provides persuasive evidence that telecommunications treaties are regarded as suspended among belligerents during international armed conflict. Similarly, domestic communications laws, and specifically 47 USC 502, do not prohibit properly authorized military information operations. It is clear, then, that CNA, as first authorized by the President in the FY 2000 Unified Command Plan, and implemented through the JIOWC and the NIPC, can be employed in a manner consistent with domestic law, as well as customary and conventional international law principles.

Finally, when CNA is lawfully employed in response to asymmetric attacks on our critical infrastructure, we must be aware that the international system will tend to ignore the original aggression, often purposefully masked in extent to shield our resulting vulnerability, while focusing on the more visible defensive response. If, however, we are to discourage the low-intensity portion of the aggressive attack spectrum, including cyber terrorism, it is essential that we understand the need for a full range of computer network defense and deterrence measures against cyber attack.

The international legal system can effectively contribute to such deterrence if, but only if, we make a clear distinction between the treatment of cyber aggression on the one hand, and computer-generated defensive responses, which can and must include CNA. That is, we must strengthen the international legal system to strongly condemn all acts of aggression, whether a cyber attack such as employed by the Russians in Moonlight Maze or the violent acts of war seen in the targeting of the warship *USS Cole* in Aden Harbor, in the 1998 attacks on our embassies in Nairobi and Dar es Salaam, and in the heinous attacks on 9/11. Just as importantly, the system must be strengthened to strongly support and legally embrace defensive computer generated digital data warfare responses to such aggression. Under such a strengthened system, CNA will provide an important new arrow in our quiver of available responses to aggression under the law of armed conflict.

Chapter Eighteen

War Powers in the Age of Terror

The 2011 Libya Operation

The recent hostilities in Libya between government forces of the late Colonel Khadafi and insurgents have once again raised issues concerning whether a U.S. president can insert combat forces for more than sixty days without securing Congressional approval. For more than thirty-five years, the War Powers Resolution[1] has required that all presidents meet the criteria for compliance which includes prior consultation with Congress, fulfillment of reporting requirements, and the securing of Congressional authorization within sixty days of the introduction of forces.[2]

The War Powers Resolution has been much maligned, both by President Nixon at the time, and by each succeeding president. In fact, every president acting under the Resolution has taken the position that it is an unconstitutional infringement on the president's authority as Commander-in-Chief.[3]

In brief, the War Powers Resolution states that the president's authority as Commander-in-Chief to introduce military forces into hostilities or imminent hostilities may only be exercised pursuant to a declaration of war; specific statutory authority; or a national emergency created by an attack on the United States or its forces.[4]

Key provisions are contained in sections 4(a)(1), 4(a)(2), 4(a)(3) and sections 5(b), (c). Section 4(a)(1) requires that the president consult with the Congress in every possible instance prior to introducing U.S. Forces into hostilities or imminent hostilities. This section also mandates the president report to Congress any introduction of U.S. forces into hostilities or imminent hostilities within forty-eight hours of that occurrence. Section 4(a)(2) carries this requirement one step further by providing that the president must report to Congress whenever U.S. forces enter foreign territory equipped for combat. Section 4(a)(3) adds the requirement that the president report to Congress whenever the U.S. substantially enlarges our forces equipped for combat already in a foreign nation. Once an initial report is presented, under 4(a)1, Congress must authorize the use of forces within sixty days (or ninety in exigent circumstances) under section 5(b) of the Resolution or the forces must be withdrawn.[5]

It is the latter requirement, ignored in Libya in May 2011, that this chapter is directed. This chapter examines the Libya crisis in 2011, reviews U.S. involvement, and places the War Powers requirements in context with other presidential requirements during armed interventions. It queries whether, through his actions in Libya, President Obama has provided a restructuring of presidential prerogatives concerning the use of force politically and legally helpful to future chief executives. Equally significant, it questions whether President Obama has redefined the construct of "hostilities" under the Resolution if no U.S. ground forces are introduced.

THE LIBYA CRISIS

In February 2011, in the midst of world concerns related to regime brutality against civilians in Tunisia and Egypt, later described as the Arab Spring, protests also began in Benghazi in western Libya. Citizens there sought governmental reforms and the end of the forty-year reign of Colonel Khadafi.[6] The response by the Khadafi government was swift and deadly. Government forces strafed, shelled, and bombed civilian protestors in Benghazi and several other western cities, causing many to flee to Egypt.[7] The United Nations acted quickly. On February 26, 2011, the Security Council (UNSC) unanimously adopted UNSC Resolution 1970, which "(e)xpress(ed) grave concern at the situation in the Arab Jamahiriya," "condemn(ed) the violence and use of force against civilians," and "(d)eplored the gross and systematic violation of human rights in Libya."[8] The Resolution called upon member states to take "the necessary measures" to prevent arms transfers "from and through their territories or by their nationals, or using their flag vessels or aircraft," to freeze the assets of Khadafi and certain other close associates of the regime, and to "facilitate and support the return of humanitarian agencies and make available humanitarian and related assistance" in Libya.[9] While important, this Resolution did not authorize member states to use military force against Khadafi's regime.

The passage of UNSC Resolution 1970 had no noticeable effect. In fact, Khadafi's forces escalated the violence against civilians in the west of Libya.[10] This caused the Council of the League of Arab States to call upon the Security Council on March 12, 2011, "to take the necessary measures to impose immediately a no-fly zone on Libyan military aviation" and to "establish safe areas in places exposed to shelling as a precautionary measure that allows the protection of the Libyan people and foreign national residing in Libya, while respecting the sovereignty and territorial integrity of neighboring states."[11]

When Khadafi's forces ignored these resolutions and made plans for an assault on Benghazi on March 17, 2011,[12] the United Nations finally acted in a meaningful way. In Resolution 1973, the Security Council, by vote of 10-0,[13] imposed a no-fly zone over Libya and authorized the use of military force to protect civilians.[14] The Security Council determined that the "situation" in Libya "continues to constitute a threat to international peace and security" and demanded the immediate establishment of a cease-fire and a complete end to violence and all attacks against, and abuses of civilians."[15] In paragraph 4, Resolution 1973 authorized member states, acting unilaterally or through regional organizations, "to take all necessary measures....to protect civilians and civilian populated areas under threat of attack in the Libyan Arab Jamahiriya, including Benghazi, while excluding foreign occupation force of any form on any part of Libyan territory."[16] Resolution 1973 further authorized member states to enforce "a ban on all (unauthorized) flights in the airspace in the Libyan Arab Jamahiriya in order to help protect civilians" and to take "all measures commensurate to the specific circumstances" to inspect vessels on the high seas suspected of violating the arms embargo imposed on Libya by UNSC Resolution 1970.[17]

Despite statements indicating compliance by Libya's Foreign Minister, Kadafi's forces continued their attacks and deaths of civilians mounted.[18]

UNITED STATES INVOLVEMENT

Although involved in New York in the drafting of Security Council Resolution 1970 through the office of UN Ambassador Susan Rice, the executive branch did not initially take the United States' lead in actions to curb Libyan violence.[19] It was the United States Senate through the Committee on Foreign Relations that passed Senate Resolution 85 by unanimous consent on March 1, 2011.[20] Resolution 85, shepherded by Senators Kerry and Lugar, "strongly condemn[ed] the gross and systematic violations of human rights in Libya, including violent attacks on protesters demanding democratic reforms," "call[ed] on Muammar Khadafi to desist from further violence," and "urg[ed] the United Nations Security Council to take such further action as may be necessary to protect civilians in Libya from attack, including the possible imposition of a no-fly zone over Libyan territory."[21]

Following the passage of United Nations Security Council Resolution (UNSCR) 1973 on March 17, 2011, authorizing a no-fly zone, President Obama gave the United States' position on March 18. He stated that for

Khadafi to avoid military intervention, he (Khadafi) needed to: implement an immediate cease fire, including ending all attacks on civilians; halt his troops advance on Benghazi; pull his troops back from three other cities; and ensure the provision of water, electricity, and gas to all areas.[22] President Obama further defined those U.S. national interests impacted by Colonel Khadafi's continued attacks on his own citizens. The President stated:

> Left unchecked, we have every reason to believe that Khadafi would commit atrocities against his people. Many thousands could die. A humanitarian crisis would ensue. The entire region could be destabilized, endangering many of our allies and partners. The calls of the Libyan people for help would go unanswered. The Democratic values that we stand for would be overrun. Moreover, the words of the international community would be rendered hollow.[23]

When Resolution 1973 was observed to have no visible effect (despite an initial Libyan government statement that they would honor the requested cease-fire), the United States, with the support of coalition partners, launched airstrikes against Khadafi to enforce UNSC Resolution 1973. The President explained his actions in a March 21, 2011, letter to Congressional leadership as follows:

> At approximately 3:00 pm Eastern Daylight Time, on March 19, 2011, at my direction, U.S. military forces commenced operations to assist an international effort authorized by the United Nations (UN) Security Council and have undertaken with the support of European allies and Arab partners, to prevent a humanitarian catastrophe and address the threat posed to international peace and security by the crisis in Libya. As part of the multilateral response authorized under UN Security Council Resolution 1973, U.S. military forces, under command of the Commander, U.S. Africa Command, began a series of strikes against air defense systems and military airfields for the purposes of preparing a no-fly zone. These strikes will be limited in their nature, duration, and scope. Their purpose is to support an international coalition as it takes all necessary measures to enforce the terms of UN Security Resolution 1973. These limited U.S. actions will set the stage for further action by other coalition partners.[24]

It was the intent of the United States, he said, to "seek a rapid, but responsible, transition of operations to coalition, regional, or international organizations that are postured to continue activities as may be necessary to realize the objectives of UN Security Council Resolutions 1970 and 1973."[25]

WAR POWERS AS INTERPRETED BY THE OBAMA PRESIDENCY

When President Obama ordered U.S. military support for the UN-sanctioned no-fly zone on March 19, 2011,[26] he was triggering requirements of the War

Powers Resolution, passed over President Nixon's veto in 1973.[27] In the thirty-eight years of its existence, eight presidents have submitted more than 130 reports pursuant to its requirements.[28] In his decision of March 19, 2011, to use military force in Libya, President Obama was making two determinations. First, as reported in the OLC analysis of April 1, 2011, he concluded he "had the constitutional authority to direct the use of military force in Libya because he could reasonably determine that such use of force was in the national interest." Second, he claimed that "[p]rior congressional approval was not constitutionally required to use military force in the limited operations under consideration."[29]

This determination to use military force in Libya without seeking prior Congressional approval must be examined in the context of the War Powers Resolution,[30] a statute intended "to fulfill the intent of the framers of the Constitution of the United States."[31] The 1973 statute provides that, in the absence of a declaration of war, the president must report to Congress within forty-eight hours of taking certain actions, including introduction of U.S. forces "into hostilities or into situations where imminent involvement in hostilities is clearly indicated by the circumstances."[32]

The heart of the Resolution is codified at 50 USC 1544(b), however. While the War Powers Resolution recognizes the president's unilateral authority to deploy armed forces, it also requires that the president must terminate such use of force within sixty days (or ninety days for military necessity) unless Congress extends the deadline, declares war, or "enact[s] a specific authorization."[33] It is this issue which presents itself most significantly in the Libya involvement.

When President Obama failed to seek Congressional approval for the operation on May 19, 2011, sixty days after the initiation of hostilities, he argued he was acting consistently with his March 21, 2011, letter report to Congress on the limited nature of U.S. involvement.[34] In that letter report, he had explained that these actions were part of "the multilateral response authorized under UN Security Council Resolution 1973" and that "these strikes will be limited in their nature, duration, and scope."[35] Further, he added that "their purpose is to support an international coalition as it takes all necessary measures to enforce the terms of UN Security Council Resolution 1973. These limited U.S. actions will set the stage for further action by other coalition partners."[36]

When the House called upon President Obama to justify his course in not seeking Congressional authorization after sixty days of military involvement, the Obama Administration released an Office of Legal Council (OLC) memorandum denying a violation of his war powers requirements.[37] The memorandum provided the rationale that "war" within the meaning of the Constitution's "Declare War Clause" does not encompass all military engagements, but only those that are "prolonged and substantial . . . , typically involving exposure of U.S. military personnel to significant risk over a substantial period."[38] The Libya intervention, the memorandum argued, did not implicate the prerogatives of Congress because the United States role was limited; unlikely to expose any U.S. persons to attack; and was likely to end soon."[39]

The House of Representatives, led by Speaker Boehner, was far from satisfied. The House passed a resolution on June 3, 2011, rebuking President Obama for failing to provide Congress with a "compelling rationale" for the military campaign in Libya, but stopped short of demanding he withdraw U.S. forces from the operation.[40] This reprimand followed the House's rejection of a more stringent resolution proposed by Democrat Representative Dennis Kucinich. That resolution would have required that President Obama remove forces from participation in Libya within fifteen days.[41] The Democrat-controlled Senate took no action.

THE OBAMA ADMINISTRATION'S RESPONSE IN HISTORICAL PERSPECTIVE

The immediate issue raised by the Libyan intervention is whether section 4(a)(1) (consultation with Congress) and section 5(b) (required authorization by Congress) of the War Powers Resolution trigger a time limitation on continued armed involvement unless Congress provides authorization to remain. On the one hand, Congressional concurrence strengthens the president's hand in his foreign policy actions. On the other, failure of the president to seek Congressional approval may strengthen his posture in terms of flexibility compared to his options under the Resolution.

Recent presidential reporting provides insights into the interpretation of the Resolution.[42] In Bosnia, for example, President Clinton directed U.S. participation in UN actions without seeking prior Congressional approval, at least with respect to no-fly zones, enforcement of safe-havens, airlift of humanitarian supplies into Sarajevo, and naval monitoring of sanctions.[43] In October 1995, war powers were raised again in the Balkans as President Clinton authorized the assignment of 20,000 combat troops to the NATO-led force.[44] The follow-on contingent of 8,500 for the Stabilization Force (SFOR), again led by NATO, was the subject of a Congressional vote in 1998 that continued the authorization and rejected a resolution that would have forced removal of U.S. armed forces from Herzegovina and Bosnia.[45]

The following year, after President Clinton ordered U.S. forces into Kosovo under NATO leadership,[46] litigation was filed in Federal District Court in Washington, D.C., challenging his use of the military absent prior Congressional authorization. This litigation was dismissed for lack of standing.[47] Meanwhile, the House of Representatives, on May 6, 1999, defeated an amendment to the fiscal year 1999 Defense Supplemental Appropriations bill that would have prohibited funds for U.S. forces to enter former Yugoslavia, except in time of war.[48] Congress subsequently passed legislation that approved supplemental appropriations for the Kosovo operation.[49]

Similarly, in Iraq after 1991, three situations raised war powers issues. The first resulted from Baghdad's refusal to cease repression of Kurdish and Shiite groups.[50] The second concerned violations of the April 3, 1991, ceasefire accord.[51] The third incident related to the Iraqi deployment of missiles in the no-fly zone in violation of Resolution 687, and the threat these posed to coalition aircraft.[52]

In each instance in Iraq, to include the current conflict and that in Afghanistan, the president has reported to Congress "consistent with" the War Powers Resolution, not "pursuant to" it. This was true in Haiti, Bosnia, Kosovo, and Somalia, as well. The Congress agreed to disagree with this language and has nevertheless provided authorization and funding under section 5(b) of the Resolution. What makes U.S. military involvement in Libya so different is the president's failure to seek authorization for a *continued* military presence beyond the sixty-day requirement.

WAR POWERS AND "HOSTILITIES" — A NEW DIALECTIC IN LIBYA

As controversial as war powers issues have been, President Obama is the first Commander-in-chief to determine that bombing and blockading an adversary is not engagement in "hostilities." Section 2(a) of the War Powers Resolution states:

> 2(a). It is the purpose of the joint resolution to fulfill the intent of the framers of the Constitution of the United States and insure that the collective judgment of both the Congress and the president will apply to the introduction of the United States' armed forces into hostilities, or into situations where imminent involvement in hostilities is clearly indicated by the circumstances, and to the continued use of such forces in hostilities or in such situation.

When military action reached its sixtieth day on May 19, 2011, President Obama showed no inclination to seek the approval of Congress for the continuation of the Libya mission. While it is true that "hostilities" are not defined in the War Powers Resolution, and the United States had no ground forces in Libya, nevertheless, U.S. forces have been enforcing a no-fly zone, conducting bombing raids, firing cruise missiles, directing lethal drone strikes, and have maintained a tight naval blockade. These are all acts of war, and constitute involvement in "hostilities," in any nation's lexicon. Moreover, while the United States has now taken on a supporting role under NATO leadership, our military leaders lead NATO, and the War Powers

Resolution clearly states that the "introduction of U.S. forces" applies in these circumstances.[53] The United States' participation in the NATO-led effort has included drone attacks, aerial refueling of allied combat aircraft, electronic jamming, search and rescue missions, and other assistance to the "kinetic operations" defined by President Obama to be outside the definition of "hostilities."

One of the unfortunate realities about being a superpower, and the United States is one (and possibly the only one), is that it possesses capabilities and resources not available elsewhere. The United States, as Professor Robert Chesney points out, "has close air support and quick response capabilities—including, but not limited to, armed drones—that the allies could not replicate, and without which the [Libya] operation might fail."[54] More interesting, though, is the obvious result of the new White House definition of "hostilities" to embrace intensity, frequency, and risk to U.S. personnel. President Obama is likely creating a dangerous precedent that could severely limit Congressional prerogatives in the War Powers process and frustrate the framers' intent.

WAR POWERS AND THE FUTURE

Current legal and policy planning for future operations could also be greatly altered by the new definition of "hostilities."[55] If a serving or future president can argue that a lethal but singular strike on the nuclear weapons capability of a potential adversary is justified without Congressional notification or approval, neither the War Powers statute nor Constitutional parity between branches of government would any longer have relevance.

Of concern as well is the White House view that senior U.S. military commanders assigned to NATO or a UN structure are no longer subject to the constraints of section 8(c) of the War Powers Resolution.[56] This could provide a president absolute license to support these operations militarily while avoiding the strictures of the Resolution. Equally troubling for the airmen flying bombing missions, sailors enforcing a naval blockade, or U.S. personnel maintaining a no-fly zone, changing the definition will in no way diminish the risks they are exposed to in executing their mission.

Chapter Nineteen

The War on Terror and Media Access

As Sebastian Junger implies in his 2010 book on the complete experience of war,[1] being embedded with our forces in Afghanistan has a special meaning for combat correspondents far beyond a limited definition of being placed within a U.S. military unit. For Junger, it meant a front row seat for the show where young Americans proved their mettle and where adrenaline ran wild. In this chapter, the development of the military-media relationship is explored and some observations are offered concerning the development of the law and policies that dictate how the media can and must operate in conflicts such as Iraq and Afghanistan.

In the nearly thirty years since the United States intervened in Grenada in 1983, the Department of Defense (DoD) has engaged in a careful process to balance the requirement that the government conduct effective military operations, with the requirement that the public, via a free press, be independently informed about the actions of its government. This process, initiated largely because of adverse press reaction to tighter restrictions on media coverage resulting from military frustrations with the press in Vietnam, was marked by a series of negotiations following United States interventions in Grenada, Panama, and the First Gulf War.

In the decade following the First Gulf War, this process was placed in abeyance as the United States and many of its European allies were engaged in peacekeeping operations under UN auspices. The multinational UN operations in Somalia, Rwanda, and the Balkans, for example, often left U. S. leaders and forces without independent control over either information or operational decision making.[2] Somalia marked the nadir of this phenomenon.[3] With the NATO Kosovo Operation in 1998, the United States and its coalition partners were able to restore strict maintenance of operational security and once again exercised effective control and limits on media access.[4]

Following the al Qaeda attacks on New York and Washington, DC, on September 11, 2001, and with the advent of Operations Enduring Freedom (OEF) and Iraqi Freedom (OIF), the Secretary of Defense promulgated clear guidance on the policies and procedures on embedding news media during operations in the USCENTCOM area of responsibility. The embedded media would "live, work and travel as part of the units with which they are embedded to facilitate maximum, in-depth coverage of U.S. forces in combat and related operations."[5]

This chapter establishes the framework for debate, reviews the historical currents underlying the present policy regarding press access, examines several conflicts (Grenada, Panama, Desert Storm, and Haiti) that have shaped that policy, reviews the litigation arising from these and other operations, and comments on the "agreement on war coverage guidelines" negotiated over a period of eight months between the press and the Department of Defense following the First Gulf War. Finally, the current process of embedding reporters in Afghanistan, and previously in Iraq, is reviewed, with an emphasis on the responsibility of U.S. commanders to ensure a full understanding of combatant operations by the media.

FRAMEWORK FOR DEBATE

The United States intervention in Grenada in 1983 marked a turning point in the relations between the working press and U.S. military officials. The exclusion of media from Grenada during the first two days of that operation resulted in a ten-year battle between the media and the government to establish reasonable limits on press access to U.S. military operations. Following the 1983 intervention, immediate demands were leveled by the national media organizations to accommodate the Fourth Estate (the press) in combat operations. Two arguments, one historical and one constitutional, were advanced to justify the presence of reporters on the battlefield. These arguments, found within the 1984 Statement of Principles on Press Access to Military Operations,[6] urged that, historically, United States reporters "have always been allowed to cover U.S. troops in action."[7] The journalists also argued that the presence of the press in combat serves the citizens' right to know. The thrust of this claim is tied to the democratic values attributed to a free press as a pillar of American strength.[8] The Sidle Panel, commissioned by the Secretary of Defense to address the press's concerns related to Grenada, assuaged the press initially, but the pool concept it approved was later found by journalists to be inadequate.[9]

The attempt to find compromise after Grenada, and the resulting press frustrations with the pool concept and its limited access to combat operations during the 1989 Panama intervention and the Desert Storm operation that followed, ultimately led to the 1992 negotiations which resulted in new Department of Defense combat coverage principles. The negotiators from the press finally agreed "that the guidelines offer the kind of coverage the citizens of a democracy are entitled to have."[10] The implementation of the negotiated agreement evolved into a lengthy process concluding with the publication of two DoD directives in 1996, and the issuance of a statement entitled "Principles of Information" by Secretary Cohen on April 1, 1997.[11]

The agreed-upon principles at the heart of these documents include: (1) open and independent coverage as the principal means of covering U.S. military operations; (2) the use of a pool when it provides the only feasible means of access to a military operation, when space is limited, or for a specific event; (3) the credentialing of journalists and the requirement to abide by security ground rules, with non-observance leading to a loss of accreditation; (4) access for journalists to all major units, although special operations units may have some restrictions; (5) the non-interference with reporting by public affairs officers; (6) the responsibility of the military to provide transport and communications facilities for pool journalists; (7) the application of these principles to the national media pool; and (8) the agreement by both parties to disagree on the issue of security review.[12]

Although agreement on these principles provided an important first step in resolving long-standing differences between the military and the media, it left as many unanswered questions as it resolved. An important unresolved issue is the meaning and extent of "open and independent coverage" in the first principle above. While reporters would like to believe it means that they can go where they want, when they want, and report on what they want, operational security (OPSEC) and the security of the force have always dictated otherwise. Nevertheless, the DoD directive requires that commanders grant reporters the maximum access possible to the battlefield.[13] The Secretary of Defense's guidance for OEF and OIF is consistent in calling for the media to "have long-term, minimally restrictive access."[14]

Another major issue left unresolved after the First Gulf War and which remains unresolved is the question of security review. The Department of Defense has remained adamant that it must retain authority to impose security review where operationally required, while the press finds no circumstances that would warrant such extreme measures. All find agreement, however, that certain ground rules to ensure the security of the operation and the safety of the force.[15]

HISTORICAL CURRENTS

Until the American Civil War, the United States military had neither cause nor capability to censor reports of the working press. There was neither a corps of American war correspondents nor a means to transmit information in a sufficiently timely manner that its dissemination could affect either actions on the battlefield or public opinion. What news that was transmitted came in the form of long-delayed personal letters from soldiers to their loved ones.[16] With the advent of the telegraph in the early 1800s, however, everything changed.[17]

Although the Mexican-American War of 1846–1847 saw the emergence of the modern war correspondent,[18] the Civil War was the first major American conflict involving large numbers of reporters. This led to the first concerted government effort at censorship. As Matthew Jacobs explains:

> The American Civil War engendered a great deal of censorship on both sides, particularly in the North where the population was divided in its support of the conflict. The North adopted voluntary censorship but did not issue guidelines, resorting largely to post publication punishment. After the *New York Journal of Commerce* and the *New York World* published a forged letter from Abraham Lincoln about plans to expand the draft, these publications were suspended for two days. Similarly, General Ambrose Burnside shut down the Chicago Tribune for three days, until President Lincoln countermanded the order with a telegram warning that censorship would do more harm than good. . . . The South, for its part, kept a close watch on the press but did not punish or prosecute any newspapers. Despite the formal restrictions, Civil War reporting in both the North and the South was plentiful and often critical of the respective governments.[19]

Contrary to the broad coverage describe above, President Lincoln placed far greater restrictions on media reporting within the border states. The President permitted his Secretaries of State and War to censor at will these slave states, which had not seceded but which held dubious loyalties to the Union.[20] President Lincoln commented at the time: "Must I shoot a simple soldier who deserts, but not touch a hair on a wily agitator who induces him to desert."[21] Censorship measures included placing all telegraph lines under military supervision, thus limiting the ability of correspondents to send stories without submitting them to prior review.[22]

Whatever the tensions that had developed between the media and the government during the Civil War were dissipated during the Indian Wars that occupied our military over the next thirty years. Reporters, although not in great numbers, accompanied General George Crook and General George Custer in their efforts to quell Indian uprisings. Largely because the views of reporters paralleled those of the military in having little sympathy for, or understanding of, marauding bands of Indian warriors, relations improved and censorship was minimal.[23]

With competition among newspapers growing, provocation by agitating editors became a major impetus for greater censorship in the Spanish-

American War. In the era of yellow journalism represented by newspaper barons like William Randolph Hearst, official government policy for the first time permitted prepublication review of incoming dispatches as key telegraph offices were monitored.[24] Grant Squires, for example, was appointed military censor in New York.[25] There were other instances of carefully controlled censorship during this conflict, as well. After the battleship *Maine* was blown up, severe controls on information were imposed in the area of operations.[26] Similarly, John J. Pershing excluded the press entirely from the successful pacification campaign he was waging on Mindoro Island in the Philippines, and General Shafter banished all Hearst reporters from captured Santiago.[27] American naval censorship was also imposed in 1914 at Vera Cruz by U.S. leaders following U.S. intervention there.[28]

The late entry by the United States into World War I brought with it two factors that greatly influenced the tight control of military information during that conflict. The first was a carefully instituted information security program already established by the British and French forces. The second was the choice of General John J. Pershing as commander of the American Expeditionary Force in Europe.[29] As he had been on Mindoro much earlier, Pershing was very comfortable with limited access for the media. Although not going as far as the British and French had initially gone in 1914 in banning all reporters from accompanying their forces, Pershing attempted to ensure operational security through several means. First, he limited accredited correspondents to thirty-one; second, he imposed rigorous prepublication censorship; and third, he restricted reporters' access to the lines where combatant activities were taking place.[30] Any reporter publishing a story without prepublication review had his credentials withdrawn immediately.[31] Although these restrictions were relaxed by mid-1918, their impact was nevertheless significant.

During World War II, different security considerations in different theaters of operation resulted in the inconsistent application of information controls. The 1942 Code of Wartime Practices was issued by the new Office of Censorship, but compliance by newsmen with its terms was voluntary.[32] In the Pacific, General MacArthur used heavy censorship to ensure that only his message was published.[33] This was also true for a short period in North Africa, where a tight lid was placed over negotiations between the Free and Vichy French. Conversely, news reporting in Europe was nearly unrestricted, although all publications had to be pre-cleared. Gottschalk reports that the media was given ready access to the battlefields in France and Italy, with five hundred newsmen accredited in London on D-Day.[34] Some stories that would be published today were censored. An example was the four hundred friendly fire deaths resulting from the loss of twenty transports over Bari to American guns.[35] Nevertheless, the press was present at the November 1942 invasion of North Africa, the July 1943 invasion of Sicily, the November

1943 invasion of Tarawa, the January 1944 invasion of Kwajalein Atoll, the October 1944 invasion of the Philippines, and the February 1945 invasion of Iwo Jima.[36]

With MacArthur in command in Korea, reporting the Korean War was not easy. By December 1950, General MacArthur had imposed full censorship on all journalists, and in January 1951, all accredited U.S. reporters were placed under the jurisdiction of the U.S. military forces within the UN Command.[37] The determination on censorship, surprisingly, was considered the lesser of two evils by the working press. Until this action, reporters had to guess whether their stories would incur the wrath of the command, and possible expulsion by MacArthur.[38] Despite these restrictions, U.S. correspondents were often seen on the front lines and accompanied UN forces into Inchon.[39]

The Vietnam conflict represented a new era for journalists, and for the military in dealing with the media. As the author can attest, this was a difficult and frustrating period for the U.S. military and press alike.[40] Phillip Knightly accurately places the conflict in perspective when he explains that there was no focus, no simply explained cause, no easily identifiable foe, no threat to U.S. territory, and therefore, no national feeling of patriotism.[41] Contrary to the Cuban missile crisis in 1962, however, when reporters were not allowed on ships or aircraft deployed for purposes of the quarantine of Cuba, or to set foot on the Guantanamo Naval Base,[42] journalists could travel relatively freely in South Vietnam.[43]

Unlike World War II and the Korean War, there was no formal security review or censorship applied to journalists during the Vietnam conflict.[44] The United States Mission in Saigon did issue guidelines covering "the release of combat information" in 1965. The guidelines "requested" that reporters not release information concerning specific U.S. casualty figures, troop movements, and order of battle information until it was clear the Viet Cong had the information. At least two reporters had their accreditation revoked for thirty days for failing to follow the guidelines.[45]

While stories were neither censored nor reviewed for security, "[c]ensorship at the source reached its apogee in the Vietnam War. . . [Reporters] who did not have the trust of senior officers . . . were given little information."[46] Several reporters fell into this category. William G. Ackerly correctly explains:

> The core of the military-media feud lay in the central contradictions of the policies pursued by Presidents Kennedy, Johnson and Nixon. Each president sought to avoid making Vietnam the central focus of U.S. policy, but each also feared that no U.S. president could "lose Vietnam" without adverse political repercussions. Thus, the U.S. military was told by the White House to avoid "losing Vietnam"—at the lowest possible cost, militarily and politically. The only problem was that this "lowest cost" kept getting more and more expen-

sive, especially in terms of American lives. And the American press was there to see it. The press covered the government's attempts to simultaneously appease society's "hawks" and "doves."[47]

The concerns of the press during the height of the Vietnam conflict centered on the quality of information provided by the military at daily briefings (the famous "five o'clock follies") and government secrecy generally, rather than access issues.[48] For the young military officers fighting the war without the total commitment of their government, however, the frustration was directed at a press constantly criticizing the conduct of the war, without acknowledging or understanding the limitations on operations created by policy considerations in Washington. For these officers, the perceived unfair press criticism of the U.S. role was the most significant factor in the erosion of public support for the war.[49] These same officers would hold senior positions during the next encounter in which the interests of the Fourth Estate clashed with those of the military—Grenada.

THE MODERN ERA OF MILITARY-PRESS RELATIONS

Operation Urgent Fury,[50] the 1983 United States invasion of the island nation of Grenada in the Caribbean, marked a new chapter in press-military relations. When army and marine forces entered Grenada in the early morning hours of October 25, 1983,[51] no correspondents were present and none had been advised of the operation in advance. When the American people were advised of the intervention the following day, the statement provided by Secretary of Defense Weinberger concerning the lack of press coverage included the comment that the military commander in the field had made the decision because of the difficulty of guaranteeing the safety of press representatives and the need to maintain secrecy during the initial phases of the intervention.[52]

The press was not allowed access until the third day of the operation, October 27, when fifteen reporters were escorted ashore by the military for a few hours.[53] The press ban was not fully removed until October 30, when 168 correspondents were allowed on the island and authorized to remain indefinitely, although without military support services.[54]

The press was outraged. Anthony Lewis demanded to know "[w]hat feared knowledge was President Reagan trying to keep from the American people on Grenada?"[55] The Managing Editors of the Associated Press condemned the government action as "inexcusable."[56] Walter Cronkite argued that "[t]his is our foreign policy and we have a right to know precisely what is happening, and there can be no excuse in denying the people that right."[57] Conversely, George Will opined:

People can reasonably differ about when journalists should have been allowed into Grenada. But journalists have earned a certain coolness from officials making life and death decisions. Many journalists advocate an "adversary" stance toward their government, denying any duty to weigh the consequences of what they print or broadcast. But incantation of the words "the public's right to know" is no substitute for thinking. Someone must make judgments. Many journalists assert a moral as well as a constitutional right to the status of—strictly speaking—irresponsibility.[58]

The media seethed for months, and then on January 10, 1984, the major news organs issued a joint statement[59] calling for recognition of the "historic principle" that reporters "should be present at U.S. military operations" but acknowledging the media's responsibility to "reaffirm their recognition of the importance of U.S. military mission security and troop safety."[60] In response to the media's criticism, the Chairman of the Joint Chiefs of Staff (JCS), General Vessey, created a panel headed by Major General Winant Sidle, to make recommendations to him on the issue of "How do we conduct military operations in a manner that safeguards the lives of our military and protects the security of the operations while keeping the public informed through the media?"[61] Although the initial plan for this study called for representatives from the working press and from the military, the major media organizations, while desiring to cooperate, determined it would be "inappropriate for media members to serve on a government panel."[62] General Sidle thus called upon experienced retired members of the press and journalism professors who were expert in military-media relations. The panel, meeting at Fort McNair in Washington, DC, in February 1984, set into principle the significant lesson from Grenada, as stated by the U.S. Commander, Admiral Joseph Metcalf, that the press ban had been counterproductive because the American people were denied the full appreciation that "in both a military and strategic sense, all objectives were realized."[63]

The Sidle Report, structured as a statement of principles and a series of recommendations, emphasized as a basic tenet that "it is essential that the U.S. news media cover U.S. military operations to the maximum degree possible consistent with mission security and the safety of U.S. forces."[64] The major recommendations were presented in two sections, with the second section providing an explanation of panel comments on each recommendation. The substance of the report declared (1) the need for early public affairs planning, concurrent with operational planning; (2) recognition of the need for a national media pool, but of minimal duration with full coverage restored as soon as feasible; (3) a recommendation to develop a pre-established and constantly updated accreditation list of correspondents in case of a military operation for which a pool is required; (4) acceptance by the press of basic security ground rules as a basic condition to media access; and (5) consideration in military public affairs planning for adequate logistics, transportation, and equipment support for all media members assigned. A final recommendation concerned measures necessary for improved military-media understanding and cooperation, to include increased education concerning the media's role in service schools, more frequent and regularized meetings between senior military and press representatives to address current problems, and the need to explore the special problems of ensuring military security when real-time or near-real time news media audiovisual coverage is available on the battlefield. [65]

The Department of Defense wasted no time in moving to implement the recommendations in the Sidle Panel Report. After instructing operational commanders to plan for public affairs in all future operational planning, the Department of Defense (DoD) implemented plans for a DoD News Media Pool. [66] The initial plan called for four television reporters, one camera reporter, and one sound technician, two news agency reporters, and one magazine correspondent. Following protests from the nation's newspapers, a newspaper was added. [67] The plan called for rotating the one newspaper slot among eight leading dailies.

In addition to four planned tests of the national pool orchestrated by DoD, [68] the pool was used for the first time in a real operation in Operations Earnest Will and Praying Mantis as part of our ship escort plan for Kuwaiti vessels in the Persian Gulf in 1987–1988. The pool was viewed as a success in those operations because no media were in the area with access to military operations, reporters could not travel to the scene without military assistance, and the capacity of navy ships in the area to accommodate the press was extremely limited. [69] A year later, in a pool created to cover Operation Nimrod Dancer in Panama when the United States moved military reinforcements into that country because of the unlawful nullification of the national election results in May 1989, criticism, rather than praise, was voiced. In Panama, reporters already had access to the area, and the creation of a mandatory national media pool restricted, rather than enhanced, access. [70] Again in 1989, criticism was voiced during Operation Just Cause, when a similar pool was established, as U.S. forces entered Panama City in December to restore order, save lives, and protect U.S. interests under the Panama Canal Treaty. [71] In Panama, the pool concept was a failure. Pool reporters were not transported into the area of hostilities until the combat was nearly over, and when they did arrive, they were given army briefings rather than access to the front lines. [72] To make matters worse, those reporters already assigned in Panama were restricted to Howard Air Force Base to ensure early access to the pool which the Department of Defense was unable to deliver in time for the fighting. [73]

The media concerns following Operation Just Cause led the Department of Defense's Assistant Secretary for Public Affairs, Pete Williams, to request Fred Hoffman, longtime Associated Press Pentagon correspondent and former Deputy Assistant Secretary of Defense for Public Affairs in the Reagan Administration, to head a panel to review the press concerns that had arisen during Operation Just Cause and to make recommendations on how greater press accommodation, consistent with mission security, could be effected.[74] Of the seventeen recommendations offered by Mr. Hoffman in his report, five were accepted for immediate implementation, six were agreed to in principle but required some refinement, and six were taken under consideration, with the recognition that they would require "further consideration and coordination with the Joint Chiefs of Staff, the Unified Commands, and the media pool members."[75] The five recommendations the Assistant Secretary agreed to act on immediately included the following:

> The ASD(PA) [Assistant Secretary of Defense for Public Affairs] must be prepared to weigh in aggressively with the Secretary of Defense and the JCS Chairman where necessary to overcome any secrecy or other obstacles blocking prompt deployment of a pool to the scene of action. . . .
>
> After a pool has been deployed, the ASD(PA) must be kept informed in a timely fashion of any hitches that may arise. He must be prepared to act immediately, to contact the JCS Chairman, the Joint Staff Director of Operations, and other Senior officers who can serve to break through any obstacles to the pool. The ASD(PA) shall call upon the Defense Secretary for help as needed. . . .
>
> The ASD(PA) should study a proposal by several of the Panama poolers that future pools deploy in two sections. The first section would be very small and would include only reporters and photographers. The second section, coming later, would bring in supporting gear, such as satellite uplink equipment. . . .
>
> The national media pool should never again be herded as a single unwieldy unit. It should be broken up after arrival at the scene of action to cover a wider spectrum of the story and then be reassembled periodically to share the reporting results. . . .
>
> During deployments, there should be regular briefings, for pool newsmen and newswomen by senior operations officers so the poolers will have an up-to-date and complete overview of the progress of an operation they are covering.[76]

This commitment on the part of DoD was followed by the March 30, 1990 dissemination of a new JCS publication,[77] which provided new planning requirements for public affairs. Under this guidance to the regional joint operational commanders (CINCs), the CINCs are required to coordinate all public affairs decisions, guidance, and activities with DoD Public Affairs and JCS to ensure the accredited media, if the pool is no longer operational, gain the greatest possible access to information. As the DoD later reported to the

Congress after the First Gulf War, this JCS publication required the CINCs to issue the appropriate public affairs instructions, after coordination with ASD(PA) and JCS, and implement public affairs policy, to include providing transportation and communication equipment support for the National Media Pool, unless unavoidable military necessity (safety or mission essential considerations) required all available resources.[78]

The 1990 guidance was tested only five months later when Saddam Hussein invaded tiny Kuwait in the Persian Gulf.[79] The immediate U.S. response, sanctioned by the United Nations, was Operation Desert Shield. During this initial operation, the press accommodations worked well enough and appeared to satisfy the media, as well as the military. This was largely because no American or European reporters were in Saudi Arabia, the deployment for U.S. and allied forces was in the early stages, and the media could not have otherwise gained access. Moreover, the military gained from the positive stories of U.S. training and deployment.

As the climate shifted from one of watchful waiting to offensive military operations, however, the press chafed under the requirements of pool restrictions imposed for Desert Storm. The DoD and JCS had approved guidelines which specified:

> To the extent that individuals in the news media seek access to the U.S. area of operations, the following rules apply: Prior to or upon commencement of hostilities, media pools will be established to provide initial combat coverage of U.S. forces. U.S. news media personnel present in Saudi Arabia will be given the opportunity to join CENTCOM media pools, provided they agree to pool their products. News media personnel who are not members of the official CENTCOM media pools will not be permitted into forward areas. Reporters are strongly discouraged from attempting to link up on their own with combat units. U.S. commanders will maintain extremely tight security throughout the operational area and will exclude from the area of operations all unauthorized individuals.[80]

The U.S. Central Command (CENTCOM) Guidelines also provided for prepublication review by the CENTCOM public affairs staff of any articles written after the inception of hostilities. The guidelines stated:

> In the event of hostilities, pool products will be subject to review before release to determine if they contain sensitive information about military plans, capabilities, operations, or vulnerabilities . . . that would jeopardize the outcome of the operation or the safety of U.S. or coalition forces. Material will be examined solely for its conformance to the attached ground rules, not for its potential to express criticism or cause embarrassment.[81]

Many in the press cried foul and demanded they be given greater access to the battlefield than provided by CENTCOM pools, urging that denial of unfettered access to news was akin to a constitutional violation.[82] Criticisms also included the claim that that prepublication review was a prior restraint, amounting to censorship, for which no extreme circumstances could be shown where national security was believed to be in peril.[83] Other journalists, however, felt the media restrictions were reasonable and necessary to protect the troops. Paul Kamenar, writing in *Legal Times* on January 28, 1991, reminded his readers that

> the free speech clause of the First Amendment is not absolute and does not protect the publication, for example, [from charges] of obscenity, so too are we reminded of Chief Justice Charles Evans Hughes oft-quoted observation in Near v. Minnesota that the First Amendment's guarantee of freedom of speech does not bar the government from preventing the publication of sailing dates of transports or the number and location of troops.[84]

While the public at large was more amused than concerned about press complaints in the First Gulf War, finding the televised daily command briefings by CENTCOM from Dhahran, Saudi Arabia, informative, Secretary of Defense Cheney did take the media concerns seriously. After the Desert Storm cease-fire, DoD asked all pool journalists for comments on military-press arrangements. A letter from seventeen news executives began a process of negotiation. Over the course of eight months, Assistant Secretary Williams engaged in a series of negotiating sessions with representatives of *Time*, the *Washington Post*, Knight-Ridder, ABC, and the Associated Press. The Services and CINCs also offered thoughtful and balanced views on the media concerns. Their comments focused on practicalities but noted the lack of accountability for the consequences of the publication of information that would have immediate adverse effects on U.S. operations.[85]

The negotiations[86] resulted in nine principles that the Defense Department and the media representatives could agree upon.[87] The news organizations originally proposed ten principles. The tenth, dealing with security review stated: "News materials—words and pictures—will not be subject to security review." The Pentagon proposed instead the following principle: "Military operational security may require review of news material for conformance to reporting ground rules."[88] The fundamental disagreement could not be bridged, just as it has not to this day. Nevertheless, Louis D. Boccardi, president and chief executive officer of the Associated Press, who had organized the original meeting with Secretary Cheney, which led to the negotiations, said of the 1992 guidelines: "It is the consensus of our group that the guidelines offer the promise of the kind of coverage the citizens of a democracy are entitled to have, while they also recognize the need for security ground rules in combat zones."[89]

On the whole, the media seemed satisfied.[90] There was, of course, a small group led by *Harper's* editor, John MacArthur, who attacked the principles as a sellout of the First Amendment.[91] However, the mainstream press, led by *Time* magazine's Washington Bureau Chief, defended the principles.[92]

The 1992 agreed-upon principles were not praised by the CINCs because of their continuing concern with the consequences of publication of information that would have immediate adverse effects on U.S. operations. Nevertheless, there was a recognition that these largely hortatory principles were not inconsistent in any meaningful way with the functioning of the National Media Pool or with the way press arrangements actually worked during the First Gulf War. There was a recognition, as well, that in future conflicts, the CINC's public affairs officers would continue to provide guidelines on reportable information, access, story filing, logistics, and other matters tailored to the particular situation.

The decade of the 1990s was the decade of UN peacekeeping and peace enforcement under both Chapter VI (peacekeeping with consensual entry), Chapter VII (peace enforcement with all necessary means), and Chapter VIII of the UN Charter (enforcement through regional organizations) as in Bosnia and Kosovo[93] with a NATO command structure. Because these operations involved multilateral forces and command structures in which U.S. military leaders could not control the information flow exclusively, and thus operational security effectively, these are not addressed here except in a cursory fashion.[94] In Somalia during UN Operations UNOSOM I and II, for example, the opportunity to enforce even the smallest modicum of press restraint in favor of operational security did not exist. In addition, reporters in Somalia seldom understood the military operational context of what they were reporting. That was reflected in 1993, when U.S. Army Rangers clearly won a highly publicized protracted firefight in Mogadishu, but that fact was lost among the casualty figures and other images that were broadcast live on television.

The 1990s' significant exception occurred in Haiti. Operation Uphold Democracy in 1994 was the last major operation prior to 9/11 in which the U.S. military controlled both operational security and press relations. In the Haiti operation, army leaders within the XVIII Airborne Corps and Joint Task Force (JTF) 180 took the lead in educating their unit commanders on what to expect from the press,[95] while thoroughly briefing the press in advance of the deployment of forces.[96]

As General Shelton and Lieutenant Colonel Vane have pointed out, "what made the Haiti operation unique was the concept of merging the media into operational units before the invasion began."[97] General Shelton explained at the time: "It was evident to [public affairs] planners and the JTF commander that what was missing from America's recent military operations were reporters who would participate in and cover the final planning and initial assault by U.S. troops."[98]

The leaders of Joint Task Force 180 in Haiti, careful observers of the U.S. experience in Somalia, were acutely aware of the principle within Army Field Manual 100-5 that: "Dramatic visual presentation can rapidly influence public—and therefore—political opinion so that the political underpinnings of war and operations other than war may suddenly change with no prior indication to the commander in the field."[99] They were convinced from Somalia that an uneducated press was no ally. For this reason, the army leadership had committed itself to the nine principles within the 1992 Statement of Principles, largely replicated in the 2008 Statement of Principles currently in force,[100] in both their planning and their execution, with the result that the operation stands as a model of good media relations. The proof lay in the lack of leaks, the stories emphasizing the military's professionalism in a complex operation, and the fact that the media really seemed to understand what they were reporting. The excellent coverage of numerous civil-affairs initiatives and of the great assistance provided by our forces in the slow process of nation building in Haiti marked a military-press relationship unusual in military operations overseas.

It was the merging of media representatives within military units in Haiti that we have seen replicated in both Operation Enduring Freedom and Operation Iraqi Freedom. In neither operation were journalists required to embed. There were, however, inherent journalist risks if they did, and inherent safety risks if they did not. Those who did not seek embed status were exposed to far greater dangers, but gained a deeper insight and the opportunity to interview a greater range of individuals. As Bill Katovsky and Timothy Carlson explain with respect to Iraq:

> Embedded and unilateral journalists covered the same war, but they experienced it in different ways. An embed's point of view was narrow and restricted. It depended on where the unit was camped and what it was doing. An enterprising unilateral might manage a broader perspective and talk to more sources, including Iraqis, but he or she often lacked the means and opportunity to get close to combat.[101]

The consensus among reporters in Afghanistan and Iraq in Operations Enduring Freedom and Iraqi Freedom is that the process of embedding, despite its limitations, allowed the American people to enjoy unparalleled coverage of these operations.[102] Never had the press been presented with such access. More importantly, the Pentagon went a long way toward restoring the trust considered breached during the Vietnam conflict.[103]

RESOLVING PRESS RESTRICTIONS IN THE COURTS

Paralleling the tortuous path just described, the same issues—lack of access and pre-publication review—were focused upon in the federal courts. In the legal context, just as in the political context, those press restrictions necessary to ensure the security of the operation and the safety of the troops were preserved. Following the conclusion of Operation Urgent Fury in Grenada where all media had been excluded during the first sixty hours of the operation, publisher Larry Flynt of *Hustler* magazine filed suit in Federal District Court in Washington, DC, seeking both declaratory and injunctive relief against Secretary Weinberger, [104] while alleging the exclusion of *Hustler* reporters from the island during the initial phase of the operation had violated his First Amendment rights. [105]

The government response was that since the restrictions complained of had been lifted, the suit should be dismissed as moot. [106] Flynt argued that the legal claims fell within an exception to the mootness doctrine, namely, "capable of repetition yet evading review," first articulated by the Supreme Court in 1911 in *Southern Pacific Terminal Company vs. ICC*. [107] Judge Oliver Gash, however, found that there was no reasonable expectation that the situation would be repeated, as required by the Supreme Court in *Southern Pacific Terminal*, for application of the exception. [108] Furthermore, Judge Gash stated that even if the challenge represented a live controversy, although he had doubts Flynt's constitutional rights had been violated, he would exercise (the court's) equitable jurisdiction and decline to enter an injunction. [109] He found that the relief sought by plaintiff "would limit the range of options available to the commanders in the field in the future, possibly jeopardizing the success of military operations and the lives of military personnel and thereby gravely damaging the national interest." [110] The court thus dismissed as moot both the request for injunction, as well as the request for declaratory relief, finding there was no "fixed and definite federal policy at issue." [111]

One week after the start of Operation Desert Storm, the Department of Defense was again sued over its policies of controlling access, this time through a pool arrangement. In *The Nation Magazine v. U.S. Department of Defense*, [112] five journalists, nine publications, a national radio network, and a news agency challenged the Department of Defense press restrictions in the Desert Storm theater of operations. They asked the United States District Court for the Southern District of New York to declare that the "defendants' creation and promotion of a pool of journalists is unconstitutional," to order "the defendants to provide the press access where U.S. forces were deployed or engaged in overt operations," and to enjoin the "defendants from preventing, hindering, obstructing, delaying, or exercising a prior restraint on conduct constituting freedom of the press by plaintiffs and other members of the U.S. press."[113]

After finding the legal question of press access to the battlefield to be a novel one,[114] the District Court found that a minimal constitutional right of access is at least implicated by the First Amendment:

> [T]here is support for the proposition that the press has at least some minimal right of access to view and report about major events that affect the functioning of government, including, for example, an overt combat operation. As such, the government could not wholly exclude the press from a land area where a war is occurring that involves the country. But this conclusion is far from certain.[115]

The court then determined that the plaintiffs had standing and that the claim for injunctive and declaratory relief did not present a nonjudiciable political question.[116] Judge Sand further found that the press restriction issues as a whole were not moot because they "were capable of repetition, yet evading review," with the proviso that pooling rules were likely to be different and differently applied in subsequent conflicts.[117] With respect to the particular claims of the plaintiffs, the court found the request for injunctive relief to be moot since "the regulations have been lifted and the press is no longer constrained from traveling throughout the Middle East, [and] there is no longer any presently operative practice for this court to enjoin."[118] With regard to the request for declaratory relief, the court declined to decide the question in the abstract, stating: "prudence dictates we leave the definition of the exact parameters of press access to military operations abroad for a later date when the full record is available, in the unfortunate event that there is another military operation."[119]

Finally, the court also declined the plaintiffs' equal protection challenge to the pools. Judge Sand elicited little disagreement among the plaintiffs "that DoD may place time, place and manner restrictions on the press upon showing that there is a significant governmental interest."[120] Nevertheless, when he urged plaintiffs, in light thereof, to suggest alternatives to utterly unfettered access, they refused and adhered to an absolute "no limitation" approach. The court thus dismissed the complaint, declining to decide an unfocused controversy.[121]

There have been no significant decisions *in the military context* on prepublication review or prior restraint. During Desert Storm as well as during the post–9/11 conflicts in Afghanistan and Iraq, challenges on this basis were likely not raised because, at worst, prepublication review (prior restraint) just delayed the stories. Another rationale for the lack of litigation in this area, either after the First Gulf War or during Operations Enduring Freedom or Iraqi Freedom, is that it would be imprudent to subject the prior restraint doctrine to a legal test at a time when the contemporary judiciary is relatively conservative.[122]

While the government may validly take measures to prevent publication of the number and location of troops in wartime,[123] "content based exclusion" of protected speech may be enforced only if the government shows that the exclusion "is necessary to serve a compelling state interest and that it is narrowly drawn to achieve that end."[124] Nevertheless, in the First and Second Gulf Wars and in Afghanistan, acceptance of the ground rules constituted an agreement on the part of either pool members (in Gulf I) or those embedded (currently) that the information controlled therein was properly restricted by the justification of a "compelling" governmental interest.

THE WAY FORWARD

The Vietnam War, in the view of many who were military participants, was an aberration in military-press relations. There were few restrictions on the media related to access to geographical areas, but restrictions at the source, through withheld and inaccurate information, soured the press. This occurred at the same time that efforts of U.S. forces to implement a flawed political agenda were turning the nation against a continued role in Vietnam.[125] Concomitantly, the military distrust of the media for a perceived lack of accountability in Vietnam carried through Grenada, Panama, and Desert Storm.

The serious negotiations between the Department of Defense and respected representatives of the media in 1992 brought the process back into balance. Subsequently, the integration of the press into combatant units in Operation Uphold Democracy in Haiti, coupled with the media's clear understanding and enforcement of the security of the operation, gave a new equilibrium to military-press relations. While there were those who argued that one-sided operations like Uphold Democracy did not offer a fair assessment of military-media relations that only major conflict could provide, it was telling that the press as a whole, and the military, accepted and incorporated the new principles in their planning.

In 1996, the Department of Defense implemented the 1992 principles in directives, with the further experience of Somalia, Haiti, and Rwanda to draw upon.[126] The 1996 directives were republished in 2000, prior to the 9/11 attacks, and retained the earlier principles.[127] The current directive, published in 2008,[128] retains all the elements of its predecessors while redrafting, but not changing substantively, the Statement of Principles.[129]

Although the current DoD directive incorporates each of the principles first negotiated in 1992 with the media, there are those in the press who will argue that providing a numerical limitation on the number of reporters allowed to accompany the force for specific types of operations should also be incorporated. They would argue that that this would serve both military and media interests by affording both the opportunity to better prepare for accommodating the press in specific types of operations, and for the press to ensure it has experienced reporters assigned for such contingencies. With regard to experience, the current directive does not change the minimal requirement for accreditation—that the correspondent be associated with a news organization. Requiring that only experienced reporters are assigned would enhance reporting and ensure that the most accurate picture is provided the American people.

It is also significant that none of the DoD directives cited, including the current 2008 version, adequately address differences in press coverage standards imposed by the Statement of Principles versus those imposed by the UN or other foreign governments in multinational operations, such as we are currently engaged in Afghanistan. The UN standards, and those of some European nations, are far more rigid, yet seldom enforced. The U.S. press standards, conversely, are more realistic, while capable of enforcement through revocation of accreditation.

Despite the minor deficiencies noted, the military-media negotiating process, to include the Sidle Panel in 1984, the Hoffman Panel in 1990, the media negotiations with Assistant Secretary of Defense Pete Williams in 1992, and the current (2008) directive, informed by our experience with embedding, has resulted in an understandable and reasonable accommodation of operational and journalism interests. The courts have not been a major player in this process, largely because of their conservative tenor, public support for the military versus the media, and the prior history of court decisions indicating a lack of eagerness to address First Amendment access or prior restraint in the military context. We can certainly expect future debate on these issues, as occurred after the McCrystal affair, but as long as our young men and women are sent to battle to defend the American people, including the American media, operational security and the safety of our forces will be carefully balanced with the right to be independently informed.

Chapter Twenty

Future Perspectives in Addressing Terror Violence

The most serious discourse today concerns the military capabilities and intentions of nonstate actors, acting either for themselves, for religious elites, or as surrogates for state sponsors. During the Cold War with the former Soviet Union, the major threat was clearly the fear of miscalculation by the Soviets. Today, that threat has been recharacterized in terms of deliberate aggression against the United States by nontraditional actors willing to take suicidal risks to inflict premeditated, brutal savagery on innocent civilians. The goal of the attackers is not to force regime change directly, but rather to force those important policy changes that can influence regime change.

Commitment to national security is only as valid as the military, economic, and political policies and plans that shape the areas and people from which these threats originate. The problem has always been to determine which policies, and how applied, can make the greatest contribution to countering the threat—a threat now represented by social and religious systems that foster or at least condone aggressive response to differing religious and social values. This has never been more true than in Afghanistan and in Iraq. Security, then, means more than simply protecting the land on which we live; it embraces a comprehensive understanding of the appropriate response to human aspirations for improved conditions of life, for equality of opportunity, and for justice and freedom. Where these interests are thwarted for peoples or groups within a particular state or region by armed protagonists representing narrow, restrictive interests, as in Afghanistan, our response must be one measured by the effective institutionalization of order.

The intersection between armed conflict and law has always been difficult, but until September 11, 2001, Americans had a clearer understanding of when they were, or were not, at war. Today's struggle against terror-violence is different, largely because of the religious element injected so deeply in its bosom. We have always, as a nation, been competent to deal with repressive practices of states, whether Communism, Fascism, or Nazism. But when addressing religiously controlled despotism, as seen in the Middle East and Southwest Asia, it is impossible to understand and address such behavior without understanding the religious and cultural roots.

The United States was jolted into an awareness of the changing character of aggression when its embassy in Tehran was seized on November 4, 1979, by Iranian militants who enjoyed the support of Ayatollah Khomeini's revolutionary government.[1] The 1983 terrorist attack on the marine battalion on the green line at the Beirut International Airport was followed in March 1986 by the bombing of a discotheque in Berlin by Libyan terrorists acting on President Kaddafi's orders. The United States responded to the Libyan attack by launching defensive strikes on military targets in Tripoli and Benghazi. The use of force directed by President Reagan in 1986 was preceded by conclusive evidence of Libyan responsibility for other prior acts of terrorism against the United States, with clear evidence that more were planned.[2]

In August 1998, al Qaeda terrorists bombed the U.S. embassies in Nairobi and Dar es Salaam, with significant loss of life. This was followed in October 2000 with a terrorist attack on the *USS Cole* in Yemeni waters. Finally, in September 2001, al Qaeda began a campaign of vitriol against the United States with attacks in New York and Washington, DC, with spill-over in Afghanistan, Iraq, and Yemen.

An examination of authorized responses to terrorist violence requires an understanding that terrorism is a strategy that does not adhere to any of the military or legal norms reflected in the Geneva Conventions of 1929 and 1949 or the Hague Conventions of 1899 and 1907. In fact, the fundamental characteristic of terrorism is reflected in its violation of the principles of discrimination, necessity, and proportionality. The only norm for terrorist violence is effectiveness. While traditional international law requires clear discrimination among those affected by an attack and proportion in an attack's intensity, the nature of terrorism is such that success is measured by the extent and duration of destructiveness, with no concern for those affected. In the contemporary language of defense economics, they wage countervalue rather than counterforce warfare.

A clear understanding of the terrorist mindset is important because the only credible response to terrorism is deterrence. There must be—as in the case of our current response against al Qaeda and the Taliban in Afghanistan and the insurgents and al Qaeda earlier in Baghdad—an assured, effective response that imposes unacceptable costs on perpetrators and those who make their activities possible. For domestic intruders, like Jose Padilla, the criminal law may suffice. For those operating outside the United States, the U.S. reaction must counter the terrorist's strategy within the parameters of international law, and more specifically, the law of armed conflict. Those who suggest otherwise neither understand the inherent flexibility of international law nor the cost of violating that law.

The thrust of the U.S. strategy in response to international terrorism, beginning with President Reagan's articulation of NSDD 138 in April 1984, has been to reclaim the initiative lost while the United States pursued a reactive policy toward unconventional threats such as terrorist violence. With the signing of NSDD 138, followed by President Clinton's issuing of PDD 62, and President Bush's declaration of the Bush Doctrine in the 2002 and 2006 National Security Strategies, preemptive self-defense measures have been authorized through carefully drawn national rules of engagement that ensure that our forces do not absorb the first hit where clear indicators of enemy attack are detected.

The inherent right of self-defense has provided the policy framework for all U.S. ROE. Within that framework, the concept of "necessity" in the counterterrorism context has always required that a hostile act occur or that a terrorist unit demonstrate hostile intent. The implementation of national guidance through promulgation of the 1980, 1986, and the current 1994 ROE, frequently amended since then, has greatly assisted in providing both clarity and flexibility of action for our theater commanders. The approval in each instance by the sitting Secretary of Defense has ensured consistency in the way all military commanders, wherever assigned, have addressed terrorist threat situations while providing the mechanism for the automatic amending of ROE or the issuance of supplemental measures upon the occurrence of specified conditions or events.

The thrust of the road map articulated in the 2002 and 2006 National Security Strategies, if it is to be effective, has to reclaim the initiative lost while the United States pursued a reactive policy to incidents of unconventional warfare under a prior presidency which neither deterred terrorists nor engaged in effective response. The key to an effective, coordinated policy to address the threat posed by those willing to target critical infrastructure in New York and at the Pentagon is the commitment to hold those accountable responsible under the law of armed conflict.

Full implementation of an effective National Security Strategy, as in that articulated by Presidents George W. Bush and Reagan, should lead to increased planning for protective and defensive measures to address this challenge to our national security, and where deterrence fails, to respond in a manner that eliminates the threat, rather than, as prior to the articulation of NSDD 138 by President Reagan, treating each incident after the fact as a singular crisis provoked by international criminals. By treating terrorists and others attempting to destroy critical infrastructure as participants in international coercion where clear linkage can be tied to a state actor, the right of self-defense against their sponsor is triggered, and responding coercion (political, economic, or military) may be the only proportional legal response to the threat. It would seem that our current president shares this perspective as reflected in his liberal use of drone aircraft to minimize the scourge of terrorism.

Notes

1. WAR ON TERROR

1. 2 J. Moore, DIGEST OF INTERNATIONAL LAW 404 (1906). This mission against the Seminoles in 1818 followed by four years President Madison's dispatch of General Jackson to Florida in 1814 to address a similar uprising by a consortium of tribes.

2. *Id.*

3. *Id.* at 409–414. The *Caroline* incident, often called the *Caroline* "case," was not resolved through the judicial process but, rather, through diplomatic correspondence.

4. 1 C. Hyde, INTERNATIONAL LAW 240 (2d ed. 1945).

5. 2 J. Moore, *supra* note 1, at 412.

6. *Participation in the North Atlantic Treaty of States Not Members of the United Nations*, Hearings Before the Senate Comm. on Foreign Relations on the North Atlantic Treaty, 81st Cong., 1st Sess. 101–02 (1949).

7. For a more complete discussion of this issue, see W. Thomas Mallison, *Limited Naval Blockade or Quarantine Interdiction: National and Collective Self-Defense Claims Valid Under International Law*, 31 GEO. WASH. L. REV. 335 (1962).

8. *See discussion in* James P. Terry, *The Iranian Hostage Crisis: International Law and U.S. Policy*, 31 JAG Jl 31 (1982).

9. UNSCR 457, Dec. 4, 1979.

10. Thirteen of 15 members of the Security Council voted in favor of the U.S. draft resolution calling for sanctions. East Germany and the Soviet Union voted *no*.

11. The arguments made on behalf of the United States by Mr. Civiletti and Mr. Owen for interim measures are reported verbatim in U.S. DEP'T OF STATE, SEL. DOC. NO. 15 (1979), at 2.

12. ORDER of December 15, 1979, U.S. V. IRAN, Provisional Measures, 1979, I.C.J. 16–17.

13. *President Imposes Oil Ban*, WASHINGTON POST, Nov. 13, 1979, at A-1. Although imposing an oil ban, the Carter Administration elected not to risk being embarrassed in the United Nations by a Security Council veto and lack of support in the General Assembly for a request made under the "Uniting for Peace" rationale. Unfortunately, by not exhausting this possible remedy to force compliance with the Court's decision, other options may have been precluded. There was one other possible rationale for not invoking Security Council assistance under Article 94. Since the Security Council, although a political body, would effectively be acting as an appellate court in reviewing and acting in the International Court of Justice's decision, it is quite possible that portions of the decision favorable to the United States might

not have been supported by the Council. In that case, certain United States options would have been precluded and a possible United States veto of Security Council action might have become necessary. Since the invocation of Article 94 is discretionary and the Court's decision is effective without further implementation, it could be that the Carter Administration determined it would preserve the greatest number of options by simply impressing on the world community the importance of the May 24, 1980, decision.

14. *Id.*, at A-1, A-16.

15. A discussion of these claims can be found in U.S. DEP'T OF STATE CUR. POL. NO. 179 (1980), at 2.

16. Exec. Order No. 12,170, 3 C.F.R. 457 (1979).

17. INTERNATIONAL EMERGENCY ECONOMIC POWERS ACT, 50 U.S.C. 1702 (Supp. III 1979). This law had been enacted in anticipation of emergency situations involving nations not on a war footing with the United States. Preceding legislation, the Foreign Assets Control Regulations, permitted the freezing of assets only of those nations with which the United States was at war. When difficulties with Cuba required similar protection in the late 1950s, the Cuban Assets Control Regulations were enacted. The 1977 Emergency Economic Powers legislation precludes the need for specific legislation each time the interests of American creditors are threatened and allows for implementation of protective measures despite the absence of a declaration of war.

18. CUR. POL. NO. 179, *supra* note 15, at 2.

19. *See Iran's Embassy Staff Cut*, WASHINGTON POST, Dec. 13, 1979, at A-1.

20. Exec. Order No. 12,205, 3 C.F.R. 248 (1980).

21. Exec. Order No. 12,211, 3 C.F.R. 253 (1980).

22. *Id.*

23. CUR. POL. NO. 179, *supra* note 15, at 2.

24. Of our allies, Great Britain proved to be the major surprise; Parliament refused to implement Prime Minister Thatcher's proposed sanctions and only agreed to suspend contracting with Iran from the date of the isolation measures. All contracts negotiated between November 4, 1979, and May 17, 1980, remained in effect, including those long-term contracts negotiated in anticipation of possible sanctions. As a result, the impact on Iran and the appearance of solidarity among the allies was severely reduced. Conversely, the United States received unexpected support from Japan and Portugal. Japan, ninety percent dependent on foreign fossil fuels, announced in late May that it would purchase no further Iranian crude at the announced price of $35 a barrel, $7 more at the time than Saudi Arabian crude. The degree to which this determination by Japan was based on American efforts to impose sanctions on Iran as opposed to the economics of the situation is difficult to determine. At the same time, Portugal denounced the Iranian actions and announced an intent to apply all the U.S.–requested measures. This was unexpected since the United States had recently been critical of human rights policies in Portuguese territories.

25. *Russia Supports Iran*, WASHINGTON POST, April 15, 1980, at A-1. For a contrary interpretation of the importance of this Soviet announcement, *see* U.S. DEP'T OF STATE, CUR. POL. NO. 165 (1980) at 2, wherein President Carter is quoted as discounting the Soviet promise of assistance to Iran. Carter stated that the Soviet transportation routes were insufficient to offset the impact of a blockade or boycott.

26. *Id.* at A-1.

27. *See* Richard Lillich, *Forcible Self Help by States to Protect Human Rights*, 53 IOWA L. REV. 325 (1967), for the argument that neither customary international law nor Article 51 of the Charter prohibits such acts of intervention. Interestingly, the International Court of Justice largely ignored the American rescue attempt of April 1980, finding it irrelevant to the determination of whether Iran's conduct in seizing the diplomatic hostages and entering the diplomatic premises violated international law. UNITED STATES v. IRAN, International Court of Justice (1980), at 40–41.

28. *See* U.S. DEP'T OF STATE CUR. POL. NO. 170 (April 1980), at 2–4, for a full explanation of the purpose and plan of the rescue mission, including the thinking that went into the decision to abort.

29. Secretary of Defense Harold Brown later claimed that it had been predetermined that fewer than six RH-53 helicopters would make the mission impossible. *Id.* at 3.

30. *Id.*

31. VIENNA CONVENTION ON DIPLOMATIC RELATIONS of 1961, 500 U.N.T.S. 95 (hereinafter VIENNA CONVENTION). Article 29 of the Convention provides: "The person of a diplomatic agent shall be inviolable. He shall not be liable to any form of arrest or detention. The receiving state shall treat him with due respect and shall take all appropriate steps to prevent any attack on his person, freedom or dignity."

32. Id. at Article 37 which, in pertinent part, provides:

1. The members of the family of a diplomatic agent forming part of his household shall, if they are not nationals of the receiving State, enjoy the privileges and immunities specified in Articles 29 to 36.
2. Members of the administrative and technical staff of the mission, together with members of their families forming part of their respective households, shall, if they are not nationals of, or permanently resident in the receiving State, enjoy the privileges and immunities specified in Articles 29-35, except that the immunity from civil and administrative jurisdiction of the receiving state specified in Paragraph 1 of Article 31 shall not extend to acts performed outside the course of their duties.

33. *See* E. Denza, DIPLOMATIC LAW: COMMENTARY ON THE VIENNA CONVENTION ON DIPLOMATIC RELATIONS 135 (1976).

34. Order of December 15, 1979, *supra* note 12, at 19.

35. It is interesting to note that the ICJ ruling in the United States' favor with respect to reparations (12-3) indicated that an award could only be fully determined by that court when the full extent of damages was known. U.S. v IRAN, *supra* note 27, at 43.

36. DAMES & MOORE V. REGAN, 453 U.S. 654 (1981).

37. WASHINGTON STAR, Jan. 29, 1981, at A-12, col. 3.

38. NATIONAL SECURITY DECISION DIRECTIVE 138, April 3, 1984.

39. *Quoted* in *Preemptive Anti-Terrorism Raids Allowed*, THE WASHINGTON POST, Apr. 16, 1984, at A-19.

40. Robert C. McFarlane, *Terrorism and the Future of Free Society*, Speech delivered at the National Strategic Information Center, Defense Strategy Forum, Washington, DC, March 25, 1985.

41. George Shultz, *Terrorism and the Modern World*, Speech to Park Avenue Synagogue, New York City, October 25, 1984, at 23.

42. Hugh Tovar, *Low Intensity Conflict: Active Responses in An Open Society*, Paper prepared for the CONFERENCE ON TERRORISM AND OTHER "LOW INTENSITY" OPERATIONS: INTERNATIONAL LINKAGES, Fletcher School of Law and Diplomacy, Medford, MA, April 1985, at 24.

43. *See discussion* in James Terry, *Countering State-Sponsored Terrorism*, NAVAL LAW REVIEW (Winter 1986) 159, 180.

44. *See* Kempster, *Cables Cited as Proof of Libyan Terror Role*, L.A. TIMES, Apr. 15, 1986, at 5, col. 5 (city ed.).

45. *Targeting a Mad Dog*, NEWSWEEK, Apr. 21, 1986, at 25.

46. *Transcript of Address by Reagan on Libya*, N.Y. TIMES, Apr. 15, 1986, at A-10, col. 1 (city ed.).

47. *Libyans Accused of Worldwide Plots*, N.Y. TIMES, April 15, 1986, at A-11, col. 4 (city ed.).

48. *Id..*

49. *See* Bernstein, *European Community Agrees on Libya Curbs*, N.Y. TIMES, Apr. 22, 1986, at A-8, col. 6 (city ed.).

50. Exec. Order No. 13010, 61 Fed. Reg. 37347.

51. Classified document described by Robert C. McFarlane in *Terrorism and the Future of a Free Society* (Speech at the National Strategic Information Center, Defense Strategy Forum, Washington, DC: March 25, 1985). *See discussion* in James P. Terry, *An Appraisal of Lawful*

Military Response to State-Sponsored Terrorism, NAVAL WAR COLLEGE REVIEW, May–June 1986, at 58.

52. Presidential Decision Directive 62, COMBATING TERRORISM, May 22, 1998. Richard A. Clarke, longtime senior National Security Council staff member, was appointed the first National Security Coordinator. In early 2004 during the 9/11 Commission hearings following the attacks on the World Trade Center and the Pentagon, Clarke testified that his strong advice to the Clinton and Bush Administrations to take the threat of bin Laden seriously was not heeded sufficiently. In one embarrassing moment, former National Security Advisor Sandy Berger attempted to remove draft memoranda from the National Archives that showed the recommendations of Clarke that were not acted on during the Clinton Administration.

53. Presidential Decision Directive 63, CRITICAL INFRASTRUCTURE PROTECTION, May 22, 1998. *See* W. Gary Sharp, Sr., CYBERSPACE AND THE USE OF FORCE (2001), at 201–204, for a comprehensive review of the major elements of PDD 63 and the requirements that have been imposed upon the various Departments of Government and the private sector under this directive.

54. George W. Bush, THE NATIONAL SECURITY STRATEGY OF THE UNITED STATES, The White House, March 16, 2006 (hereinafter 2006 NSS).

55. George W. Bush, THE NATIONAL SECURITY STRATEGY OF THE UNITED STATES, The White House, February 2002.

56. P. Baker, *Bush to Restate Terror Strategy: 2002 Doctrine of Preemptive War to be Reaffirmed,* WASH. POST, March 16, 2006, at A-1.

57. 2006 NSS, *supra* note 54, at 12.

58. *Id.* at 19.

59. *Id.* at 23.

2. LEGAL REQUIREMENTS FOR UNCONVENTIONAL WARFARE

1. 1949 Geneva Conventions and 1977 Additional Protocols are reproduced in John N. Moore, G. Roberts, and R. Turner (eds.), NATIONAL SECURITY LAW DOCUMENTS (1995).

2. All major news outlets reported on February 1, 2008 that two women with mental disabilities were used as bomb couriers for al Qaeda in a Baghdad pet market bombing resulting in significant loss of Iraqi lives.

3. *Id*, Common Art. 3, at 185.

4. *See discussion* in Waldemar Solf and E. Cummings, *A Survey of Penal Sanctions Under Protocol I to the Geneva Conventions of August 12, 1949*, CASE W. UNIV. JL.INT'L L. (Spring 1977) at 205.

5. Article 1(2) of Protocol I states that "civilians and combatants remain under the protection and authority of the principles of international law derived from established custom, from the principles of humanity and from the dictates of public conscience."

6. UN Charter art. 2, para. 4.

7. *See* League of Nations Covenant, art. 12.

8. Myres McDougal and F. Feliciano, LAW AND MINIMUM WORLD ORDER 142–43 (1961).

9. *See* Definition of Aggression, G.A. Res. 3314, 29 U.N. GAOR Supp. (No. 31) at 142, U.N. Doc. A/9631 (1974); Declaration on Principles of International Law Concerning Friendly Relations and Cooperation Among States in Accordance with the Charter of the United Nations, G.A. Res. 2625, 25 U.N. GAOR Supp. (No. 28) at 121, U.N. Doc. A/8028 (1970) [hereinafter cited as Declaration on Friendly Relations].

10. The Declaration on Friendly Relations includes the following provisions:

> "Every State has the duty to refrain from organizing or encouraging the organization of irregular forces or armed bands, including mercenaries, for incursion into the territory of another State."

"Every State has the duty to refrain from organizing, instigating, assisting or participating in acts of civil strife or terrorist acts in another State."

"No State shall organize, assist, foment, finance, incite or tolerate subversive, terrorist or armed activities directed towards the violent overthrow of the regime of another State."

Declaration on Friendly Relations, *supra* note 9, at 122–23.

11. "By accepting the respective texts [of the Declaration on Friendly Relations], states have acknowledged that the principles represent their interpretation of the obligations of the Charter." Resinstock, *The Declaration of Principles of International Law Concerning Friendly Relations: A Survey*, 65 AM. JUR. INT'L L. 713, 715 (1971).

12. Definition of Aggression, *supra* note 9, at 142.

13. Included in the list of acts of aggression are: "(g) The sending by or on behalf of a State of armed bands, groups, irregulars, or mercenaries, which carry out acts of armed force against another State of such gravity as to amount to the acts listed above, or its substantial involvement therein." Definition of Aggression, *supra* note 9, at 143.

14. A fundamental purpose of the UN Charter is to "maintain international peace and security." UN Charter, art. 1, para. 1. Article 5, Paragraph 2, of the Definition of Aggression provides: "A war of aggression is a crime against international peace. Aggression gives rise to international responsibility." Definition of Aggression, *supra* note 9, at 144.

3. STATE-SPONSORED TERRORISM

1. The most oft-cited are the Hague Conventions of 1899 and 1907, the Genocide Convention of 1948, and the Geneva Conventions of 1949.

2. Albert Soboul, THE FRENCH REVOLUTION 1789-1799, trans. Alan Forrest and Colin Jones (New York: Random House, 1975), 385.

3. Hannah Arendt, THE ORIGINS OF TOTALITARIANISM (New York: Harcourt Brace Jovanovich, 1973), 464.

4. Report of the Ad Hoc Committee on International Terrorism, UN Doc. A/9028 (1973).

5. *Id.*, at 17.

6. *See*, *e.g.*, Amnesty International Annual Report 2000/2001 (2001).

7. Felix Gross, *Political Violence and Terror in 19th and 20th Century Russia and Eastern Europe* in J. Kirkham, S. Levy, and W. Crotty, eds. A REPORT TO THE NATIONAL COMMISSION ON THE CAUSES AND PREVENTION OF VIOLENCE, vol. 8 (Washington: U.S. Gov. Printing Office, 1969) 428–32.

8. Paul Wilkinson, POLITICAL TERRORISM (New York: John Wiley, 1975) 126.

9. Hannah Arendt, *supra* note 76, at 474.

10. *Id.* at 458.

11. T. R. Gurr, WHY MEN REBEL (Princeton: Princeton University Press, 1970) 213.

12. Maurice Merleau-Ponty, HUMANISM AND TERROR: AN ESSAY ON THE COMMUNIST PROBLEM, trans. J. O'Neill (Boston: Beacon Press), 39.

13. *See* W. Thomas and Sally V. Mallison, *The Concept of Public Purpose Terror in International Law: Doctrines and Sanctions to Reduce the Destruction of Human and Material Values*, HOWARD LAW JOURNAL, vol. 18, (1974), 12–28.

14. UN Doc. A/8791/Add. 1 (1972).

15. UN Doc. A/PV. 2037 (1972), at 61.

16. Address by Secretary of State William P. Rogers, UN General Assembly, September 25, 1972, Press Release USUN 104 (1972).

17. *See* Resolution 3034 in UN Doc. A/RES. /3034(XXVII), of Dec. 18, 1972.

18. William Hannay, *International Terrorism: The Need for a Fresh Perspective*, INTERNATIONAL LAWYER, vol. 8 (1974), at 273.

19. In an earlier unpublished study completed by this author, the various conventions drafted by these organizations and their relative effectiveness are discussed. *See* James Terry, *Methodological Options for the Control of International Terrorism* (1979).

20. *See* A. Dallin and G. Breslauer, POLITICAL TERROR IN COMMUNIST SYSTEMS (Stanford: Stanford University Press, 1970). The authors detail the use of terror and conclude that it serves as a useful tool for motivation where positive benefits such as material inducements are lacking, noting: "Organized terror now serves to ensure compliant behavior during . . . a period of change, and to this extent, political terror, however painful or distasteful, has a rational basis." Id. at 7. *See also* Robert Conquest, THE GREAT TERROR: STALIN'S PURGE OF THE THIRTIES (New York: McMillan, 1968).

21. The systematic and ritualized use of terror in primitive societies has been studied exhaustively in E. V. Walter, TERROR AND RESISTANCE: A STUDY OF POLITICAL VIOLENCE (London: Oxford University Press, 1969).

22. The generally accepted view among representatives from former colonies is that colonial and "settler" regimes (such as Rhodesia, South Africa and Israel) have a virtual monopoly on true terrorism. This was emphasized by one of the panelists on terrorism at a meeting of the American Society of International Law, where it was said: "I assume therefore, at least for the weak members of the international community—which happens to coincide with the third world component—that terrorism in international relations, irrespective of how we define terrorism, is largely an attribute of the strong." Address by Professor Ibrahim Abu-Lughod of Northwestern University, American Society of International Law, April 12, 1973.

23. MERIP Reports, no. 59 (August 1977), at 22.

24. *Protection of Human Rights in Occupied Territories*, UN Office of Public Information Document OPI/582 (1977), at 5.

25. *Id.*

26. *See Treatment of the Palestinians in Israeli-Occupied West Bank and Gaza: Report of the National Lawyers Guild 1977 Middle East Delegation* (1978).

4. THE LAW OF SELF-DEFENSE AS APPLIED TO THE TERRORIST THREAT

1. Report of DoD Commission on Beirut International Airport Terrorist Act of 23 October 1983, at 129 (Dec. 20, 1983), *reprinted in* AM. FOREIGN POL'Y DOCUMENT 122, at 349, col. 2 (1983).

2. *See, e.g.*, Rovine, *Contemporary Practice of the United States Relating to International Law,* 68 AM. J. INT'L L. 720, 736 (1974) (statement of then-Acting Secretary of State Dean Rusk).

3. UN Charter, art. 51.

4. 5 Marjorie Whiteman, DIGEST OF INTERNATIONAL LAW sec. 25, at 971-72 (1965).

5. George Shultz, *Low Intensity Warfare: The Challenge of Ambiguity*, U.S. DEP'T OF STATE CURRENT POLICY NO. 783, at 1 (Jan. 1986).

6. U.N. Charter, art. 2, para. 4.

7. Myres McDougal, *The Soviet-Cuban Quarantine and Self-Defense*, 57 AM J. INT'L L. 697, 600 (1963).

8. Following the 1837 *Caroline* incident, Secretary of State Daniel Webster, in formulating an oft-cited principle of customary preemptive self-defense, said that there must be a demonstrated "necessity of self-defense, instant, overwhelming, leaving no choice of means and no moment of deliberation." It is clear, however, that the Webster formulation was *not* applied by the British in the decision to destroy the *Caroline*, at least with respect to the element requiring "no moment of deliberation." The U.S. Department of State has properly criticized Secretary Webster's formulation as follows: "This definition is obviously drawn from consideration of the right of self-defense in domestic law: the cases are rare indeed in which it would fit an international situation."

9. NATIONAL SECURITY DECISION DIRECTIVE 138, White House, Washington, DC, April 3, 1984.

10. U.S. Defense Official Noel Koch *quoted* in *Preemptive Anti-Terrorism Raids Allowed*, THE WASHINGTON POST, Apr. 16, 1984, at A-19.

11. Robert C. McFarlane, *Terrorism and the Future of Free Society*, Speech delivered at the National Strategic Information Center, Defense Strategy Forum, Washington, DC, March 25, 1985.

12. Classified document described by Robert C. McFarlane in *Terrorism and the Future of a Free Society, supra. See discussion* in James P. Terry, *An Appraisal of Lawful Military Response to State-Sponsored Terrorism*, NAVAL WAR COLLEGE REVIEW, May-June 1986, at 58.

13. Presidential Decision Directive 62, COMBATING TERRORISM, May 22, 1998. Richard A. Clarke, longtime senior National Security Council staff member, was appointed the first National Security Coordinator.

14. George W. Bush, THE NATIONAL SECURITY STRATEGY OF THE UNITED STATES, The White House, March 16, 2006. (hereinafter 2006 NSS)

15. George W. Bush, THE NATIONAL SECURITY STRATEGY OF THE UNITED STATES, The White House, February 2002.

16. 2006 NSS, *supra* note 14, at 12.

17. *Id.* at 19.

18. *Id.* at 23.

5. THE DEVELOPMENT OF RULES OF ENGAGEMENT

1. J. Ashly Roach, *Rules of Engagement*, NAVAL WAR C. REV., Jan.–Feb. 1983, at 46.

2. Joint Chiefs of Staff Peacetime Rules of Engagement for U.S. Seaborne Forces (May 1980).

3. Joint Chiefs of Staff Peacetime Rules of Engagement for U.S. Forces (June, 1986).

4. *See* J. P. Terry, *Countering State-Sponsored Terrorism: A Law-Policy Analysis*, NAVAL LAW REVIEW, Winter 1986, at 159.

5. Chairman of the Joint Chiefs of Staff Instruction 3121.01, *Standing Rules of Engagement for U.S. Forces*, Oct. 1, 1994, as amended Dec. 22, 1994, and thereafter. The most recent amendment to this CJCS Instruction is CJCSI 3121.01B, June 13, 2005.

6. Amendments have permitted U.S. military response to attacks on, and intrusions into, our critical defense and intelligence computer networks (CND) and have authorized computer network attack (CNA) on enemy computer networks where necessary to protect vital U.S. national infrastructure from imminent attack. The most recent amendments to Chairman JCS Instruction 3121.01 were approved in 2006. *See guidance regarding critical infrastructure in* PDD 63, May 22, 1998. *See also* J. P. Terry, *Responding to Attacks on Critical Computer Infrastructure: What Targets? What Rules of Engagement?* NAVAL LAW REVIEW (1999); J. P. Terry, *The Lawfulness of Attacking Computer Networks in Armed Conflict and in Self-Defense in Periods Short of Armed Conflict: What Are the Targeting Constraints?* MILITARY LAW REVIEW (2001).

7. *Id.*

6. USE OF FORCE BY THE PRESIDENT

1. *See discussion* of the actions of Presidents Madison, Polk, McKinley, Lincoln, Wilson, Roosevelt, Truman, George H. W. and George W. Bush vis-à-vis the Congress in James Terry, *The President as Commander in Chief,* AVE MARIA LAW REVIEW (Spring 2009).

2. U.S. Constitution, Article I, section 8.

3. U.S. Constitution, Article II, section 2.

4. *See, e.g.*, Edward Corwin, THE PRESIDENT: OFFICE AND POWERS, 1787-1957, 198–201 (1957).

5. *Id.*

6. President Howard Taft *quoted in* Quincy Wright, THE CONTROL OF AMERICAN FOREIGN RELATIONS, 309 (1922).

7. Corwin, *supra* note 4 at 201.

8. *See* the discussion in the Senate Committee on Foreign Relations, *Report on the National Commitments Resolution*, S. Rept. No. 91-129, 91st Congress, 1st. Sess. (1969); *U.S. Commitments to Foreign Powers*, Hearings before the Senate Committee on Foreign Relations, 90th Congress, 1st Sess. (1967), 16–19.

9. Gulf of Tonkin Resolution, H.R. J. Res. of Aug. 10, 1964, Pub. L. No. 88-408, No. 2, 78 Stat. 384.

10. Dean Acheson, PRESENT AT THE CREATION (New York: 1969) 414, 415.

11. *See* Department of State, Historical Studies Division, *Armed Actions Taken by the United States Without a Declaration of War*, 1789-1967 (Res. Proj. No. 806A (Washington: 1967)).

12. *Id.*

13. *See* J. Terry, *Intervention in Panama*, NAVAL WAR COLLEGE REVIEW (Winter 1990).

14. *Fleming v. Page*, 9 How. (50 U.S.) 603, 615 (1850).

15. *Madsen v. Kinsella*, 343 U.S. 341, 348 (1952).

16. *Totten v. United States*, 92 U.S. 105 (1876).

17. *Mitchell v. Harmony*, 13 How. (54 U.S.) 115 (1852); *United States v. Russell*, 13 Wall. (80 U.S.) 623 (1871); *Totten v. United States*, *supra* at 105; 40 Ops. Atty. Gen. 250, 253 (1942).

18. *Cf.* the Protocol of August 12, 1898, which foreshadowed the Peace of Paris, 30 Stat. 1742, and President Wilson's Fourteen Points, which were incorporated into the Armistice of November 11, 1918.

19. *Fleming v. Page*, 9 How. (50 U.S.) 603, 615 (1850).

20. Santiago v. Nogueras, 214 U.S. 260 (1909). Within occupied territory, *see Dooley v. United States*, 182 U.S. 222, 230-31 (1901).

21. Joseph Story, COMMENTARIES ON THE CONSTITUTION OF THE UNITED STATES 546–47 (1833, reprinted 1987).

22. Cong. Rec., 79th Cong., 1st sess., vol. 91, pt. 8, Nov. 26, 1945, at 10967.

23. Cong. Rec. 79th Cong., 1st. sess., vol. 91, July 27, 1945, at 8127–28.

24. Cong. Rec. 79th Cong., 1st sess., vol. 91, July 26, 1945, at 8065.

25. *Special Message to the Congress Regarding United States Policy for the Defense of Formosa*, January 24, 1955, in PUBLIC PAPERS OF THE PRESIDENTS: DWIGHT D. EISENHOWER, 1955 (1999) at 209–210.

26. *Id.* at 209; Pub. L. 4, 84th Cong. (69 Stat. 7) (1955).

27. *See discussion* in William Goldsmith, THE GROWTH OF PRESIDENTIAL POWER, vol. 3 (1974), at 1872–74.

28. *See generally* James Terry, *The Vietnam War in Perspective*, NAVAL LAW REVIEW (2007) at 79.

29. Legislation includes the War Powers Resolution, Pub. L. 93-148, 87 Stat. 555 (1973), 50 U.S.C. 1541-48; the National Emergencies Act, Pub. L. 94-412, 90 Stat. 1255 (1976), 50 U.S.C. 1601-51 (establishing procedures for presidential declaration and continuation of national emergencies and providing for a bicameral congressional veto); the International Emergency Economic Powers Act, Pub. L. 95-223, 91 Stat. 1626 (1977), 50 U.S.C. 1701-06 (limiting the great economic powers conferred on the President by the Trading With the Enemy Act of 1917, 40 Stat. 415, 50 U.S.C. App. 5(b), to times of declared war, and providing new and more limited powers, with procedural restraints, for non-wartime emergencies); and see the Foreign Sovereign Immunities Act of 1976, Pub. L. 94-583, 90 Stat. 2891, 28 U.S.C. 1330, 1602-11 (removing from executive control decisions concerning the liability of foreign sovereigns to suit).

30. Pub. L. No. 88-408, 78 Stat. 384 (1964).

31. *Id.*

32. *See* Robert Turner, *The Authority to Use the Armed Forces*, Chap. 17 in John Norton Moore and Robert F. Turner, NATIONAL SECURITY LAW, 2d ed.(2005), at 871.

33. *See* Memorandum by the State Department Legal Advisor Leonard C. Meeker, *The Legality of the United States Participation in the Defense of Vietnam*, March 4, 1966, *reproduced in* STATE DEPARTMENT BULLETIN 474 (1966). The Memorandum is addressed in more detail in James Terry, *The Vietnam War in Perspective*, NAVAL LAW REVIEW (2007) at 73.

34. *Id.*

35. The bombing initiative, in fact, had that effect. North Vietnam returned to the negotiating table in January 1973 and quickly signed a cease-fire agreement.

36. *See discussion* in Richard E. Grimmett, *Foreign Policy Roles of the President and Congress* (1999), at http://fpc.stste.gov/6172.htm.

37. Pub. L. No. 93-52, 87 Stat 130 (1973). Congress, under pressure from peace groups, withdrew funding in May 1973, and prohibited the expenditure of appropriated funds "to finance directly or indirectly combat activities by United States military forces in or over or from off the shores of North Vietnam, South Vietnam, Laos or Cambodia."

38. *See discussion* in Turner, *supra* note 32, at 873.

39. These actions by the Congress to provide funding limitations are addressed in Grimmett, *supra* note 36.

40. *See* James P. Terry, *Operation Desert Storm: Stark Contrasts in Compliance with the Rule of Law*, NAVAL LAW REVIEW (1993) for a thorough discussion of the events leading up to the attack and the conduct of operations thereafter.

41. The prior UNSC Resolutions were 660, 661, 662, 664, 665, 666, 667, 669, 670, 674, and 677.

42. S. J. Res. 2 (1990).

43. *See discussion* in James P, Terry, *The President as Commander in Chief,* AVE MARIA LAW REVIEW (Spring 2009).

44. The capture of W.O. Durant and the UN inability to control the situation in Mogadishu may have been the final straw for the U.S. Senate in passing the Byrd Amendment limiting U.S. funding.

45. The Byrd Amendment, section 8156 of the FY 94 Defense Appropriations Act, provided that any funds appropriated for DoD may be obligated for expenses incurred only through March 31, 1994, for "the Operations of U.S. Armed Forces in Somalia."

46. The Kempthorne Amendment, although less onerous than the Byrd Amendment, restricted funding for U.S. military personnel in Somalia on a "continuous basis" after September 30, 1994.

47. The Nunn-Mitchell Amendment also provided specific direction in paragraph (f)(1)(B) for the President to submit a plan to Congress on the manner in which the Bosnian Army would be trained by U.S. and allied forces outside Bosnian territory. The Amendment, however, had to be read in light on UNSC 713 which called "upon all States to refrain from any action which might contribute to increasing tension or impeding or delaying a peaceful and negotiated outcome to the conflict in Yugoslavia." Implementation of this training was viewed by many as making the U.S. a party to the conflict, just as the *USS New Jersey*'s fire missions on behalf of the Lebanese Armed Forces in 1983 was seen as taking the U.S. over the line and into the conflict, thus legally (if not morally) justifying the attack on the Marine Barracks at Beirut International Airport.

48. THE PEACE POWERS ACT would have eliminated the War Powers Resolution's 60 day clock; would have severely limited the payment of assessments to the UN for peacekeeping; would have required 15 days advance notification to Congress before voting in the UNSC on peacekeeping; and would have precluded foreign command of U.S. forces.

49. The NSRA would, in part, have demanded credits against our CIPA assessment for voluntary activities; would have limited the use of DoD funds for UN peacekeeping activities; would have restricted the sharing of intelligence with the UN; and would have added significant restrictions and reporting requirements on placing American forces under UN operational control.

50. In Operation Desert Storm, a brigade of the 82d Infantry Division and a Marine Corps Artillery unit from the 12th Marines were assigned to the command of French and British forces, respectively, to allow their advance at the same pace as other coalition forces.

51. Civilized behavior on the battlefield is defined within the four Geneva Conventions for the Protection of the Victims of War, dated August 12, 1949, addressed Wounded and Sick in Armed Forces in the Field (Geneva I), 6 U.S.T 3115; Wounded, Sick and Shipwrecked Members of Armed Forces at Sea (Geneva II), 6 U.S.T. 3219; Treatment of Prisoners of War (Geneva III), 6 U.S.T. 3517; and Protection of Civilian Persons in Time of War (Geneva IV), 6 U.S.T. 3317. The four Conventions were ratified by the United States on July 14, 1955.

52. President Clinton issued PRESIDENTIAL DECISION DIRECTIVE (PDD) 62, *Combating Terrorism*, on May 22, 1998. PDD 62 made the same points as President Reagan's NSDD 138 and mirrored President Bush's 2003 statements in a speech at West Point.

53. NATIONAL SECURITY DECISION DIRECTIVE 138, April 3, 1984.

54. *Quoted* in *Preemptive Anti-Terrorism Raids Allowed*, THE WASHINGTON POST, Apr. 16, 1984, at A-19.

55. Robert C. McFarlane, *Terrorism and the Future of Free Society*, Speech delivered at the National Strategic Information Center, Defense Strategy Forum, Washington, DC, March 25, 1985.

56. George Shultz, *Terrorism and the Modern World*, Speech to Park Avenue Synagogue, New York City, October 25, 1984, at 23.

57. *See* Phillip Taubman, *The Shultz-Weinberger Feud*, THE NEW YORK TIMES MAGAZINE, April 14, 1985, at 3.

58. Hugh Tovar, *Low Intensity Conflict: Active Responses in An Open Society*, Paper prepared for the CONFERENCE ON TERRORISM AND OTHER "LOW INTENSITY" OPERATIONS: INTERNATIONAL LINKAGES, Fletcher School of Law and Diplomacy, Medford, Mass., April 1985, at 24.

59. The rules of land warfare are found primarily in HAGUE CONVENTION IV of 1907.

60. Abraham Miller, *Terrorism and Hostage Taking: Lessons from the Iranian Crisis*, 13 RUT.-CAM. L. J. 513, 523 (1982).

61. George Shultz, Address before the Low-Intensity Warfare Conference, National Defense University, Washington, DC: January 15, 1986.

62. *See* J. P. Terry, *Al Qaeda and Taliban Detainees—An Examination of Legal Rights and Appropriate Treatment*, Chapter XXVI in INTERNATIONAL LAW AND THE WAR ON TERROR (2003) at 441.

63. *See discussion in* J. P. Terry, *The Iranian Hostage Crisis: International Law and U.S. Policy*, 31 JAG Jl 31 (1982).

64. Presidential Decision Directive 62, COMBATING TERRORISM, May 22, 1998. Presidential Decision Directive 63, CRITICAL INFRASTRUCTURE PROTECTION, May 22, 1998.

7. COVERT ACTION AND THE WAR ON TERROR

1. The Intelligence Reform and Terrorism Prevention Act of 2004 (hereinafter the Intelligence Reform Act), Pub. L. 108-458 (2004).

2. The intelligence community is defined at 50 U.S.C. 401(a)(4).

3. The intelligence community also includes the National Geospatial-Intelligence Agency (NGA), Federal Bureau of Investigation (FBI), Army Intelligence, Navy Intelligence, Air Force Intelligence, Marine Corps Intelligence, Coast Guard (CG), Treasury Department, Energy Department, and the Drug Enforcement Agency (DEA). 50 U.S.C. 401(a)(4).

4. *Supra* note 1.

5. These firewalls between intelligence and law enforcement were fashioned by Jamie Gorelick, then Deputy Attorney General.

6. *See* James Terry, *Eliminating Piracy on the High Seas: Legal and Policy Considerations*, J.F.Q., July 2009.

7. NGA was previously named the National Imagery and Mapping Agency (NIMA). NIMA was renamed the National Geospatial-Intelligence Agency (NGA) by the FY2004 Defense Authorization Act, P.L. 108-136.

8. P.L. 93-559 (1974). The "appropriate committees of Congress" was interpreted to include the Committees on Armed Services, Foreign Relations (Senate) and Foreign Affairs (House), and Appropriations of each house of Congress, a total of six committees.

9. The Senate Select Committee on Intelligence was established in 1976. The House Permanent Select Committee on Intelligence was established in 1977.

10. P.L. 96-450 (1980).

11. See W. Michael Reisman and James E. Baker, REGULATING COVERT ACTION (1992), at 131–32.

12. *Id.*

13. *Id.*

14. National Security Decision Directive (NSDD) 286 (1987).

15. *Id.*

16. Memorandum of Disapproval issued by President George H. W. Bush, Nov. 30, 1990.

17. P.L. 102-88 (1991), 50 U.S.C. 501 *et seq.* The heart of this 1991 legislation is found in section 501(a)(1), which requires that the president keep the intelligence committees fully and currently informed of the intelligence activities of the United States, and in section 503(a), which states the president may not authorize the conduct of a covert operation unless the president determines that such is necessary to support "identifiable foreign policy objectives" of the United States and that determination shall be set forth in a finding.

18. P.L. 108-36.

19. *Id.*

20. *See* Helen Fessenden, CQ WEEKLY, *Intelligence: Hill's Oversight Role at Risk*, Mar. 27, 2004, at 734.

21. P.L. 110-417, sec. 1208 (2009).

22. When serving as Legal Counsel to the Chairman, JCS from 1991–1995, the author reviewed all findings on behalf of the Chairman.

23. See Joint Explanatory Statement of the Committee of Conference, H.R. 1455, July 25, 1991 [hereinafter "Joint Statement"].

24. *See* P.L. 102-88, 1105 Stat. 429 (1991), codified at Sec. 503(a) of the National Security Act of 1947, 50 U.S.C. 413b, 50 U.S.C. 501 *et seq.*

25. *Id*, sec. 501(a)(1).

26. *Supra* note 23.

27. *Id.*

28. Sec. 503(e), Intelligence Oversight Act of 1991, P.L. No. 102-88, 105 stat. 429.

29. *Id.* at Sec. 503(e)(1).

30. *Id.* at Sec. 503(e)(2).

31. *Id.* at Sec. 503(e)(3).

32. *Id.* at Sec. 503(e)(4).

33. *See* Joint Statement, *supra* note 23.

34. *See* Sect. 102(c), National Security Act, 50 U.S.C. 403-4(h) (formerly 50 U.S.C. 403(c)).

35. *See, e.g.,* Rhodes v. United States, 156 Cl.Ct 31, *cert den.,* 371 U.S. 821 (1962); Torpats v. McCone, 300 F.2d 914(DC Cir.) *cert. den.* 371 U.S. 886 (1962).

36. Sect. 403(g), Central Intelligence Agency Act of 1949, 50 U.S.C. 403a, *et seq.*

37. *See* Snepp v. United States, 444 U.S. 507 (1980) *(per curium).*

38. Intelligence Authorization Act of 1997, 104 P.L. 104-293, sect, 402, 110 Stat. 3461 (1996).

39. National Security Act, *supra* note 34.

40. The Economic Espionage Act of 1996, P.L. No. 104-294, 110 Stat. 3488 (1996).

41. Annex 4 to the Hague Rules of 1899 requires that those participating in armed conflict be members of a defined military force, wear recognizable uniforms, carry arms openly, and operate within the laws of warfare.

42. Mary E. O'Connell, *International Law and the Use of Drones,* lecture at the Royal Institute of International Affairs in London, Oct. 21, 2010.

43. *See* Gary Solis, *CIA Drone Attacks Produce America's Own Unlawful Combatants*, Wash. Post, Mar. 12, 2010.

44. Harold H. Koh, *The Obama Administration and International Law*, Annual Meeting of the American Society of International Law, March 25, 2010.

8. HABEAS CORPUS AND THE DETENTION OF ENEMY COMBATANTS

1. 339 U.S. 763 (1950).

2. *Id.* at 768.

3. The habeas statute states that "Writs of habeas corpus may be granted by the Supreme Court, any justice thereof, the district courts and any circuit judge within their respective jurisdictions." 22 USC 2241(a).

4. *See Peyton v. Rowe*, 391 U.S. 54, 59, 88 S.Ct. 1549, 20 L. Ed. 2d. 426 (1968).

5. The phrase, *habeas corpus*, refers to the common law writ of habeas corpus, or the "Great Writ." *Preiser v. Rodriguez*, 411 U.S. 475, 484-85 and n.2, 93 S.Ct. 1827, 36 L.Ed. 2d. 439 (1973), citing *Ex Parte Bollman*, 8 U.S. (4 Cranch) 75, 95, 2 L.Ed. 554 (1807). .

6. *See* Alan Clarke, *Habeas Corpus: The Historical Debate*, 14 N.Y.L. Sch. Jl Hum. Rts. 375, 378 (1998); William F. Duker, A CONSTITUTIONAL HISTORY OF HABEAS CORPUS 17 (1980).

7. Clarke, *supra* at 6, at 379.

8. The Norman Conquest took place in the 11–12th centuries.

9. Supra note 6 at 380.

10. *Id.*

11. *See discussion* in Gerald L. Newman, *Habeas Corpus, Executive Detention, and the Removal of Aliens*, 98 COLUM. L. REV. 961, 970-71 (1998).

12. Clarke, *supra* note 6 at 380.

13. *Bushell's Case*, Vaughan 135, 136, 124 Eng. Rep. 1006, 1007 (1670).

14. *See* Rex A. Collins, *Habeas Corpus for Convicts—Constitutional Right or Legislative Grace*, 40 CAL. L. REV. 335, 339 (1952)

15. Max Rosenn, *The Great Writ—A Reflection of Societal Change*, 44 OHIO ST. L. JL. 337, 338, n. 14 (1983). .

16. Erwin Chemerinsky, *Thinking about Habeas Corpus*, 37 CASE W. RES. L. REV. 748, 752 (1987).

17. U.S. Const., art. 1, sec. 9, cl. 2.

18. Act of Sept. 24, 1789, ch. 20, sec. 14, 1 Stat. 73, 81.

19. Duker, *supra* note 6 at 149.

20. Act of Mar. 3, 1863, 12 Stat. 755. *See also* James Terry, *The President as Commander in Chief*, AVE MARIA LAW REV. (Spring 2009), for a discussion of the circumstances underlying Lincoln's decision.

21. *See* Duker, *supra* note 6, at 178, n. 190.

22. Act of July 1, 1902, ch. 1369, 32 Stat. 691.

23. *See discussion* in *Duncan v. Kahanamoku*, 327 U.S. 394, 307-08, 66 S.Ct. 606, 90 L.Ed. 688 (1946).

24. *Supra* note 1 at 768. This replicates the situation in Guantanamo.

25. 317 U.S. 1 (1942).

26. *Id.*

27. *Quirin*, 317 U.S. at 20–24.

28. *Id.* at 25. The German saboteurs were convicted by the Military Commission and executed.

29. 335 U.S. 188 (1948).

30. *Id.* at 189.

31. *Id.* at 190, 192.

32. Id. at 193.

33. *See Padilla v. Rumsfeld*, 542 U.S. 426 (2004).

34. LEASE OF LANDS FOR COALING AND NAVAL STATIONS, Feb. 23, 1903, U.S.-Cuba, Art.III, T.S. No. 418. The leasehold has no termination date.

35. 355 U.S. App. D.C. 189, 321 F.3d 1134 (D.C. Cir. 2003). The D.C. Circuit affirmed the district court's dismissal of various claims, habeas and non-habeas, holding, with regard to the habeas claims, that "no court in this country has jurisdiction to grant habeas relief, under 28 U.S.C. 2241, to the Guantanamo detainees." 321 F. 3d at 1141. Regarding the non-habeas claims, the court noted that "'the privilege of litigation' does not extend to aliens in military custody who have no presence in 'any territory over which the United States is sovereign." *Id.* at 1144.

36. *Rasul v. Bush*, 542 U.S. 466 (2004); *Padilla v. Rumsfeld*, 542 U.S. 426 (2004); *Hamdi v. Rumsfeld*, 542 U.S. 507. (2004).

37. *Boumediene v. Bush*, 128 S. Ct. 2229 (2008); 2008 WL 2369628 (U.S.); 76 USLW 4391, 76 USLW 4406.

38. *Id.*

39. *Id.*

40. 355 U.S. App. D.C. 189 (D.C. Cir. 2003).

41. These are unlawful alien combatants but not technically *enemy aliens* since they do not represent any country with which the United States is at war.

42. *Rasul*, 542 U.S. at 470.

43. *Rasul*, 542 U.S. at 483–84.

44. 28 U.S.C. 1331.

45. 28 U.S.C. 1350.

46. *Rasul*, 542 U.S. at 484–485.

47. *Supra* note 265.

48. Id., at 441–43, 450–51.

49. *Id.*

50. *Id.* at 435. Secretary Rumsfeld's office was in the Eastern District of Virginia at the Pentagon.

51. *Hamdi v. Rumsfeld*, 542 U.S. 507 (2004).

52. *Hamdi*, 542 U.S. at 510.

53. *Hamdi*, 542 U.S. at 525.

54. *Hamdi*, 542 U.S. at 533. Hamdi was later released from confinement and returned to Saudi Arabia, having served three years of incarceration without charge.

55. Pub. L. No. 109-148, 119 Stat 2680 (2005). Signed into law December 30, 2005.

56. *Eisentrager, supra* note 1.

57. Detainee Treatment Act, sec. 1005 (e)(1).

58. Detainee Treatment Act, sec. 1005(e)(2), (e)(3).

59. 126 S. Ct. 2749, 165 L.Ed. 2d. 723 (2006)

60. 126 S. Ct. at 2769.

61. Pub. L. No. 109-366, 120 Stat. 2600 (2006). The President signed the Military Commissions Act into law on October 17, 2006.

62. Sec. 7, Military Commissions Act, *supra.*

63. *See, e.g.*, 152 Cong. Rec. S.10357 (daily ed. Sept. 28, 2006) (statement of Sen. Leahy) ("The habeas stripping provisions in the bill go far beyond what Congress did in the Detainee Treatment Act . . . . This new bill strips habeas jurisdiction retroactively, even for pending cases."); *id.* at S10367 (statement of Sen. Graham) ("The only reason we are here is because of the *Hamdan* decision. The *Hamdan* decision did not apply . . . the Detainee Treatment Act retroactively, so we have about 200 and some habeas cases left unattended and we are going to attend them now."); *id* at S10403 (statement of Sen. Cornyn) ("[O]nce . . . section 7 is effective, Congress will finally accomplish what it sought to do through the Detainee Treatment Act last year. It will finally get the lawyers out of Guantanamo Bay. It will substitute the blizzard of litigation instituted by *Rasul v. Bush* with a narrow DC Circuit-only review of the CSRT hearings.")

64. 476 F.3d 981 (2007).

65. *Id.* at 987.
66. *Id.*
67. *Id.*
68. *Id.* at 985.
69. *Id.*
70. *Boumediene v. Bush*, 127 S. Ct. 1478 (2007).
71. *Boumediene v. Bush*, 2007 U.S. 8757; 75 U.S. L.W. 3707, June 29, 2007.
72. *Boumediene v. Bush, supra* note 37.
73. *Id.* at 2234.
74. *Id.* at 2234–35.
75. Id. at 2235, 2276.
76. *Id.* at 2237.
77. *Id* at 2275.
78. *Id.* at 2280.
79. *Id.* at 2279–80.
80. *Id* at 2302.
81. *Id.*
82. The Suspension Clause in Article I, sec. 9, cl. 2, directs that "[t]he Privilege of the Writ of Habeas Corpus shall not be suspended, unless when in Cases of Rebellion or Invasion the public Safety may require it."
83. *See INS v. St. Cyr*, 533 U.S. 289, at 301 (2001).
84. *Boumediene, supra* note 296, at 988.
85. In *id*, at 988, the appellants cited three cases for this proposition: *Lockington's Case*, Bright. (N.P.) 269 (Pa. 1813); *The Case of Three Spanish Sailors*, 96 Eng. Rep. 775 (C.P. 1779); and *Rex v. Schiever*, 97 Eng. Rep. 551 (K.B. 1759).
86. *See id.*
87. 97 Eng. Rep. (2 Burr.) 587 (K.B. 1759).
88. *Supra* note 64 at 989.
89. *Supra* note 1 at 768.
90. *Id.*
91. *Supra* note 64 at 990–91.
92. *Boumediene, supra* note 37.
93. *Id.*
94. Pub. L. No. 109-148, 119 Stat 2680 (2005). Signed into law December 30, 2005.
95. Pub. L. No. 109-366, 120 Stat. 2600 (2006). The President signed the Military Commissions Act into law on October 17, 2006.
96. *Supra* note 269.
97. *See Padilla*, 542 U.S. at 426.
98. *Rasul*, 542 U.S. at 478–79.
99. *See Rasul*, 542 U.S. at 506. *See also Boumediene*, 128 S.Ct. 2306-07. In his dissent in both cases, Justice Scalia raises this and other concerns.

9. TORTURE AND THE INTERROGATION OF DETAINEES

1. *See* Memorandum for John Rizzo, Acting Gen. Counsel, CIA, from Steven G. Bradbury, Principal Deputy Assistant Att'y Gen., Dept. of Justice, Office of Legal Counsel, *Re: Application of 18 U.S.C 2340 – 2340A to Certain Techniques That May Be Used in the Interrogation of a High Value al Qaeda Detainee* at 4 (May 10, 2005) [hereinafter *Techniques*] (declassified and disclosed by the Obama Admin., Apr. 16, 2009).
2. United Nations Convention Against Torture and Other Cruel, Inhuman or Degrading Treatment or Punishment, Dec. 10, 1984, 1465 U.N.T.S. 85 (entered into force for U.S. Nov. 20, 1994 ("Convention Against Torture" or "CAT").
3. *Techniques, supra* note 1, at 3.

4. *See* Memorandum for John Rizzo, Acting Gen. Counsel, CIA, from Steven G. Bradbury, Principal Deputy Assistant Att'y Gen., Dept. of Justice, Office of Legal Counsel, *Re:Application of United States Obligations Under Article 16 of the Convention Against Torture to Certain Techniques that May Be Used in the Interrogation of High Value al Qaeda Detainees*, (May 30, 2005) [hereinafter *Obligations*] (declassified and disclosed by the Obama Administration, Apr. 16, 2009), at 15.

5. *Techniques, supra* note 1, at 1.

6. *See* President Barack Obama, Address to Joint Session of Congress (Feb. 24, 2009), http://www.whitehouse.gov/the_press_office/remarks-of-president-barack-obama-address-to-joint-session-of-congress. *See also* Exec. Ord. No. 13,492, 74 Fed. Reg. 4897, 4898 (Jan. 22, 2009).

7. *Supra* note 1.

8. *Id.* at 10–11 (citations omitted). The reporting emphasized that this was but a small portion of the intelligence obtained through interrogations of Khalid Shaykh Muhammad and Abu Zubaydah.

9. George W. Bush, President of the United States, President Discusses Progress in War on Terror to National Guard (Feb. 9, 2006), http://georgewbush-whitehouse.archives.gov/news/releases/2006/02/20060209-2.html.

10. Ali Soufan, *My Tortured Decision,* N.Y. Times, Apr. 22, 2009, http://www.nytimes.com/2009/04/23/opinion/23soufan.html?_r=3&ref=opinion.

11. *Id.*

12. *Id.*

13. *See What Went Wrong: Torture and the Office of Legal Counsel in the Bush Administration: Hearing Before the S. Comm. On the Judiciary*, 111th Cong. (2009). http://judiciary.senate.gov/hearings/testimony.cfm?id=3842&wit_id+7904.

14. *Supra* note 6.

15. Jane Meyer, *The Black Sites,* The New Yorker, Aug. 13, 2007, http://www.newyorker.com/reporting/2007/08/13/070813fa_fact_mayer?printable=true.

16. David Rose, *Tortured Reasoning*, Vanity Fair, Dec. 16, 2008, http://www.vanityfair.com/magazine/2008/12/torture200812?printable=true&currentPage=all.

17. *See Obligations, supra* note 4, at 12 (*citing* Fax from Assoc. Gen. Counsel, CIA, for Daniel Levin, Acting Assistant Att'y Gen., Dept. of Justice, Office of Legal Counsel, *Re: Background Paper on CIA's Combined Use of Interrogation Techniques* at 4 (Dec. 30, 2004) [hereinafter *Background Paper*]). The Background Paper, which was cited in many of the documents declassified and released by the Obama Administration on April 16, 2009, has not been declassified and released.

18. *Obligations, supra* note 4, at 12.

19. *Id.* (citing *Background Paper, supra* note , at 13).

20. *Techniques, supra* note 1, at 7.

21. *Id.* at 7–8.

22. *Id.* at 7.

23. *Id.*

24. *Id.*

25. *Id.*

26. *See e.g.*, B. Kunderman et al., *Sleep Deprivation Affects Thermal Pain Thresholds but not Somatosensory Thresholds in Healthy Volunteers*, 66 Psychosomatic Med. 932 (2004).

27. *Id.*

28. *See* S. Hakki Onen et al., *The Effects of Total Sleep Deprivation, Selective Sleep Interruption, and Sleep Recovery on Pain Tolerance Thresholds on Healthy Subjects*, 10 J. Sleep Research 35, 41 (2001); *id* at 35–36 (discussing other studies).

29. *See Techniques, supra* note 1, at 11–13. The procedures are explained at length.

30. *Obligations, supra* note 4, at 13 (quoting *Background Paper, supra* note, at 5).

31. *Techniques, supra* note 1, at 8–9; *Obligations, supra* note 4, at 14 (citing *Background Paper, supra* note, at 5–7).

32. *Obligations, supra* note 4, at 8–9.

33. *Techniques, supra* note 1 at 8, 33.

34. *Id.* at 8
35. *Obligations, supra* note 4 at 8.
36. *Techniques, supra* note 1 at 8.
37. *Id* at 9.
38. *Id.*
39. *Id.* at 8–9.
40. *Id.* at 8.
41. *Id.*
42. *Id.*
43. *Obligations, supra* note 4 at 8.
44. *Id.* at 14 (citing *Background Paper, supra* note, at 7).
45. *Id.*
46. *Id.* (citing *Techniques, supra* note 1, at 8).
47. *Techniques, supra* note 1, at 8
48. *Obligations, supra* note 4, at 14.
49. *Id.*
50. *Techniques, supra* note 1, at 9.
51. *Id.* at 10.
52. *Obligations, supra* note 4, at 15.
53. *Techniques, supra* note 1, at 9.
54. *See* Office of Medical Services (OMS) Guidelines on Medical and Psychological Support to Detainee Rendition, Interrogation and Detention (Dec. 2004). (OMS *Guidelines*) The CIA's OMS carefully evaluated detainees before any enhanced technique was authorized in order to ensure that the detainee "[was] not likely to suffer any severe physical or mental pain or suffering as a result of interrogation." *OMS Guidelines* at 9.
55. *Techniques, supra* note 1, at 9.
56. *Id.*
57. *Id.*
58. *Id.*
59. *Id.*
60. *Id.* at 6.
61. *Id.* at 13.
62. Id. at 13.
63. *See* Report of CIA Inspector General, *Counterterrorism Detention and Interrogation Activities (Sept 2001-Oct 2003)*, No. 2003-7123-IG (May 7, 2004) (*IG Report*), at 15 ("Airflow is restricted. . . . and the technique produces the sensation of drowning and suffocation.").
64. *Techniques, supra* note 1, at 13.
65. *Obligations, supra* note 4, at 29. The three detainees upon whom the waterboard technique was used were Khalid Shaykh Mohammed, Abu Zubaydah, and Al-Nashiri. *Id.*
66. *Id.* at 14.
67. *Obligations, supra* note 4, at 37.
68. *See id.*
69. Convention Against Torture, *supra* note 2.
70. *Id.* at art. 1, para. 1.
71. *Id.* at art. 16, para. 1.
72. Declaration on Protection from Torture, G.A. Res. 3452 art. 1, ¶2, U.N. GAOR, 30th Sess., Supp. No. 34, U.N. Doc. A/1034 (Dec. 9, 1975).
73. S. Exec. Doc. No. 101–30, at 36 (1990).
74. 136 Cong. Rec. 36198 (1990).
75. *See discussion* in *Obligations, supra* note 4, at 16.
76. *Id.*
77. 2 Eur. Ct. H.R. 25 (ser. A) (1978).
78. *Id.* at 59.
79. *Id.* at 79–80.
80. *Id.* at 61.
81. *Id.* at 79–80.

82. Supreme Court of Israel: Judgment Concerning the Legality of the General Security Service ' s Interrogation Methods, 38 I.L.M. 1471, (Sept. 9, 1999); also available at H.C. 5100/94, The Public Committee Against Torture in Israel v. Israel (Sept. 9, 1999), available at http://www.derechos.org/human-rights/mena/doc/torture.html.

83. *Id.* at 1474–76.

84. *See id.* at 1482–84.

85. Geneva Convention Relative to the Treatment of Prisoners of War, Aug. 12, 1949, 6 U.S.T. 3217, 75 U.N.T.S. 135.

86. *Id.* The preamble to Common Article 3 [hereinafter Art. 3 Preamble] provides:

In the case of *armed conflict not of an international character occurring in the territory of one of the High Contracting Parties*, each party to the conflict shall be bound to apply, as a minimum, the following provisions:

1. *Persons taking no active part in the hostilities, including members of Armed forces* who have laid down their arms and those placed hors de combat by sickness, wounds, *detention*, or any other cause, shall in all circumstances be *treated humanely*, without any adverse distinction founded on race, colour, religion, or faith, sex, birth or wealth, or any other similar criteria. To this end the following acts are and shall remain prohibited at any time and in any place whatsoever with respect to the above mentioned persons.

(a) Violence to life and person, in particular murder of all kinds, mutilation, cruel treatment and *torture*;

(b) Taking of hostages;

(c) Outrages upon personal dignity, in particular, *humiliating and degrading treatment.* . . .

Id. (emphasis added).

87. *Id.*

88. *Hamdan v. Rumsfeld*, 548 U.S. 557 (2006).

89. Geneva Convention Relative to the Treatment of Prisoners of War, *supra* note 85.

90. *What Went Wrong?: Torture and the Office of Legal Counsel in the Bush Administration, Hearing Before the Subcomm. on Admin. Oversight and the Courts, Wednesday,* 111th Cong. 17–18 (2009) (statement of Robert Turner, Assoc. Director, Center for National Security Law, University of Virginia School of Law).

91. A. John Radsan, *The Collision Between Common Article Three and the Central Intelligence Agency,* 56 Cath. U. L. Rev. 959, 972 (2007).

92. *But cf.* Fionnuala Ní Aoláin, *Hamdan and Common Article 3: Did the Supreme Court Get it Right?,* 91 Minn. L. Rev. 1523, 1556 (2007) ("Because of the apparent absence of a nexus between al-Qaeda and any sovereign State, some legal scholars seem to have viewed this as a conflict not of an international character.")

93. *See, e.g.*, Jean S. Pictet, International Committee of the Red Cross: Commentary to the Convention (I) Relative to the Amelioration of the Condition of the Wounded and Sick in Armed Forces in the Field 39–43 (1952) (where "civil war" is used well over a dozen times, along with "armed conflicts . . . of an internal character," "insurrections," "social or revolutionary disturbances," and conflicts "within the borders of a state.").

94. *Id.*

95. G.I.A.D. Draper, *Humanitarian Law and Internal Armed Conflict,* 13 GA. J. INT'L 7 COMP. L. 253, 268 (1983). ("No convention dealing with the law of war made any reference to conduct in *internal armed conflicts* until the four Geneva Conventions of 1949.")

96. *See, e.g.*, Fionnuala Ní Aoláin, *Hamdan and Common Article 3,* 91 Minn. L. Rev. 1523 at 1558 ("[A] 'formal' legal application issue arises when applying Common Article 3: the provision only textually applies to armed conflicts occurring in the territory of a state party. This issue raises the question of whether Common Article 3 applies in transnational contexts. A formalistic approach would suggest that a conflict must be either an interstate (international) conflict or an internal conflict taking place in the territory of a specific state."); *See also* Alberto T. Muyot & Ana Theresa B. Del Rosario, The Humanitarian Law on Non-International Armed Conflicts 14–15, 27–28 (1994).

97. *Hamdan v. Rumsfeld*, 548 U.S. 557 (2006).

98. *Hamdan v. Rumsfeld*, 415 F.3d 33, 41 (D.C. Cir. 2005).

99. *Hamdan*, 548 U.S. at 630.

100. *See Constitutional and International Law Implications of Executive Order 13440 Interpreting Common Article 3 of the 1949 Geneva Conventions: Hearing on U.S. Interrogation Policy and Executive Order 13440 Before the S. Select Comm. on Intelligence*, 110th Cong. 1 (2007) (statement of Robert F. Turner, Associate Director, Center for National Security Law, University of Virginia School of Law).

101. Convention Against Torture, *supra* note 2, Art 4.

102. S.Rep. No. 103–107, at 58 (1993).

103. *See* H.R. Rep. No. 103–482, at 229 (1994) (Conf. Rep.).

104. *See* S.Rep., *supra* note 102, at 58–59.

105. *Id.*

106. An individual convicted of torture faces a fine or confinement up to 20 years or both. For those acts resulting in a victim's death, a defendant may be sentenced to life imprisonment or death. 18 U.S.C. § 2340A(a) (2004). When death does not result, the statute of limitations is 8 years; where death results, there is no statute of limitations. 18 U.S.C. § 3286(b) (2002); 18 U.S.C. § 2332b(g)5(B) (1996). Section 2340A, as originally enacted, did not provide for the death penalty. The 1994 Omnibus Crime Bill, Pub. L. No. 103–322, sec. 60020, 108 Statute 1979, amended section 2340A to provide for that punishment. *See* H.R. Conf. Rep. No. 103–711, at 388 (1994) (Conf. Rep.), noting that the act added the death penalty as a penalty for torture.

107. 18 U.S.C. § 2340(1), 2340A (2004).

108. *See* S. Exec. Doc. No. 101–30, at 6 (1990), which states: "For an act to be 'torture,' it must . . . cause severe pain and suffering, and be intended to cause severe pain and suffering."

109. 18 U.S.C. § 2340A(c) (2004).

110. 28 U.S.C. 1350 (2000).

111. *Id.*

112. *See Xuncax v. Gramajo*, 886 F. Supp. 162, 176 n. 12 (D. Mass. 1995).

113. *See, e.g., Ortiz v. Gramajo*, 886 F. Supp. 162 (D. Mass. 1995); Kadic v. Karadzic, 70 F.3d 232 (2d Cir. 1995).

114. 18 U.S.C. § 2441(2006).

115. 18 U.S.C. § 2241(c)(3) (2006).

116. *Cf.*, Hamdi v. Rumsfeld, 542 U.S. 507, 518 (2004) (plurality opinion) (describing important incidents of war).

117. U.S. Department of Justice, *Placing of United States Armed Forces Under United Nations Operational or Tactical Control*, 20 Op. Off. Legal Counsel 182, 185 (1996).

118. U.S. Const. art. I, § 8 cl. 10.

119. Pub. L. No. 109–366, 120 Stat. 2600 (2006).

120. 548 U.S. 557 (2006).

121. U.S. Const. art. I, § 8, cl. 14.

122. Pub. L. No. 109–148, 119 Stat. 2863 (2005).

123. Authorization for Use of Military Force, Pub. L. No.107–40, 115 Stat. 224 (2001).

124. *Id.* pmbl.

125. *Id.* § 2(a) (emphasis added).

126. 117 Cong Rec. 31557 (1971) (statement of Rep Mikva).

127. Most notably water boarding.

128. *See* Peter Finn, Joby Warrick & Julie Tate, *How a Detainee Became an Asset*, WASH. POST, Aug. 29, 2009, at A1, A6. (Note, however, that former FBI agent Soufan claimed, *supra* note 341, that the information was secured not from the harsh interrogation administered but rather through traditional interrogation methods).

129. *See* Art. 3, *supra* note 86.

130. *Johnson v. Eisentrager*, 339 U.S. 763 (1950).

131. Interview by George Stephanopoulos with President-Elect Barack Obama, *This Week* on ABC (Jan. 11, 2009) *available at* http://abcnews.go.com/ThisWeek/Economy/story?id=6618199&page=1.

132. S.Amdt. 1556: To prohibit cruel, inhuman, or degrading treatment or punishment of persons under the custody or control of the United States Government, S. 1042, 109th Cong.

(2006), *available at* http://www.govtrack.us/congress/amendment.xpd?session=109& amdt=s1556.

133. *Id.*

134. *See* Cathy Young, *Torturing Logic*, Reason, March 2006, at http://www.reason.com/ news/show/33263.html.

135. *See* Charles Krauthammer, *The Truth About Torture*, The WEEKLY STANDARD, Dec. 5, 2005, *available at* http://www.weeklystandard.com/Content/Public/Articles/000/000/006/ 400rhqav.asp.

136. *Supra* note 132.

137. *See* Anne Kornblut, *New Unit to Question Key Terror Suspects*, WASH. POST, Aug. 24, 2009, at A1, A5.

10. FEDERAL COURT OR MILITARY COMMISSION

1. The remaining four are Walid Muhammad Salih Mubarak Bin'Attash, Ramzi Binal-shibh, Ali Abdul Aziz Ali, and Mustafa Ahmed Adam al Hawsawi.

2. Pub. L. No. 109-366, 120 Stat. 2600 (2006). The president signed the Military Commissions Act into law on Oct. 17, 2006.

3. *Illinois v. Gates,* 462 US. 213, 238 (1983).

4. *See discussion* in M. E. Bowman, *National Security and the Fourth and Fifth Amendments*, in John N. Moore and Robert F. Turner, eds., NATIONAL SECURITY LAW, (2005), at 1059, *et seq.*

5. Detention, Treatment, and Trial of Certain Non-Citizens in the War Against Terrorism sec. 1(a), 66 Fed. Reg. 57,833 (Nov. 16, 2001).

6. See James P. Terry, *Habeas Corpus and the Detention of Enemy Combatants in the Global War on Terror*, JOINT FORCE QUARTERLY (Jan. 2008).

7. *Rasul v. Bush*, 542 U.S. 466 (2004).

8. Detainee Treatment Act of 2005, P.L. 109–148 (Title X).

9. *Hamdan v. Rumsfeld*, 126 S. Ct. 2749 (2006), *rev'g* 415 F. 3d 33 (D.C. Cir 2005).

10. The procedural rules for court martial proceedings are set forth in the Uniform Code of Military Justice, 10 U.S.C. 801, *et seq.*

11. *Hamdan*, at 2794.

12. E.O. 13492, *Review and Disposition of Individuals Detained at the Guantanamo Naval Base and Closure of Detention Facilities*, 74 Federal Register 4897, Jan. 22, 2009 (hereinafter Executive Order).

13. *Id.* at sec. 4. The Attorney General is required to coordinate with the SecDef, SecState, SecHS, DNI, and the Chairman, JCS.

14. *Id.*

15. DOJ/DoD Press Release, Departments of Justice and Defense Announce Forum Decisions for Ten Guantanamo Bay Detainees, Nov. 13, 2009, http://www.justice.gov/opa/pr/2009/ November/09-ag-1224.html (hereinafter Press Release).

16. *Id.*

17. U.S. Constitution, Art. 2, sec. 2, cl. 1. *See* James P. Terry, *The President as Commander in Chief*, AVE MARIA LAW REVIEW 391 (2009).

18. *See* 10 USC 821. Statutory offenses for which military commissions may be convened are limited to aiding the enemy, 10 USC 904, and spying, 10 USC 906. These offenses are explicitly included in the MCA.

19. UCMJ, 10 U.S.C. 801, *et seq.*

20. *See* William Winthrop, MILITARY LAW AND PRECEDENTS 831 (2d ed., 1920) (describing the distinction between courts-martial and military commissions).

21. Military Order No. 1, 2001, Nov. 13, 2001, *published as* Detention, Treatment, and Trial of Certain Non-Citizens in the War Against Terrorism sec. 1(a), 66 Fed. Reg. 57,833 (Nov. 16, 2001).

22. The United States first used military commissions during the occupation of Mexico in 1847, and made heavy use of them in the Civil War and in the Philippine Insurrection.

23. *See Ex Parte Quirin*, 317 U.S. at 38 (1942), *Ex Parte Milligan*, 71 U.S. (4 Wall) 2, 123 (1866) (noting a service member "surrenders his right to be tried by the civil courts").

24. *Hamdan*, at 2796–2797 (plurality opinion).

25. *Id.*

26. *Reprinted* at 41 I.L.M. 725 (2002). Military Commission Order No. 1, was issued in March 2002 and revised on August 31, 2005.

27. *Hamdan*, 2797.

28. P.L. 109–366, 120 Stat. 2600, codified at chapter 47a of Title 10 U.S. code.

29. 10 U.S.C. 948a (as added by the MCA).

30. MCA, sec. 4 (amending 10 U.S.C 821).

31. *Boumediene v. Bush*, 128 S.Ct. 2229 (2008). *See also* James Terry, *Habeas Corpus and the War on Terror*, chapter 3 in John Norton Moore and Robert F. Turner, eds., LEGAL ISSUES IN THE STRUGGLE AGAINST TERROR (2010).

32. *See* Michael John Garcia, *Boumediene v. Bush: Guantanamo Detainees' Right to Habeas Corpus*, CRS Report RL34536 (2008).

33. Kiyemba v. Obama, 2009 WL 935637 (Oct. 20, 2009).

34. Art. I, sect. 8, cl. 10, U.S. Constitution.

35. Pub. L. No. 109-366, 120 Stat. 2600 (2006). The president signed the Military Commissions Act into law on Oct. 17, 2006.

36. 548 U.S. 557 (2006).

37. Art. I, sect. 8, cl. 14, U.S. Constitution.

38. P.L. 109–148, 119 Stat. 2680 (2005). Signed into law December 30, 2005.

39. Authorization for Use of Military Force, Pub. L. 107–40, 115 Stat. 224 (2001).

40. *Id*, preamble.

41. *Id.*, sect 2(a).

42. Title XVIII of the National Defense Authorization Act for Fiscal Year 2010, P.L. 111–84 (2009).

43. *Id.*

44. These include Omar Khadr, a Canadian citizen captured as a teenager and charged before a military commission for allegedly throwing a hand grenade that killed a U.S. medic in Afghanistan; abd al-Rahim al-Nashiri, whose military commission charges related to the October 2000 attack on the *USS Cole* were previously withdrawn in February 2009; Ahmed Mohammed Ahmed Haza al Darbi, who is accused of participating in an al Qaeda plot to blow up oil tankers in the Straits of Hormuz; and two other detainees about whom no further information has been provided.

45. *See* U.S. Constitution, Amend. V ("No person shall be held to answer for a capital, or otherwise infamous crime, unless on presentment or indictment of a Grand Jury, *except* in cases arising in the land or naval forces") (italics added).

46. *See, e.g., Ex Parte Quirin*, 317 U.S. 1, 40 (1942) ("we must conclude that sec. 2 of Article III and the Fifth and Sixth Amendments cannot be taken to have extended the right to demand a jury trials at military commission, or to have required that offenses against the law of war not triable by jury at common law be tried only in the civil courts."); *Whelchel v. McDonald*, 340 U.S. 122 (1950) ("The right to trial by jury guaranteed by the Sixth Amendment is not applicable to trials by courts martial or by military commissions").

47. *Weiss v. United States*, 510 U.S. 163, 177 (1994).

48. *See also Chappel v. Wallace*, 462 U.S. 296, 301 for a similar interpretation.

49. *See generally* CRS Report RL 33688, The Military Commissions Act of 2006: Analysis of Procedural Rules and Comparison with Previous DoD Rules and the Uniform Code of Military Justice (2007).

50. U.S. Const., Amend. VI.

51. *McMann v. Richardson*, 397 U.S. 759, 771 n. 14 (1970); *Powell v. Alabama*, 287 U.S. 45, 71–72 (1932); *Glasser v. United States*, 315 U.S. 60, 70 (1942),

52. Fed. R. Crim. P., Rule 44.

53. Fed. R. Crim P., Rule 44a.

54. *See* 10 U.S.C. 949a, 949c (as amended by P.L. 111–84, sec. 1802 (2009))
55. 10 U.S.C. 949c (as amended by P.L. 11–84, sec. 1802 (2009).
56. RCM, 502(d).
57. RCM, 506(c)
58. U.S. Const., Amend. V.
59. *Bram v. United States*, 168 U.S. 532, 542 (1887); *Miranda v. Arizona*, 384 U.S. 436, 444–45 (1966).
60. *Brown v. Mississippi*, 297 U.S.278, 285–87 (1936); *Dickerson v. United States*, 530 U.S. 428, 434 (2000).
61. *See Miranda v. Arizona, supra.* The Miranda requirement applies anytime federal officials have a suspect in custody. The warning typically begins with "You have a right to remain silent . . ." before the statement is taken. In the context of terrorist suspects' statements, at least one court has held that *Miranda* applies in Article III courts even if the questioning took place outside of the United States. *See United States v. Bin Laden*, 132 F. Supp. 2d 168, 173–79 (S.D.N.Y. 2001).
62. 467 U.S. 649 (1984).
63. *Id.* at 657–658. The court reasoned that requiring police to determine whether to take the time to give Miranda warnings "in a matter of seconds" was impracticable under the circumstances.
64. *United States v. Josef*, 327 F. 3d 56, 145 (2d Cir 2003), *cert denied*, 540 U.S. 933 (2003).
65. *Id.* at 145–46. *See also United States v. Abu Ali*, 528 F.3d 210, 232, 234 (4th Cir. 2008). In *Abu Ali*, a case involving a defendant who had been arrested and questioned by Saudi officials for assisting terrorists in an attack, the 4th Circuit upheld statements made to the Saudi interrogators, despite a lack of Miranda warnings, because the court found the statements were voluntary.
66. *Supra* note 64.
67. P.L. 111–84, sec. 1040 (2009).
68. 10 USC 948r(a) (as amended by P.L. 111–84, sec. 1802 (2009).
69. 10 U.S.C. 948r(b) (as amended by P.L. 111–84, sec. 1802 (2009).
70. 10 U.S.C. 948r(c) (as amended by P.L. 111–84, sec. 1802 (2009). The military commission must consider the totality of the circumstances, including "(1) The details of the statement, accounting for the circumstances of the conduct of military and intelligence operations during hostilities; (2) The characteristics of the accused, such as military training, age and education level; and (3) The lapse of time, change of place, or change in identity of the questioners between the statement sought to be admitted and any prior questioning of the accused." 10 U.S.C. 948r(d) (as amended by P.L. 111–84, sec. 1802 (2009).
71. Fed. R. Evid. 802.
72. Fed. R. Evid. 801(D), 803.
73. Fed. R. Evid. 807
74. *United States v. Dumeisi*, 424 F. 3d 566 (7th Cir. 2005).
75. Fed. R. Evid. 801(D)(2).
76. Mil. Comm R. Evid. 802–803.
77. *Id.*
78. *Id.* at 803(c)
79. U.S. Const., Amend. VI.
80. *Klopfer v. North Carolina*, 386 U.S. 213, 226 (1967).
81. 407 U.S. 514, 519 (1972).
82. *Id.*
83. *Id.* at 519.
84. 18 U.S.C. 3161.
85. 18 U.S.C. 3161(b), (c).
86. *See Verdugo-Urquidez v. United States*, 494 U.S. 259, at 268, 270–71(1990)
87. 18 U.S.C. 3161(h)(8)(A) .
88. *Id.*
89. *See United States v. Marion*, 404 U.S. 307, at 424 (1971).

90. U.S. Const. Amend. VI.
91. P.L. 95–456, *codified at* 18 USC app. 3 sec. 1–16.
92. 18 U.S.C. app. 3, sec. 3; Fed. R. Crim. P. 16(d)(1).
93. *See* 10 U.S.C. 949p-1, *et seq.*(as added by P.L. 111–84, sec. 1802 (2009)
94. 10 U.S.C. 949p-6(c) (as added by P.L. 111–84, sec. 1802 (2009)
95. 10 U.S.C. 949p-6(a)(3) (as added by P.L. 111–84, sec. 1802 (2009)
96. *Id.*
97. 18 U.S.C. 3161(b), (c).

11. THE INTERNATIONAL CRIMINAL COURT AND THE TRIAL OF TERROR-RELATED CRIMES

1. *See generally* Roger S. Clark & Madeleine Sann, eds., THE PROSECUTION OF INTERNATIONAL WAR CRIMES (1996).
2. *See Ex Parte Milligan*, 71 U.S. (4 Wall.) 2 (1866), for the premise that courts not properly established under the Constitution "can exercise no part of the judicial power of the country."
3. *See, e.g., U.S. v. Pascasco*, 37 M.J. 1012, *rev. den.* 45 M.J. 6 (1993). Under 18 USC 3161, a federal prosecutor must indict within 30 days of arrest and bring the defendant to trial within 70 days of indictment.
4. 524 U.S. 666 (1998).
5. The NATO experience in Bosnia under a similar court structure reflects the requirement for such oversight.
6. *See discussion* of these three interventions and their legal and moral authority under the Charter in J. Terry, THE REGULATION OF INTERNATIONAL COERCION (2005).
7. There are 105 states that have ratified the Rome Statute, including most NATO nations.
8. Most notably the late Senator Jesse Helms of the Senate Foreign Relations Committee, and Chairman Henry Hyde of the House International Relations Committee.
9. Statement of the President: Signature of the International Criminal Court Treaty, The White House (Camp David), December 31, 2000.
10. Letter from John R. Bolton, former Under Secretary of State for Arms Control and International Security, U.S., to Kofi Annan, Secretary-General (May 6, 2002).
11. Pub. L. No. 107-206 (2006); 22 U.S.C. 7401-7433 (2003). (The earlier version was named the American Service-Members Protection Act, hence ASPA).
12. The author served as Deputy Assistant Secretary of State for Regional, Global and Functional Affairs in the Bureau of Legislative Affairs during this period and shepherded this legislation through the Congress.
13. Article 98 of the Rome Statute provides for bilateral agreements in which protections between participating nations for their individual forces in UN operations, to include immunity from referral to the ICC, can be previously negotiated.
14. The United States presently has negotiated 104 of these Article 98 agreements (97 are in force).

12. HIGH SEAS TERROR AND THE ELIMINATION OF PIRACY

1. UNSC Res. 1851 (2008).
2. UN Doc. 9541, 16 Dec. 2008, at 10.
3. *See Pirate Washes Ashore with Cash*, at http://news.bbc.co.uk/go/pr//fr/-/2/hi/africa/7824353.stm of 12 January 2009.
4. *Id.*

5. *Id.*

6. *See* SC Doc. 9541, *supra* note 2, at 2–3.

7. Sec. 3.5.2, ANNOTATED SUPPLEMENT TO THE COMMANDER'S HANDBOOK ON THE LAW OF NAVAL OPERATIONS, 222–223 (1999).

8. Sec. 101, UNITED NATIONS CONVENTION ON THE LAW OF THE SEA, *opened for signature* 10 Dec. 1982, 21 I.L.M. 1261 (hereinafter LOS Convention). Art. 15 of the CONVENTION ON THE HIGH SEAS (hereinafter High Seas Convention), defines piracy in essentially identical terms. *See* 13 U.S.T. 2312, 450 U.N.T.S. 92, Geneva, 29 April 1958.

9. Sec. 3.5.2, *supra* note 7.

10. Modern piracy is addressed by Petrie, *Pirates and Naval Officers*, NAV. WAR COLL. REV., May–June 1982, at 15. *See* also Ellen, *Contemporary Piracy*, 21 CAL. WEST. INT'L L. J. 123 (1990).

11. Art. I, sect. 8, U.S. CONSTITUTION

12. *See* 18 U.S. CODE 1651-1661 (1996) (piracy), 33 U.S.CODE 381-384 (1996) (regulations for the suppression of piracy), and 18 U.S. CODE 1654 (1996) (privateering).

13. 18 U.S.C. 1651 (1996).

14. 33 U.S.C. 381–384 (1996).

15. *Id.*

16. 18 U.S.C. 1654 (1996).

17. 18 U.S.C. 1655 (1996).

18. 18 U.S.C. 1656 (1996).

19. 18 U.S.C. 1657 (1996).

20. 18 U.S.C. 1660 (1996).

21. 18 U.S.C. 1661 (1996).

22. Art. 21, High Seas Convention, *supra* note 8.

23. Art. 107, LOS Convention, *supra* note 8.

24. *Id.*

25. *See* Sec. 3.5.3.1, ANNOTATED SUPPLEMENT, *supra* note 7.

26. Art. 19, High Seas Convention, *supra* note 8; Art 105, LOS Convention, *id.*

27. *See* e.g., UNSC Res. 733 (1992); UNSC Res. 1356 (2001); UNSC Res. 1425 (2002); UNSC Res. 1725 (2006); UNSC Res. 1744 (2007); UNSC Res. 1772 (2007); UNSC Res. 1801 (2008); UNSC Res. 1811 (2008), and the statements of the Security Council President, in particular those of July 13, 2006 (S/PRST/2006/31), December 22, 2006 (S/PRST/2006/59), April 30, 2007 (S/PRST2007/13), June 14, 2007 (/PRST/2007/19), and December 19, 2007 (S/PRST/2007/49).

28. Para. 11, UNSC Res. 1814 (2008)

29. Para. 7, UNSC Res. 1816 (2008).

30. Para. 2, UNSC Res. 1838 (2008).

31. Para. 6, *id. See also,* IMO Res. A-1002 (25) which requested that member states of the International Maritime Organization issue similar guidance to all vessels flying their national ensigns.

32. Para. 10a, UNSC Res. 1846 (2008).

33. Para. 6, UNSC Res. 1851 (2008).

34. Known as "shipriders."

35. Para. 3, UNSC Res. 1851.

36. Cong. Res. Rep. R40081, Ocean Piracy and Its Impact on Insurance, Dec. 3, 2008.

37. *Id.*

38. Statement of the Honorable Elijah Cummings, Subcommittee on the Coast Guard and Maritime Transportation, Hearing on "International Piracy on the High Seas", Feb. 4, 2009, at 1.

39. National Security Council, *Countering Piracy off the Horn of Africa: Partnership and Action Plan*, The White House, Washington DC, December 2008 (hereinafter National Strategy).

40. *Id.*, at 6.

41. *Id.*, at 8.

42. *Id.*, at 10.

43. *Id.*, at 12.
44. *Id.*
45. VAdm. Wm. Gartney, *New Counter-Piracy Task Force Established*, www.navy.mil/local/cusnc, Jan. 8, 2009,
46. *Id.*
47. *Id.*
48. (U) CFMCC CENT P 301133Z Dec. 08 (Subject: CTF 151 EXORD) (hereinafter EX-ORD).
49. Para. 2.D, EXORD.
50. Para. 2.E.1, EXORD.
51. *See* testimony of RAdm. Wm. Baumgartner, USCG, *Hearing on International Piracy on the High Seas*, before the House Subcommittee on Coast Guard and Maritime Transportation, Feb. 4, 2009, at 6.
52. *Id.*

13. OUTSOURCING DEFENSE SUPPORT OPERATIONS IN THE WAR ON TERROR

1. *See discussion* of these operations in J. P. Terry, *Operation Desert Storm: Stark Contrasts in Compliance With the Rule of Law*, NAVAL LAW REVIEW, Winter 1993.
2. *See, e.g.*, J. P. Terry, *U.N. Peacekeeping and Military Reality*, BROWN JOURNAL OF WORLD AFFAIRS, Winter/Spring 1996; J. P. Terry, *Rethinking Humanitarian Intervention After Kosovo*, THE ARMY LAWYER (August 2004).
3. *See generally*, J. P. Terry, THE REGULATION OF INTERNATIONAL COERCION, Chapter VII (2005).
4. *See, e.g.*, U.S. Army, *Logistics Civil Augmentation Program*, Department of the Army Regulation 700-137 (Dec. 16, 1985); U.S. Air Force, *Performance Based Service Contracts*, Air Force Inst. 63-124 (Apr. 1, 1999); U.S. Army, *Contractors Accompanying the Force*, Department of the Army Regulation 715-9 (Oct. 29, 1999); U.S. Army, *Logistics Civil Augmentation Program*, Army Material Command Pamphlet 700-30 (Jan. 2002); U.S. Army, *Contractors on the Battlefield*, Department of the Army Field Manual 3-100.21 (Jan. 3, 2003); DoD Inst. 3020.41, *Contractor Personnel Authorized to Accompany the U.S. Armed Forces* (Oct. 3, 2005). DoD Inst. 3020.41 requires the department to maintain by-name accountability of contractors deploying with the force, who are defined as systems support and external support contractors, and associated subcontractors, specifically authorized in their contract to deploy to support U.S. forces.
5. *See discussion* in GAO Report 07-145, *Military Operations: High Level DoD Action Needed to Address Long-Standing Problems with Management and Oversight of Contractors Supporting Deployed Forces* (Dec. 2006) at 10. *See discussion* of Gansler Report therein.
6. Testimony of Thomas F. Gimble, Acting IG, DoD, in *Combating War Profiteering: Are We Doing Enough to Investigate and Prosecute Contracting Fraud in Iraq?* Hearing before the Committee on the Judiciary, United States Senate, March 20, 2007, at 9.
7. *See discussion* of these and other LOGCAP concerns in GAO Report GAO-04-854 MILITARY OPERATIONS: DOD'S EXTENSIVE USE OF LOGISTICS SUPPORT CONTRACTS REQUIRES STRENGTHENED OVERSIGHT (July 2004).
8. *See* DoD Inst. 3020.41, *Contractor Personnel Authorized to Accompany the U.S. Armed Forces* (Oct. 3, 2005).
9. *See* GAO Report GAO-07-145, *Military Operations: High Level DoD Action Needed to Address Long-Standing Problems with Management and Oversight of Contractors Supporting Deployed Forces* (Dec. 2006), at 3–5.
10. *See* GAO Report GAO-08-436T, *Military Operations: Implementation of Existing Guidance and Other Actions Needed to Improve DoD's Oversight and Management of Contractors in Future Operations* (Jan. 24, 2008), at 2–3.

11. Prior to January, 2006, the USCENTCOM SJA's position was that PSCs could only be used for static/perimeter security. That position was enforced with respect to DoD use of PSCs until the 'direct confrontation with a uniformed enemy' opinion was issued by DoD GC in January 2006.

12. *See discussion* in DoD Instr. 3020.41, Oct. 3, 2005, *supra*.

13. DoD Deputy GC (International Affairs) Memo to SJA, USCENTCOM, *Request to Contract for Private Security Companies in Iraq*, Jan. 10, 2006, at 2 (hereinafter DoD Dep GC Memo).

14. DoD Inst. 3020.41, Oct. 3, 2005.

15. *Id.* at para. 6.3.5.

16. DoD Deputy GC Memo, *supra* note 13, at 3.

17. *See* UN Security Council Resolutions 1546 and 1637.

18. DoD Dep GC Memo, *supra* note 13, at 4.

19. *Id.*

20. *See discussion* of ROE applicable to U.S. and coalition military personnel in Iraq and Afghanistan in J. P. Terry, *"Operationalizing" Legal Requirements for Unconventional Warfare*, JOINT FORCE QUARTERLY, October 2008.

21. CENTCOM Dec 05, Subj: (U) *USCENTCOM Policy Relating to Possession and Use of Arms by All DoD Civilian Personnel and All DoD Contractors and Their Employees Present Within Iraq and Afghanistan*, para. 2.C.2.B.

22. *Id.*, para. 4.D.2.

23. DepSecDef Memorandum of 25 Sept. 2007, Subj: (U) *Management of DoD Contractors and Contractor Personnel Accompanying U.S. Armed Forces in Contingency Operations Outside the United States*, at 1.

24. *Id*, at 2.

25. *Also see* MILITARY EXTRATERRITORIAL JURISDICTION ACT OF 2000, sec. 3261, Pub. L. 106-523, Nov. 22, 2000. This provision of the Act established the right to try contractor employees for felony offenses.

26. DepSecDef Memo, *supra* note 23, at 2.

27. *Supra* note 25. Unfortunately, to date, the COCOMS have not issued any implementing guidance.

28. DoD Inst. 5525.11, *Criminal Jurisdiction Over Civilians Employed by or Accompanying the Armed Forces Outside the United States, Certain Service Members, and Former Service Members*, March 3, 2005.

29. DepSecDef Memo, *supra* note 23, at 2.

30. The same results have been reported in both Kabul and Baghdad.

31. *See* testimony of William Solis, Director, Defense Capabilities and Management, before the Subcommittee on National Security , Emerging Threats, and International Relations, Committee on Government Reform in GAO Report, *Rebuilding Iraq: Actions Still Needed to Improve the Use of Private Security Providers*, GAO-06-86T, June 13, 2006.

32. *See* T. Christian Miller, *Private Contractors Outnumber U.S. Troops in Iraq*, L.A. TIMES, July 4, 2007, at A-2.

15. ENVIRONMENTAL TERRORISM

1. General Order No. 100 (1863) signed by President Abraham Lincoln, in Dietrich Schindler and Jiri Toman, eds. THE LAWS OF ARMED CONFLICT (Leiden: Sijthoff, 1988), 3.

2. J. Goldblat, AGREEMENTS FOR ARMS CONTROL: A CRITICAL SURVEY (London: Taylor and Francis 1982), 120—21.

3. Regulations Annexed to Hague Convention IV of 1907 Respecting the Laws and Customs of War on Land, 36 Stat. 2259; TREATIES AND INTERNATIONAL AGREEMENTS SERIES (TIAS), 538; Charles I. Bevans, TREATIES AND OTHER INTERNATIONAL AGREEMENTS OF THE U.S.A., 1776-1949, Dept. of State Pub. 8407 (Washington: November 1968), 619.

4. International Military Tribunal (Nuremberg), *Judgment and Sentence*, AMERICAN JOURNAL OF INTERNATIONAL LAW, no. 41, 1947, at 172.

5. "Usufruct," as used in the Convention, means "the right of one state to enjoy all the advantages derivable from the use of property which belongs to another state."

6. *See* Art. 51, Geneva Convention I (GCI); Art. 52, GCII; Art. 131, GCIII; and Art. 148, GCIV.

7. *See* Art. 49, GCI; Art. 50, GCII; Art. 129, GCIII; Art. 146, GCIV.

8. UN Security Council Resolution 687, requiring Iraqi compensation to Kuwait, has its underpinnings in Article 3, Hague Convention IV of 1907.

9. Convention on the Prohibition of Military or Any Other Use of Environmental Modification Techniques (ENMOD Convention), signed in Geneva, 18 May 1977, entered into force, 5 October 1978; U.S. ratification, 13 December 1979; ratification deposited in New York, 17 January 1980; published in U.S. Arms Control and Disarmament Agency, ARMS CONTROL AND DISARMAMENT AGREEMENTS (Washington: 1990), 214–19.

10. *Id.*, Art. I.

11. *Id.*, at 219.

12. Though both were enacted the same year, the ENMOD Convention and the 1977 Geneva Protocol are not directly related. The 1977 Geneva Protocol I addresses both means and methods of international armed conflict and protection of victims of international armed conflict. It is therefore a melding of the Hague Law (means and methods) and the Geneva Law (protection of the victims of warfare). The ENMOD Convention addresses only restrictions on changes to the environment in a widespread, long-lasting, or severe manner (Article I) by military or any other hostile use of environmental modification techniques. While the Conference of the Committee on Disarmament (C.C.D.), an arm of the United Nations, sponsored the ENMOD Convention, the International Committee of the Red Cross (I.C.R.C.) in Geneva sponsored the negotiations on the 1977 Geneva Protocol, just as it had thirty years earlier for the 1949 Geneva Conventions.

13. *See, e.g.*: (i) Treaty Banning Nuclear Weapons Tests in the Atmosphere, In Outer Space, and Under Water, August 5, 1963, 14 United States Treaties (UST) 1313; TIAS 5433; 480 United States Treaty Series (UNTS) 43 (1963); (ii) Treaty on the Non-Proliferation of Nuclear Weapons, July 1, 1968, 21 UST 483; TIAS 6839 (1970); (iii) Additional Protocol II to the Treaty for the Prohibition of Nuclear Weapons in Latin America, February 14, 1967, 22 UST 754; TIAS 7137; 634 UNTS 364 (1971); (iv) Treaty on the Prohibition of the Emplacement of Nuclear Weapons and Other Weapons of Mass Destruction on the Seabed and the Ocean Floor and in the Subsoil Thereof, February 11, 1971, 23 UST 701; TIAS 7337 (1972); (v) Interim Agreement between the Union of Soviet Socialist Republics (now Russian Federation) and the United States of America on Certain Measures with Respect to the Limitation of Strategic Offensive Arms, with Protocol, May 26,1972, 23 UST 3462; TIAS 7504 (1972).

14. It is recognized that overly restrictive attempts to regulate weaponry and targeting parameters either to protect the environment or to induce disarmament (using environmental protection as the vehicle) raise the danger of bringing the law into disregard and weakening its legal and moral force. It is necessary to seek a realistic threshold of regulation; the present law, if enforced, provides such a threshold. It allows only that level of destruction and choice of targets necessary to restore the rights of the nation attacked. Any regime which would preclude exercise of effective self-defense options in favor of environmental protections would be honored in the breach rather than adherence.

16. DEFENSE OF CRITICAL INFRASTRUCTURE SYSTEMS FROM TERRORISTS

1. *See* Bradley Graham, *U.S. Studies New Threat: Cyber Attack*, WASHINGTON POST, May 24, 1998, at A1. The author describes OPERATION ELIGIBLE RECEIVER, conducted by the NSA and other government agencies.

2. Hon. Jamie Gorelick, Speech before the Corps of Cadets, U.S. Air Force Academy, (February 29, 1996).

3. *See* William Gertz, *Chinese Hackers Raid U.S. Computers*, WASHINGTON TIMES, May 16, 1999, at C1 for a troubling review of Chinese efforts to attack White House, State Department and other government computer systems.

4. Hague II, Hague IV, Additional Protocol I.

5. Lawrence T. Greenberg *et al.*, INFORMATION WARFARE AND INTERNATIONAL LAW (Institute for National Security Studies: Washington) 1997, at 32.

6. G.A. Res. 53/70, U.N. GAOR, 53rd Sess., U.N. Doc. A/RES/53/70 (1998).

7. *Id.*

8. *United States Explanation of Vote After the Vote*, re: G.A. Res. 53/70 (1998), *reprinted in* W. Gary Sharp, CYBERSPACE AND THE USE OF FORCE, (Aegis: Falls Church, VA 1999) at 189.

9. Chairman of the Joint Chiefs of Staff Instruction 3121.01, STANDING RULES OF ENGAGEMENT FOR U.S. FORCES, Oct. 1, 1994, *as amended* Dec. 22, 1994, and Feb. 2005.

10. U.S. Department of the Navy, THE COMMANDERS HANDBOOK ON THE LAW OF NAVAL OPERATIONS (NWP 1-14m), para. 8.1 (1997).

11. Sharp, *supra* note 8 at 205–06.

12. *See infra* Chapter I.

13. *Id.*

14. *Quoted in* R. Oppenheim, INTERNATIONAL LAW 299 (London: Longmans [8th ed. 1955]).

15. Ian Brownlee, *The Use of Force in Self-Defense*, BR. Y.B. INT'L L. 183, 207 (1961).

16. http://www.few.com/Articles/2009/06/24/DOD-launches-cyber-command.aspx

17. U.S. Department of Defense, Cyber Command Fact Sheet, May 21, 2010.

18. *Id.*

19. *Id.*

20. *Id.*

21. http://www.koreatimes.co.kr/www/news/nation/2009/12/205_56502.html.

22. http//en.wikipedia.org/wiki/United_States_Cyber_Command#Mission.

23. http://www.af.mil/news/story.asp?id=123204543.

17. THE LEGALITY OF ATTACK ON FOREIGN INFRASTRUCTURE POSING A THREAT

1. U.S. Space Command News Release No. 20–99, Oct. 1, 1999, at 1.

2. *Id.*

3. Unclassified paragraph 22(a)(12) of the FY 2000 UCP provided that USSPACECOM's responsibilities include:

> 12 (U) In coordination with the Joint Staff and appropriate CINCs,
> serving as the military lead for computer network defense (CND)
> and, effective 1 October 2000, *computer network attack (CNA)*, to
> include advocating the CND and CNA requirements of all CINCs,
> conducting CND and CNA operations, planning and developing national require-
> ments for CND and CNA, and supporting other CINCs for CND
> and CNA (emphasis added).

4. *See* DEFENSE INFORMATION AND ELECTRONICS REPORT (DIER), Oct. 22, 1999, at 1.

5. *See* DIER, Oct. 8, 1999, at 1.

6. *Id.*

7. The NIPC is located in the Hoover Building in Washington, DC. The NIPC brings together representatives from the FBI, DoD, other government agencies, state and local governments, and the private sector.

8. PDD 63, CRITICAL INFRASTRUCURE PROTECTION (1998), establishes these categories as critical infrastructure, the protection of which constitutes defense of vital national interests.

9. The NIPC works closely with USSPACECOM's JIOC and with the Critical Infrastructure Coordination Group, which answers to the National Coordinator for Infrastructure Protection.

10. UN Charter art. 2, para. 4. The Charter is codified at 59 Stat. 1031; TS 993; 3 Bevans 1153. Signed at San Francisco 26 June 1945. *Reprinted in* U.S. State Department Publication 2368, 1–20.

11. 5 Marjorie Whiteman, DIGEST OF INTERNATIONAL LAW, Sec. 25, at 971–72 (1965).

12. The law of targeting is a subset of the law of armed conflict, and the dual requirements of necessity and proportionality, the twin pillars of that body of law, are equally applicable to target selection and approval.

13. *See* Art. 51(1), Protocol I Additional to the 1949 Geneva Conventions (1977), 16 I.L.M. 1391, *reprinted in* Schindler and Toman, THE LAW OF ARMED CONFLICTS (Sijhoff: Leiden 1982) (hereinafter PROTOCOL I). Art. 51(1), defines civilian objects as "all objects which are not military objectives as defined in paragraph 2."

14. *Id.*

15. DoD General Counsel, *An Assessment of International Legal Issues in Information Operations*, May 19, 1999 at 22.

16. *See* PROTOCOL I, *supra,* Art. 52(2) .

17. Lawrence G. Downs, Jr., *Digital Data Warfare: Using Malicious Computer Code As A Weapon*, study published by National Defense University Institute for Strategic Studies (1995), at 58.

18. *Id.*

19. 18 U.S.T. 2411, T.I.A.S. 5433, 480 U.N.T.S. 43 (1967).

20. 19 U.S.T. 7570, T.I.A.S. 6599, 672 U.N.T.S. 119 (1968).

21. 24 U.S.T. 2389, T.I.A.S. 7762 (1972).

22. 28 U.S.T. 695, T.I.A.S. 8480, 1023 U.N.T.S. 15 (1975).

23. Article I, Outer Space Treaty.

24. Article IX, Outer Space Treaty.

25. The Liability Convention elaborates the general principle of international liability for damage set forth in Article VII of the Outer Space Treaty in Articles Ia, II, III, and VI. Articles IV and V of the Liability Convention address joint and several liability.

26. *See* ANNOTATED SUPPLEMENT TO THE COMMANDER'S HANDBOOK ON THE LAW OF NAVAL OPERATIONS, NWP 1-14M (1995) at 2–38.

27. DoD GC ASSESSMENT, *supra* note 15 at 22.

28. The requirements were stated previously in the 1973 INTERNATIONAL TELECOM-MUNICATIONS CONVENTION, Malaga-Torremolinos, 28 U.S.T. 2495, T.I.A.S. 8572. The Malaga-Torremolinos Convention was replaced by the 1982 INTERNATIONAL TELECOM-MUNICATIONS CONVENTION, Nairobi, 6 Nov. 1982, 32 U.S.T. 3821; T.I.A.S. 9920 (entered into force for the United States 10 January 1986).

29. *See discussion* in DoD GC ASSESSMENT, *supra* note 15 at 36–37.

30. CONVENTION (V) RESPECTING THE RIGHTS AND DUTIES OF NEUTRAL POWERS AND PERSONS IN CASE OF WAR ON LAND, signed at the Hague, 18 Oct. 1907, 36 U.S. STATUTES AT LARGE 2310–2331; 1 BEVANS 654–668; 2 AM. J. INT'L L., 1908 Supp., at 117–27.

31. Where this provision is violated, however, and a satellite node is used for aggression, the inviolability of the system from attack would arguably cease.

32. 47 USC 502 provides: "Any person who willfully and knowingly violates any rule, regulation, restriction, or condition made or imposed by the Commission under authority of this Act [47 USC 151, et seq.], or any rule, regulation, restriction, or condition made or imposed by

any international radio or wire communications treaty or convention, or regulations annexed thereto, to which the United States is or may hereafter become a party, shall, in addition to any other penalties provided by law, be punished , upon conviction thereof, by a fine of not more than $500 for each and every day during which such offense occurs."

33. *See* discussion in DoD GC ASSESSMENT, *supra* note 15 at 38.

18. WAR POWERS IN THE AGE OF TERROR

1. War Powers Resolution, Pub. L. 93-148 (Nov. 7, 1973). The views expressed are those of the author alone and do not reflect any position by a government official.

2. *Id.*, sec. 5.

3. *See generally*, James Terry, *The President as Commander-in-Chief*, AVE MARIA L. REV. (2009).

4. *Supra*, note 1.

5. *Id.*, sec. 5.

6. Colonel Khadafi, of Sirte, Libya, had ruled Libya since taking power in a 1969 tribal coup.

7. *See Authority to Use Military Force in Libya*, Office of Legal Counsel (OLC) Memorandum Opinion for the Attorney General, U. S. Department of Justice (DOJ), Apr. 1, 2011, at 1 (hereinafter OLC Memorandum Op., Apr. 1, 2011 .

8. UNSC Res. 1970, UN Doc. S/Res/1970 (Feb. 26, 2011).

9. *Id.,* paras. 9, 17, 26.

10. *See, e.g.,* African Union (AU) Communique of the 265th Mtg. of the Peace and Security Council, PSC/PR/COMM.2(CCLXV)(Mar. 10, 2011) (describing the "prevailing situation in Libya as posing a serious threat to peace and security in that country and region as a whole and reiterating AU's strong and unequivocal condemnation of the indiscriminate use of force and lethal weapons.")

11. League of Arab States, The Outcome of the Council of the League of Arab States Meeting at the Ministerial Level in its Extraordinary Session on the Implication of the Current Events in Libya and the Arab Position, Res. No. 7360 Para. 1 (Mar. 12, 2011).

12. Khadafi, in a March 17 radio address to his supporters, pledged that his forces would begin an assault on Benghazi that night and "show no mercy and no pity" to those who would not give up resistance. Khadafi stated: "We will come house by house, room by room. It's over. The issue has been decided." *See* Dan Bilefsky and Mark Landler, *Military Action Against Khadafi is Backed by UN*, NY TIMES, Mar. 18, 2011, at A–1.

13. Five Security Council Members abstained.

14. *See* UNSC Res. 1973, UN Doc. S/RES/1973 (Mar. 17, 2011).

15. *Id.*

16. *Id.*, para. 4.

17. *Id.*, paras. 6–8, 13.

18. *See* Press Release, Office of the Press Secretary, The White House, Letter From the President Regarding Commencement of Operations in Libya: Text of Letter from President Obama to Speaker Boehner and the President Pro Tempore of the Senate (Mar. 21, 2011) available at http:/www.whitehouse.gov/the-press-office-/2011/03/21/letter-president-regarding-commencement-operations-libya.

19. This is somewhat surprising in light of Khadafi's well documented state-sponsored terrorism against U.S. citizens in 1985–86. *See e.g.,* James Terry, *An Appraisal of Lawful Military Response to State-Sponsored Terrorism*, NAVAL WAR COLLEGE REV., May-June 1986.

20. S. Res. 85, 112th Cong. (as passed by the Senate, Mar. 1, 2011).

21. *Id.*, paras 2, 3, and 7.

22. Press Release, Office of the Press Secretary, The White House, Remarks by the President on the Situation in Libya (Mar. 18, 2011), available at http://www.whitehouse.gov/the-press-office/2011/03/18/remarks-president-situation-libya.

23. *Id.*

24. Letter from the President to the Speaker of the House of Representatives and the President Pro-Tempore of the Senate Regarding Commencement of Operations in Libya (March 21, 2011); available at http://www.whitehouse.gov/the-press-office/2011/03/21/letter-president-commencement-operations-libya.

25. *Id.*

26. UNSC 1973, 2011, *supra* note 14.

27. War Powers Resolution, *supra* note 1.

28. *See generally,* James Terry, The President as Commander in Chief, AVE MARIA L.REV. (2009).

29. OLC Memorandum Op., *supra* note 7 at 1.

30. *Supra* note 1.

31. *See* 50 U.S.C. 1541(a).

32. *Id.*, sec. 1543(a).

33. Id, sec. 1544(b).

34. *See* March 21 Letter to Congress, *supra* note 757.

35. *Id.*

36. *Id.*

37. OLC Memorandum, *supra* note 7.

38. *Id.*

39. *Id.*

40. *See* David A. Fahrenhold, *House Reprimands Obama Over Military Effort in Libya*, WASH. POST, June 3, 2011, at A-7.

41. *Id.*

42. President Ford submitted 4 reports; President Carter 1; President Reagan 14; President George H. W. Bush 7; President Clinton 60; President George W. Bush 39; and President Obama 5. *See* Richard F. Grimmet, CSR Rep. R41199, *The War Powers Resolution After 36 Years* (2009).

43. *Id.*, at 5.

44. *See generally* James Terry, *UN Peacekeeping and Military Reality*, BROWN JL OF WORLD AFF. (Winter/Spring 1996).

45. H. Con. Res. 227, Mar. 18, 1998. Resolution 227 would have directed the President, pursuant to Section 5© of the WPR, to remove all forces from Bosnia and Herzegovina.

46. *See* James Terry, *The Emerging Role of NATO in UN Peace Enforcement Operations*, THE LAW OF MILITARY OPERATIONS, vol. 72, INTERNATIONAL LAW STUDIES, Nav. W. Col. Press (Newport, RI 1998), at 297.

47. *See* Campbell v. Clinton, 52 F. Supp. 2d 34 (1999). Judge Paul Friedman ruled on June 8, 1999, that Representative Campbell and others lacked standing to bring the suit. The decision was affirmed by the D.C. Cir. Court of App., 203 F. 3d 19 (DC Cir. 2000), and *certiori* was denied by the Supreme Court, 531 U.S. 815 (2000).

48. HR 1664, FY 1999, Defense Supplemental Appropriations 1999.

49. HR 1141, FY 1999, Emergency Supplemental Appropriations, May 20, 1999.

50. See UNSC Res. 688, Apr. 5, 1991. The Resolution condemned the repression of the Iraqi civilian population and appealed for contributions for humanitarian relief.

51. UNSC Res. 687, April 3, 1991.

52. Pub. L. 102–1 (1991) authorized the President to use U.S. armed forces pursuant to the cease-fire to achieve implementation of previous Security Council resolutions. UNSC Resolution 687 was adopted after this. On August 2, 1991, the Senate adopted an amendment to the Defense Authorization bill for FY 1992 supporting the use of all necessary means to achieve the goals of Resolution 687.

53. Admiral James Stavridis, USN, Commands USSACEUR and NATO's military arm. Sec. 8(c) of the WPR states: "For purposes of this joint resolution, the term 'introduction of United States Armed Forces' includes the assignment of a member of such armed forces to command, coordinate, participate in the movement of, or accompany the regular or irregular military forces of any foreign country or government when such military forces are engaged, or there exists an imminent threat that such forces will become engaged, in hostilities."

54. Robert Chesney, *Primer on the Libya War Powers Resolution Compliance Debate*, Brookings Inst., July 19, 2011, at http://www.brookings.edu/opinions/2011/0617_war_powers_chesney.aspx?.p=1.

55. Jeh Johnson at DoD and Caroline Krass at Justice have advised the White House that they disagree with the new definition of 'hostilities', fashioned by Harold Koh at State and the White House Counsel's Office, for purposes of the War Powers Resolution.

56. *See* discussion in note 7, *supra*.

19. THE WAR ON TERROR AND MEDIA ACCESS

1. *See* Sebastian Junger, WAR (New York: Twelve) 2010.

2. *See* James P. Terry, *A Legal Review of U.S. Military Involvement in Peacekeeping and Peace Enforcement Operations*, 42 NAVAL L. REV. 79 (1995).

3. It is hard to forget the international array of newsmen, complete with lights and camera equipment, awaiting the arrival of U.S. Marines by sea at Mogadishu, Somalia, during operation Restore Hope.

4. *See* James P. Terry, *Rethinking Humanitarian Intervention After Kosovo*, THE ARMY LAWYER, August 2004.

5. SECDEF 101900Z FEB 03: Subj: Public Affairs Guidance (PAG) on Embedding Media During Possible Future Operations/Deployments in the U.S. Central Commands (CENTCOM) Area of Responsibility (AOR) (UNCLASS).

6. The statement was issued on January 10, 1984. The full text is reported in N.Y. TIMES, Jan. 11, 1984, at A10, col. 1.

7. *See Media Organizations Take a Stand*, EDITOR & PUBLISHER, Jan. 14, 1984, at 18.

8. *See* Henry Catto, Jr., *Dateline Grenada: The Media and the Military Go at It*, WASH. POST, Oct. 30, 1983, at C7.

9. Discussion of the Sidle Report is included in John Jeffries, *Freedom of Expression*, in NATIONAL SECURITY LAW 995 (Moore, Tipson, & Turner 1990).

10. Louis D. Boccardi, *Agreement on War Coverage Guidelines*, A.P. News Release, May 21, 1992.

11. *See* U.S. DEP'T OF DEFENSE, DIR. 5122.5, ASSISTANT SECRETARY OF DEFENSE FOR PUBLIC AFFAIRS (29 Mar. 1996) [hereinafter DOD DIR. 5122.5]; U.S. DEP'T OF DEFENSE DIR. 5400.13, JOINT PUBLIC AFFAIRS OPERATIONS (9 Jan. 1996) [hereinafter DOD DIR. 5400.13]; and William S. Cohen, Secretary of Defense, *Principles of Information* (Apr. 1, 1997) (public statement). DOD Directive 5122.5 sets policy by documenting the responsibility of the Assistant Secretary of Defense for Public Affairs to the media, and establishes, in enclosure 3, the tasks to be performed by the various echelons for accommodating reporters during operations. DOD Directive 5400.13 assigns responsibilities for the conduct of joint, combined and unilateral military operations. The 1996 statement, *Principles of Information* commits "the Department of Defense to make available timely and accurate information so that the public, Congress and the news media may and understand the facts about national security and defense strategy."

12. *See* DOD DIR. 5122.5, *supra* note 11, encl. 3. These principles, entitled *Statement of DoD Principles for News Media Coverage of DOD Operations* were first incorporated in the 19 May 1992, version of this Directive.

13. *See* DOD DIR. 5400.13, *supra* note 11.

14. SECDEF 101900Z, *supra* note 5.

15. In the ongoing operations in Iraq and Afghanistan, the ground rules, set forth in paragraph 4 of SECDEF 101900Z, *supra* note 5, provide that the following categories of information are not releasable since their publication could jeopardize operations and endanger lives: specific number of troops in units below corps/MEF level; specific number of aircraft in units at or below the air expeditionary wing level; specific numbers regarding other equipment or critical supplies (e.g., artillery, tanks, landing craft, radars, trucks, water, etc.); specific number of ships in units below the carrier battle group level; names of military installations or specific

geographic locations of military units in the CENTCOM area of responsibility, unless specifically released by the Department of Defense or authorized by the CENTCOM commander; news and imagery products that identify or include identifiable features of these locations are not authorized for release; information regarding future operations; information regarding force protection measures at military installations or encampments (except those which are visible or readily apparent); photography showing level of security at military installations or encampments; rules of engagement; and information on intelligence collection activities compromising tactics, techniques or procedures. Following these general requirements, the ground rules further provide that extra precautions in reporting will be required at the commencement of hostilities to maximize operational surprise; that during an operation specific information on friendly force troop movements, tactical deployments, and dispositions that would jeopardize operational security or lives will not be released; that information is not releasable on special operations units, unique operations methodology or tactics; that information on effectiveness of enemy electronic warfare in not releasable; that information identifying postponed or cancelled operations is not releasable; that information on missing or downed aircraft or missing vessels while search and rescue and recovery operations are underway is not releasable; that information on effectiveness of enemy camouflage, cover, deception, targeting, direct and indirect fire, intelligence collection, or security measures is not releasable; that no photographs or other visual media showing an enemy prisoner of war or detainee's recognizable face, nametag or other identifying feature or item may be taken; and that no still or video imagery of custody operations or interviews with persons in custody may be made.

16. *See* Jack A. Gottschalk, *Consistent with Security: A History of American Press Censorship*, 5 COMMUNICATIONS AND THE LAW 35, 35–36 (1983).

17. *See* Arthur Lubow, *Read Some About It*, NEW REPUBLIC, Mar. 18, 1991, at 23. Lubow describes the significant impact of the first real war correspondent, William Howard Russell of *The Times of London* during the Crimean War. Russell's vivid descriptions of the horrible battlefield conditions in the Crimea incurred the wrath of the British commander and shocked the British public. The result was the fall of a government and the end of official British tolerance for battlefield journalism.

18. *See* Joseph J. Mathews, REPORTING THE WARS 54–55 (1957). Matthews explains that for the first time, during the Mexican-American War, newspapers carried extensive coverage of war news. This was due, in part to newspaper reporters' widespread access to the war, as there were no legal restrictions on reporting. Matthews also notes there was little to distinguish a reporter from an ordinary soldier, as writing men fought and fighting men wrote. He observes that aside from the representatives of the New Orleans press, all who served as reporters appear to have attended the conflict primarily as fighters.

19. Matthew J. Jacobs, *Assessing the Constitutionality of Press Restrictions in the Persian Gulf War*, 44 STAN. L. REV. 675, 680 (1992).

20. *See* Zechariah Chafee, Jr., FREE SPEECH IN THE UNITED STATES 105 (1941).

21. *Id.*

22. *See* Mathews, *supra* note 18, at 82.

23. *See* Oliver Knight, FOLLOWING THE INDIAN WARS: THE STORY OF THE NEWSPAPER CORRESPONDENTS AMONG THE INDIAN CAMPAIGNERS 307 (1960). Knight reported that the press was accommodated because of their small number and because they shared the same negative view of Indians as did U.S. forces.

24. *See* Gottschalk, *supra* note 16, at 20.

25. *See* Frank Mott, AMERICAN JOURNALISM—A HISTORY: 1690–1960 536–37 (1962).

26. *See* Franklin Ballard, FAMOUS WAR CORRESPONDENTS 413–14 (1914).

27. *See* Drew Middleton, *Barring Reporters from the Battlefield*, N.Y.TIMES MAG., Feb. 5, 1984, at 36, 37.

28. See Gottschalk, supra note 16, at 38. Gottschalk notes that while censorship was imposed at Vera Cruz in 1914, no media restrictions were used during the U.S. Army's campaign against the Mexican revolutionary Pancho Villa in 1916.

29. *See* Matthews, *supra* note 18, at 161.

30. *Id.*, at 169.

31. *See* M. Stein, UNDER FIRE: THE STORY OF AMERICAN WAR CORRESPON-DENTS 73 (1968).

32. *See* Gottschalk, *supra* note 16, at 40.

33. *Id.*

34. *Id.*

35. *See* Matthews, *supra* note 18, at 215–16.

36. *See* Affidavit of Dale R. Spencer, Flynt v. Weinberger, 588 F. Supp. 57 (D.D.C. 1984).

37. *See* Phillip Knightly, THE FIRST CASUALTY—FROM CRIMEA TO VIETNAM: THE WAR CORRESPONDENT AS HERO, PROPAGANDIST, AND MYTH-MAKER 337 (1975).

38. *Id*. at 349.

39. *See* Stein, *supra* note 31, at 149–50.

40. The author served as a Marine Corps infantry platoon commander with 1st Battalion, Third Marines in I Corps in 1968–1969. *See* James P. Terry, *The Vietnam War in Perspective*, NAVAL LAW REVIEW (2007).

41. *See* Knightly, *supra* note 37, at 381.

42. *See Hearings on Governmental Information Plans and Policies, before a Subcommittee of the House Comm. on Governmental Operations*, 88th Cong., 1st Sess. 15, 32, 34, 61 (Part 1), 269 (Part 2) (1963). The press did accompany United States Marines during the 1965 intervention in the Dominican Republic. *See* N.Y. TIMES, Oct. 27, 1983, at A23, col. 6.

43. Despite a liberal access policy, the press was not able to go everywhere. In January 1971, in the first six days of the Dewey Canyon II Operation, a news embargo was maintained, no U.S. correspondent was permitted in the operational area, and no reports were permitted on the operation. No member of the press was on board the helicopters that raided the Son Tay POW camp or on the ships that rescued the crew of the Mayaguez. The secret bombing in Laos and Cambodia for fourteen months in 1969 and 1970 was not disclosed to the press. Later, reporters could only cover the air war in Thailand by special permission. *See 1984-Civil Liberties and the National Security State: Hearings Before the Subcomm. on Courts, Civil Liberties and the Administration of Justice of the House Comm. on the Judiciary*, 98th Cong., 1st Sess.(1983).

44. *See* Robert Waters, *The Media vs. the Military*, HARTFORD COURANT, Dec. 23, 1985, at 1.

45. *See News Policies in Vietnam: Hearings Before the Senate Comm. on Foreign Relations*, 86th Cong., 2d Sess. 68 (1966) (Statement by Asst. Sec. of Def. Arthur Sylvester).

46. Middleton, *supra* note 760, at 61.

47. William G. Ackerly, Analysis of the Pentagon's Press Pool Tests 10 (1987) (unpublished M.A. thesis, University of Kansas) (on file with the University of Kansas Library).

48. *See* Lubow, *supra* note 17, at 25.

49. *Id.*

50. *See Special Report: The Battle for Grenada*, NEWSWEEK, Nov. 7, 1983, at 66, for a detailed summary of the operation.

51. Army forces entered Grenada through a low-level parachute drop while Marines came ashore on the eastern coast and moved south.

52. *See* Jeffries, *supra* note 9, at 993–96.

53. *See U.S. Allows 15 Reporters to Grenada for Day*, N.Y. TIMES, Oct. 28, 1983, at A13, col. 5.

54. *See U.S. Eases Restrictions on Coverage*, N.Y. TIMES, Oct. 31, 1983, at A12, col. 1

55. Anthony Lewis, *What Was He Hiding?*, N.Y. TIMES, Oct. 31, 1983, at A19.

56. *See* N.Y. TIMES, Nov. 4, 1983, at A16, col. 1.

57. N.Y. TIMES, Oct. 28, 1983, at A13, col. 5.

58. NEWSWEEK, Nov. 7, 1983, at 142.

59. The text of the joint statement was reported in the N.Y.TIMES, Jan. 11, 1984, at 1, 10.

60. *Id.*

61. Question asked and explained in Major General Sidle's introduction to U.S. Dept. of Defense, Report of CJCS Media–Military Relations Panel (Sidle Panel) (1984) (available in Pentagon Library) [hereinafter Sidle Panel Report].

62. *Id.*

63. Vice Admiral Joseph Metcalf, *The Press and Grenada:1983*, in DEFENSE AND ME-
DIA IN TIME OF LIMITED WAR, SMALL WARS AND INSURGENCIES 169–70 (P.
Young, ed. 1991).

64. *See* Statement of Principles in Section I, Sidle Panel Report, *supra* note 794.

65. The *Sidle Panel Report* was signed by the following panel members: Winant Sidle,
Major General, USA (Ret); Brent Baker, Captain, USN; Keyes Beech; Scott M. Cutlip; John T.
Halbert; Billy Hunt; George Kirschenbauer, Col. USA; A.J. Langguth; Fred T. Lash, Major,
USMC; James Major, Captain, USN; Wendel S. Merick; Robert O'Brien, Colonel, USAF;
Richard S. Salant; and Barry Zorthian.

66. *See Pact Reached on Media Pool to Cover Military Operations*, WASH. POST, Oct.
11, 1984, at A1, col. 4.

67. *See Pentagon to Add Reporter from Daily Paper to Pool*, WASH. POST, Oct. 12, 1984,
at A1, col. 1.

68. The four tests were conducted in 1985 and 1986 during military exercises in Honduras;
Fort Campbell, Kentucky; off the southern coast of California; and at Twenty Nine Palms,
California. *See* Ackerly, *supra* note 47 at 31–32.

69. *See discussion* of Operation Earnest Will in P. Combelles-Siegel, THE TROUBLED
PATH TO THE PENTAGON'S RULES ON MEDIA ACCESS TO THE BATTLEFIELD:
GRENADA TO TODAY 13 (U.S. Army War College Strategic Studies Institute, 1996).

70. *See* U.S. Dept. of the Army, Public Affairs Office, Info. Memorandum, Deployment of
the DoD Media Pool on Nimrod Dancer (12 May 1989). In this Information Memorandum, the
Army concedes the pool should not have been deployed since more than a hundred reporters
were in Panama, already covering these operations.

71. *See* Fred Hoffman, *Review of Panama Pool Deployment, December 1989*, in UNDER
FIRE: U.S. MILITARY RESTRICTIONS ON THE MEDIA FROM GRENADA TO THE
PERSIAN GULF, APP. C, at 4 (J. Sharkey, ed.1991). *See also* James P. Terry, *Law in Support
of Policy in Panama*, NAVAL WAR COLLEGE REVIEW 110 (Autumn 1990).

72. *See* James Warren, *In First Battlefield Test, Media Pool Misses Mark*, CHI.TRIBUNE,
Jan. 7, 1990, Perspective sect., at 1.

73. *See* Pascale M. Combelles-Siegel, *Operation Just Cause: A Military-Media Fiasco*,
MIL. REV. (May–June 1995), at 77–85.

74. In his report to Assistant Secretary Williams, dated March 1990, Mr. Hoffman gives an
account of the operation, offers his observations about what happened, and makes 17 recommendations he believes would improve future media pool operations. *See* Fred Hoffman, *Review of Panama Pool Deployment* (March 1990) (Report on file with the Pentagon Library,
Washington, DC 20310). *See also* Hoffman, *supra* note 71, App. C.

75. Pete Williams, Assistant Secretary for Public Affairs, Memorandum for Correspondents
(March 20, 1990) on file with the Pentagon Library, Washington, DC 20310). In the Memorandum, Assistant Secretary Williams stated: "The Department of Defense is committed to the
National Media Pool and will make every effort to use the pool in a way that serves the
interests of informing the American people about military activities."

76. Hoffman, *supra* note 71.

77. JOINT CHIEFS OF STAFF, JOINT PUB. 5-02.2, ANNEX F, PLANNING GUID-
ANCE—PUBLIC AFFAIRS (30 March 1990).

78. *Id.*

79. *See* James. P. Terry, *Operation Desert Storm: Sharp Contrasts in Compliance With the
Rule of Law*, 41 NAVAL LAW REVIEW 83 (1993) for one view of how and under what
authority the United States initially responded to the Iraqi invasion of Kuwait.

80. U.S. Central Command, Public Affairs Office, Guidelines for News Media (Jan. 14,
1991).

81. *Id.*

82. The right of journalistic access to news, or to places where news is found, is one that the
Supreme Court has never recognized. *See, e.g.,* Branzburg v. Hayes, 408 U.S. 665 (1972).

83. *See, e.g.,* New York Times Co. v. United States, 403 U.S. 713 (1971) (per curiam).

84. Paul D. Kamenar, *Media Restrictions are Necessary to Protect Troops*, LEGAL TIMES, Jan. 28, 1991, at 19–20. *See* Near v. Minnesota ex rel. Olson, 283 U.S. 697, 716 (1931).l

85. Another comment raised frequently by JCS and the CINCs Public Affairs Officers was that much of the media criticism was based on false analogies to other conflicts, in which events unfolded at a much more deliberate pace and press presence developed over a considerable length of time.

86. The media representatives negotiating this Statement of Principles included Stanley Cloud of the New York Times, Michael Getler of the Washington Post, Clark Hoyt of Knight-Ridder Newspapers, George Watson of ABC News, and Jonathon Wolman of the Associated Press.

87. The nine principles, announced on 21 May 1992, by Assistant Secretary Williams, were as follows:

1. Open and independent reporting will be the principal means of coverage of U.S. military operations.
2. Pools are not to serve as the standard means of covering U.S. military operations. Pools may sometimes provide the only feasible means of early access to military operations. Pools should be as large as possible and disbanded at the earliest opportunity—within 24 to 36 hours when possible. The arrival of early-access pools will not cancel the principle of independent coverage for journalists already in the area.
3. Even under conditions of open coverage, pools may be appropriate for specific events, such as those at extremely remote locations or where space is limited.
4. Journalists in a combat zone will be credentialed by the U.S. military and will be required to abide by a clear set of military security ground rules that protect U.S. forces and their operations. Violation of the ground rules can result in suspension of credentials and expulsion from the combat zone of the journalist involved. News organizations will make their best efforts to assign experienced journalists to combat operations and to make them familiar with U.S. military operations.
5. Journalists will be provided access to all major military units. Special operations restrictions may limit access in cases.
6. Military public affairs officers should act as liaisons but should not interfere with the reporting process.
7. Under conditions of open coverage, field commanders should be instructed to permit journalists to ride on military vehicles and aircraft wherever feasible. The military will be responsible for the transportation of pools.
8. Consistent with its capabilities, the military will supply PAOs with facilities to enable timely, secure, compatible transmission of pool material and will make these facilities available whenever possible for filing independent coverage. In cases where government facilities are unavailable, journalists will, as always, file by any other means available. The military will not ban communications systems operated by news organizations, but electromagnetic operational security in battlefield situations may require limited restrictions on the use of such systems.
9. These principles will apply as well to the operations of the standing National Media Pool system.

88. U.S. Dept. of Defense, Dir. 5122.5, Encl. 3(19 May 1992). The current Principles of Information, detailed in Enclosure 2 to DoDD 5122.05, September 5, 2008, are totally consistent with the 1992 Principles. The current Principles are as follows:

a. Information shall be made fully and readily available, consistent with the statutory requirements, unless its release is precluded by current and valid security classification. The provisions of the Freedom of Information Act will be supported in both letter and spirit.
b. A free flow of general and military information will be made available, without censorship or propaganda, to the men and women of the Armed Forces and their dependents.

    c. Information will not be classified or otherwise withheld to protect the Government from criticism or embarrassment.

    d. Information will be withheld only when disclosure would adversely affect national security, threaten the safety or privacy of the men and women of the Armed Forces, or if otherwise authorized by statute or regulation.

    e. The Department of Defense's obligation to provide the public with information on its major programs may require detailed public affairs planning and coordination within the Department of Defense and within other Government agencies. The sole purpose of such activity is to expedite the flow of information to the public; propaganda has no place in DoD public affairs programs.

89. Louis D. Boccardi, Remarks found in ASD(PA) News Release No. 241–92, May 21, 1992.

90. *See* the statement of Seymour Topping, President of the American Society of Newspaper Editors and Director of Editorial Development for the 32 regional newspapers of the New York Times Company, in Robert Pear, *Military Revises Rules to Assure Reporters Access to Battle Areas*, N.Y. TIMES NAT'L, May 22, 1992, at 3. Topping stated: "We hold that if the spirit of the agreement is fully respected by both sides, the military will find no need for prior security review." It is important to note that the major criticism during the First Gulf War came from Eastern media representatives where the pressure to meet deadlines and placate editors is strongest, with Central and Western reporters not disturbed by the pool system or pre-publication review. Therefore, it was critical in 1992 that the Eastern media was satisfied with the agreement that was developed.

91. *See* John R. MacArthur, SECOND FRONT: CENSORSHIP AND PROPAGANDA IN THE GULF WAR (1992).

92. *See* Stanley W. Cloud, *Covering the Next War*, N.Y. TIMES, Aug. 4, 1992, at 19.

93. While NATO actions in Kosovo were not endorsed by the UN initially, the follow-on stabilization operation was endorsed under Chapter VIII of the Charter in two separate Security Council Resolutions.

94. *See, e.g.*, J. P. Terry, *UN Peacekeeping and Military Reality*, BROWN JOURNAL OF WORLD AFFAIRS, Winter/Spring 1996; *A Legal Review of U.S. Military Involvement in Peacekeeping and Peace Enforcement Operations*, NAVAL LAW REVIEW (1995).

95. The XVIII Airborne Corps held two separate sessions on Media Intelligence Preparation of the Battlefield (IPB), on Aug. 3 and Sept. 22, 1994, to educate their senior leaders on the media's training, background capabilities, and needs in order to enable them to incorporate the newsmen smoothly into military deployments and operations.

96. The assigned media members were thoroughly briefed prior to deployment. They received detailed information from USACOM, from the Joint Task Force Commander at Fort Bragg, and from representatives of the individual units they would cover.

97. Henry Shelton & Timothy Vane, *Winning the Information War in Haiti*, MIL. REV., Nov.–Dec. 1995, at 3, 5.

98. *Id.*, at 3.

99. *See* U.S. DEPT. OF ARMY FIELD MANUAL 100–5, OPERATIONS 1, 3(14 June 1993).

100. *See* note 88, *infra*.

101. *See* Bill Katovsky & Timothy Carlson, EMBEDDED: THE MEDIA AT WAR IN IRAQ xiv (2003).

102. *See generally* Stephen Hess & Marvin Kalb, eds., THE MEDIA AND THE WAR ON TERRORISM (2003).

103. This may have suffered a hiccup in late June 2010 when General McCrystal was totally sandbagged by a Rolling Stone reporter while delayed in Paris with his staff, resulting in his relief for cause and a pointed Secretary of Defense Memorandum dated July 2, 2010, to all Defense officials and commanders to direct all press interviews through public affairs channels. This resulted in a strong statement by Professor Hanson of the University of Maryland on the PBS Lehrer Report on July 8, 2010, concerning the Gates' memo: "I think it will definitely have a chilling effect on reporting on the U.S. military." John Burns of the New York Times was more balanced in his remarks on the same program: "And I think we need to—as Lara

Logan suggested in that clip, we need to also look—take a look at the mote, or maybe I should say the beam, in our own eye and look at the question of trust pretty carefully." Despite this incident, the reporting and the relationship between reporters and the military in these two operations has been positive.

104. *Flynt v. Weinberger*, 588 F. Supp. 59 (1983).

105. *Id.*

106. Id.

107. 219 U.S. 498 (1911). For a discussion of the "capable of repetition vet evading review" doctrine, *see* R. Greenstein, *Bridging the Mootness Gap in Federal Court Class Actions,* 35 STAN. L. REV. 897 (1983)

108. *Flynt*, 588 F.Supp. at 59.

109. *Id.* at 60.

110. *Id.*

111. *Id.* at 60–61. *See also Halkin v. Helms*, 600 F. 2d 977, 1006–09 (D.C. Cir. 1982).

112. 762 F. Supp 1558 (S.D.N.Y. 1991). *Agence France-Presse* also filed suit against DoD on 6 Feb. 1991, challenging its exclusion from the Desert Storm media pool because priority was given to entities that "principally serve the American public." It also complained that administration of the pool had been entrusted to Reuters, its principal competitor. *Agence France-Presse* asked for a TRO. The Government defended on a variety of grounds, eventually moving for joinder with *Nation Magazine*. The *Agence* suit was ultimately dismissed when *The Nation* suit was dismissed.

113. *Id.* at 1561–63.

114. *Id.* at 1561.

115. *Id.* at 1572.

116. *Id.* at 1568.

117. *Id.* at 1569.

118. *Id.* at 1570.

119. *Id.* at 1572.

120. *Id.* at 1574

121. *Id.* at 1575.

122. *See* Garry Sturgess, *Media Powers Oppose War Rules but Shun Suit*, LEGAL TIMES, Feb. 4, 1991, at 2.

123. *See Near v. Minnesota ex rel. Olson*, 283 U.S. 697, 716 (1931).

124. *Frisby v. Schultz*, 487 U.S. 474, 481 (1988).

125. *See, e.g.,* James P. Terry, *The Vietnam War in Perspective*, NAVAL LAW REV. (2007)

126. *See* DoD Dir. 5122.5, 29 Mar. 1996; DoD Dir. 5400.13, Jan. 9, 1996.

127. *See, e.g.,* DoD Dir. 5122.5, Sept. 27, 2000.

128. DoD Dir. 5122.05, Sept. 5, 2008.

129. Enclosure 2 to DoDD 5122.05, September 5, 2008, are totally consistent with the 1992 Principles. The current Principles are as follows:

a. Information shall be made fully and readily available, consistent with the statutory requirements, unless its release is precluded by current and valid security classification. The provisions of the Freedom of Information Act will be supported in both letter and spirit.

b. A free flow of general and military information will be made available, without censorship or propaganda, to the men and women of the Armed Forces and their dependents.

c. Information will not be classified or otherwise withheld to protect the Government from criticism or embarrassment.

d. Information will be withheld only when disclosure would adversely affect national security, threaten the safety or privacy of the men and women of the Armed Forces, or if otherwise authorized by statute or regulation.

e. The Department of Defense's obligation to provide the public with information on its major programs may require detailed public affairs planning and coordination within the Department of Defense and within other Government agencies. The sole purpose of such activity is to expedite the flow of information to the public; propaganda has no place in DoD public affairs programs.

20. FUTURE PERSPECTIVES IN ADDRESSING TERROR VIOLENCE

1. *See* James P. Terry, *The Iranian Hostage Crisis: International Law and U.S. Policy*, JAG JOURNAL 31–79 (Summer 1982).

2. *See* James P. Terry, *An Appraisal of Lawful Military Response to State-Sponsored Terrorism*, NAVAL WAR C. REV. (May–June 1986) at 61, 66.

Selected Bibliography and Sources

THE THREAT OF TERRORISM IN PERSPECTIVE

Baker, Peter, *Bush to Restate Terror Strategy: 2002 Doctrine of Preemptive War to be Reaffirmed,* WASHINGTON POST, March 16, 2006.

Bernstein, R., *European Community Agrees on Libya Curbs,* NEW YORK TIMES, Apr. 22, 1986.

Bush, George W., THE NATIONAL SECURITY STRATEGY OF THE UNITED STATES, The White House, February 2002.

————. THE NATIONAL SECURITY STRATEGY OF THE UNITED STATES, The White House, March 16, 2006.

Denza, R., DIPLOMATIC LAW: COMMENTARY ON THE VIENNA CONVENTION ON DIPLOMATIC RELATIONS 135 (1976).

Hyde, C., INTERNATIONAL LAW 240 (2d ed. 1945).

Kempster, R., *Cables Cited as Proof of Libyan Terror Role,* L.A. TIMES, Apr. 15, 1986,

Lillich, Richard, *Forcible Self Help by States to Protect Human Rights,* 53 IOWA LAW REVIEW. 325 (1967)

Mallison, W. Thomas, *Limited Naval Blockade or Quarantine Interdiction: National and Collective Self-Defense Claims Valid Under International Law,* 31 GEORGE WASHINGTON LAW REVIEW. 335 (1962).

McFarlane, Robert C., *Terrorism and the Future of Free Society,* Speech delivered at the National Strategic Information Center, Defense Strategy Forum, Washington, DC, March 25, 1985.

Moore, J., DIGEST OF INTERNATIONAL LAW 404 (1906).

Sharp, W. Gary Sr., CYBERSPACE AND THE USE OF FORCE (Falls Church, VA: Aegis Research Corporation, 2001).

Shultz, George, *Terrorism and the Modern World,* Speech to Park Avenue Synagogue, New York City, October 25, 1984.

Terry, James P., *The Iranian Hostage Crisis: International Law and U.S. Policy,* 31 JAG JL 31 (1982).

————. *Countering State-Sponsored Terrorism,* NAVAL LAW REVIEW (Winter 1986)

————. *An Appraisal of Lawful Military Response to State-Sponsored Terrorism,* NAVAL WAR COLLEGE REVIEW, May–June 1986,

Tovar, Hugh, *Low Intensity Conflict: Active Responses in An Open Society,* Paper prepared for the CONFERENCE ON TERRORISM AND OTHER "LOW INTENSITY" OPERATIONS: INTERNATIONAL LINKAGES, Fletcher School of Law and Diplomacy, Medford, Mass., April 1985.

LEGAL REQUIREMENTS FOR UNCONVENTIONAL WARFARE: THE OPERATIONAL CONTEXT

McDougal, Myres, and F. Feliciano, LAW AND MINIMUM WORLD ORDER 142–43 (1961).

Moore, J, G. Roberts, and R. Turner (eds.), NATIONAL SECURITY LAW DOCUMENTS (1995).

Solf, W. and E. Cummings, *A Survey of Penal Sanctions Under Protocol I to the Geneva Conventions of August 12, 1949*, CASE W. UNIV. JL.INT'L L. (Spring 1977).

STATE SPONSORED TERRORISM: THE INTERNATIONAL POLITICAL CONTEXT

Abu-Lughod, Ibrahim, Northwestern University, American Society of International Law, April 12, 1973.

Amnesty International Annual Report 2000/2001 (2001).

Arendt, Hannah, THE ORIGINS OF TOTALITARIANISM (New York: Harcourt Brace Jovanovich, 1973).

Conquest, Robert, THE GREAT TERROR: STALIN'S PURGE OF THE THIRTIES (New York: McMillan, 1968).

Dallin, A. and G. Breslauer, POLITICAL TERROR IN COMMUNIST SYSTEMS (Stanford: Stanford University Press, 1970).

Gross, Felix, *Political Violence and Terror in 19th and 20th Century Russia and Eastern Europe* in J. Kirkham, S. Levy, and W. Crotty, eds. A REPORT TO THE NATIONAL COMMISSION ON THE CAUSES AND PREVENTION OF VIOLENCE, vol. 8 (Washington: U.S. Gov. Printing Office, 1969).

Gurr, T. R., WHY MEN REBEL (Princeton: Princeton University Press, 1970).

Hannay, Hannay, *International Terrorism: The Need for a Fresh Perspective*, INTERNATIONAL LAWYER, vol. 8 (1974).

Mallison, W. Thomas and Sally V., *The Concept of Public Purpose Terror in International Law: Doctrines and Sanctions to Reduce the Destruction of Human and Material Values*, HOWARD LAW JOURNAL, vol. 18, (1974).

MERIP Report, no. 59 (August 1977).

Merleau-Ponty, Maurice, HUMANISM AND TERROR: AN ESSAY ON THE COMMUNIST PROBLEM, trans. J. O'Neill (Boston: Beacon Press, 1980).

Protection of Human Rights in Occupied Territories, UN Office of Public Information Document OPI/582 (1977).

Report of the Ad Hoc Committee on International Terrorism, UN Doc. A/9028 (1973).

Rogers, William P., UN General Assembly, September 25, 1972, Press Release USUN 104 (1972).

Soboul, Albert, THE FRENCH REVOLUTION 1789–1799, trans. Alan Forrest and Colin Jones (New York: Random House, 1975).

Treatment of the Palestinians in Israeli-Occupied West Bank and Gaza: Report of the National Lawyers Guild 1977 Middle East Delegation (1978).

Walter, E. V., TERROR AND RESISTANCE: A STUDY OF POLITICAL VIOLENCE (London: Oxford University Press, 1969).

Wilkinson, Paul, POLITICAL TERRORISM (New York: John Wiley, 1975).

THE LAW OF SELF-DEFENSE AS APPLIED TO THE TERRORIST THREAT IN IRAQ AND SOUTHWEST ASIA

McDougal, Myres, *The Soviet-Cuban Quarantine and Self-Defense*, 57 AMERICAN JOURNAL OF INTERNATIONAL LAW. 697 (1963).

McFarlane, Robert C., *Terrorism and the Future of Free Society*, Speech delivered at the National Strategic Information Center, Defense Strategy Forum, Washington, DC, March 25, 1985.

NATIONAL SECURITY DECISION DIRECTIVE 138, White House, Washington, DC, April 3, 1984.

Presidential Decision Directive 62, COMBATING TERRORISM, May 22, 1998.

Report of DoD Commission on Beirut International Airport Terrorist Act of 23 October 1983, at 129 (Dec. 20, 1983), *reprinted in* AM. FOREIGN POL'Y DOCUMENT 122, at 349, col. 2 (1983).

Rovine, J., *Contemporary Practice of the United States Relating to International Law*, 68 AM. J. INT'L L. 720, 736 (1974) (statement of then–Acting Secretary of State Dean Rusk).

Shultz, George, *Low Intensity Warfare: The Challenge of Ambiguity*, U.S. DEP'T OF STATE CURRENT POLICY NO. 783 (Jan. 1986).

Terry, James P., *An Appraisal of Lawful Military Response to State-Sponsored Terrorism*, NA-VAL WAR COLLEGE REVIEW, May–June 1986.

Whiteman, Marjorie, 5 DIGEST OF INTERNATIONAL LAW sec. 25 (1965).

THE DEVELOPMENT OF RULES OF ENGAGEMENT AND THEIR APPLICATION IN THE TERRORIST ENVIRONMENT

Chairman of the Joint Chiefs of Staff Instruction 3121.01, *Standing Rules of Engagement for U.S. Forces*, Oct. 1, 1994, as amended Dec. 22, 1994, and thereafter. The most recent amendment to this CJCS Instruction is CJCSI 3121.01B, 13 June 2005.

Joint Chiefs of Staff Peacetime Rules of Engagement for U.S. Seaborne Forces (May 1980).

Joint Chiefs of Staff Peacetime Rules of Engagement for U.S. Forces (June, 1986).

Roach, J. Ashly, *Rules of Engagement*, NAVAL WAR COLLEGE REVIEW., Jan–Feb 1983.

Terry, James P., *Countering State-Sponsored Terrorism: A Law–Policy Analysis*, NAVAL LAW REVIEW, Winter 1986.

————. *Responding to Attacks on Critical Computer Infrastructure: What Targets? What Rules of Engagement?* NAVAL LAW REVIEW (1999).

————. *The Lawfulness of Attacking Computer Networks in Armed Conflict and in Self-Defense in Periods Short of Armed Conflict: What Are the Targeting Constraints?* MILITARY LAW REVIEW (2001).

USE OF FORCE BY THE PRESIDENT: DEFENSIVE USES SHORT OF WAR

Acheson, Dean, PRESENT AT THE CREATION (New York: W.W. Norton and Co., 1969).

Department of State, Historical Studies Division, *Armed Actions Taken by the United States Without a Declaration of War*, 1789–1967 (Res. Proj. No. 806A (Washington: 1967)).

Corwin, Edward, THE PRESIDENT: OFFICE AND POWERS, 1787–1957 (New York: New York University Press, 1957).

Goldsmith, William, THE GROWTH OF PRESIDENTIAL POWER, vol. 3 (1974).

Grimmett, Richard E., *Foreign Policy Roles of the President and Congress* (1999), at http://fpc.stste.gov/6172.htp.

Gulf of Tonkin Resolution, H.R. J. Res. of Aug. 10, 1964, Pub. L. No. 88-408, No. 2, 78 Stat. 384.

Meeker, Leonard C., Memorandum by the State Department Legal Advisor, *The Legality of the United States Participation in the Defense of Vietnam*, March 4, 1966, *reproduced in* STATE DEPARTMENT BULLETIN 474 (1966).

Miller, Abraham, *Terrorism and Hostage Taking: Lessons from the Iranian Crisis*, 13 RUTGERS-CAMDEN LAW JOURNAL 513, 523 (1982).

Senate Committee on Foreign Relations, *Report on the National Commitments Resolution*, S. Rept. No. 91-129, 91st Congress, 1st. Sess. (1969); *U.S. Commitments to Foreign Powers*, Hearings before the Senate Committee on Foreign Relations, 90th Congress, 1st Sess. (1967).

Special Message to the Congress Regarding United States Policy for the Defense of Formosa, January 24, 1955, in PUBLIC PAPERS OF THE PRESIDENTS: DWIGHT D. EISENHOWER, 1955 (1999).

Story, Joseph, COMMENTARIES ON THE CONSTITUTION OF THE UNITED STATES 546–47 (1833, reprinted 1987).

Taubman, Phillip, *The Shultz-Weinberger Feud*, THE NEW YORK TIMES MAGAZINE, April 14, 1985.

Terry, James P., *Al Qaeda and Taliban Detainees-An Examination of Legal Rights and Appropriate Treatment*, Chapter XXVI in INTERNATIONAL LAW AND THE WAR ON TERROR (2003).

————. *Intervention in Panama*, NAVAL WAR COLLEGE REVIEW (Winter 1990).

————. *The President as Commander in Chief*, AVE MARIA LAW REVIEW (Spring 2009).

————. *The Vietnam War in Perspective*, NAVAL LAW REVIEW (2007).

Turner, Robert, *The Authority to Use the Armed Forces*, Chap. 17 in John Norton Moore and Robert F. Turner, eds., NATIONAL SECURITY LAW, 2d ed.(2005).

Wright, Quincy, THE CONTROL OF AMERICAN FOREIGN RELATIONS (New York: Macmillan, 1922).

HABEAS CORPUS AND THE DETENTION OF ENEMY COMBATANTS

Chemerinsky, Erwin, *Thinking about Habeas Corpus*, 37 CASE W. RES. L. REV. 748, 752 (1987).

Clarke, Alan, *Habeas Corpus: The Historical Debate*, 14 N.Y.L. SCH. JL HUM. RTS. 375, 378 (1998).

Collins, Rex A., *Habeas Corpus for Convicts—Constitutional Right or Legislative Grace*, 40 CAL. L. REV. 335, 339 (1952).

Detainee Treatment Act, Pub. L. No. 109-148, 119 Stat 2680 (2005). Signed into law December 30, 2005.

Duker, William F., A CONSTITUTIONAL HISTORY OF HABEAS CORPUS 17 (Westport, CT: Greenwood Press, 1980).

LEASE OF LANDS FOR COALING AND NAVAL STATIONS, Feb. 23, 1903, U.S.-Cuba, Art.III, T.S. No. 418.

Military Commissions Act, Pub. L. No. 109-366, 120 Stat. 2600 (2006). The President signed the Military Commissions Act into law on October 17, 2006.

Newman, Gerald L., *Habeas Corpus, Executive Detention, and the Removal of Aliens*, 98 CO-LUM. L. REV. 961, 970–71 (1998).

Rosenn, Max, *The Great Writ—A Reflection of Societal Change*, 44 OHIO STATE LAW JOURNAL. 337, 338, n. 14 (1983).

Terry, James P., *The President as Commander in Chief*, AVE MARIA LAW REV. (Spring 2009).

TORTURE AND THE INTERROGATION OF DETAINEES

Authorization for Use of Military Force, Pub. L. No.107-40, 115 Stat. 224 (2001).

Bush, George W., President of the United States, President Discusses Progress in War on Terror to National Guard (Feb. 9, 2006), http://georgewbushwhitehouse.archives.gov/news/releases/2006/02/20060209-2.html.

Constitutional and International Law Implications of Executive Order 13440 Interpreting Common Article 3 of the 1949 Geneva Conventions: Hearing on U.S. Interrogation Policy and Executive Order 13440 Before the S. Select Comm. on Intelligence, 110th Cong. 1 (2007) (statement of Robert F. Turner, Associate Director, Center for National Security Law, University of Virginia School of Law).

Declaration on Protection from Torture, G.A. Res. 3452 art. 1, ¶2, U.N. GAOR, 30th Sess., Supp. No.34, U.N. Doc. A/1034 (Dec. 9, 1975).

Draper, G.I.A.D., *Humanitarian Law and Internal Armed Conflict*, 13 GA. J. INT'L 7 COMP. L. 253, 268 (1983).

Fax from Assoc. Gen. Counsel, CIA, for Daniel Levin, Acting Assistant Att'y Gen., Dept. of Justice, Office of Legal Counsel, *Re: Background Paper on CIA's Combined Use of Interrogation Techniques* at 4 (Dec. 30, 2004).

Fionnuala Ní Aoláin, *Hamdan and Common Article 3: Did the Supreme Court Get it Right?*, 91 MINN. L. REV. 1523, 1556 (2007).

Finn, Peter, Joby Warrick & Julie Tate, *How a Detainee Became an Asset*, WASHINGTON POST, Aug. 29, 2009, at A1, A6.

Geneva Convention Relative to the Treatment of Prisoners of War, Aug. 12, 1949, 6 U.S.T. 3217, 75 U.N.T.S. 135.

Hakki Onen, S. et al., *The Effects of Total Sleep Deprivation, Selective Sleep Interruption, and Sleep Recovery on Pain Tolerance Thresholds on Healthy Subjects*, 10 J. Sleep Research 35, 41 (2001).

Kornblut, Anne, *New Unit to Question Key Terror Suspects*, WASHINGTON POST, Aug. 24, 2009, at A1, A5.

Krauthammer, Charles, *The Truth About Torture*, THE WEEKLY STANDARD, Dec. 5, 2005, *available at* http://www.weeklystandard.com/Content/Public/Articles/000/000/006/400rhqav.asp.

Kunderman, B. et al., *Sleep Deprivation Affects Thermal Pain Thresholds but not Somatosensory Thresholds in Healthy Volunteers*, 66 Psychosomatic Med. 932 (2004).

Memorandum for John Rizzo, Acting Gen. Counsel, CIA, from Steven G. Bradbury, Principal Deputy Assistant Att'y Gen., Dept. of Justice, Office of Legal Counsel, *Re: Application of 18 U.S.C 2340–2340A to Certain Techniques That May Be Used in the Interrogation of a High Value al Qaeda Detainee* at 4 (May 10, 2005) (declassified and disclosed by the Obama Administration, Apr. 16, 2009).

Memorandum for John Rizzo, Acting Gen. Counsel, CIA, from Steven G. Bradbury, Principal Deputy Assistant Att'y Gen., Dept. of Justice, Office of Legal Counsel, *Re: Application of United States Obligations Under Article 16 of the Convention Against Torture to Certain Techniques that May Be Used in the Interrogation of High Value al Qaeda Detainees*, (May 30, 2005) (declassified and disclosed by the Obama Administration, Apr. 16, 2009), at 15.

Meyer, Jane, *The Black Sites*, THE NEW YORKER, Aug. 13, 2007, http://www.newyorker.com/reporting/2007/08/13/070813fa_fact_mayer?printable=true.

Obama, President Barack, Address to Joint Session of Congress (Feb. 24, 2009), http://www.whitehouse.gov/the_press_office/remarks-of-president-barack-obama-address-to-joint-session-of-congress.

Office of Medical Services (OMS) Guidelines on Medical and Psychological Support to Detainee Rendition, Interrogation and Detention (Dec. 2004).

Pictet, Jean S., INTERNATIONAL COMMITTEE OF THE RED CROSS: COMMENTARY TO THE CONVENTION (I) RELATIVE TO THE AMELIORATION OF THE CONDITION OF THE WOUNDED AND SICK IN ARMED FORCES IN THE FIELD 39–43 (1952)

Radsan, John, *The Collision Between Common Article Three and the Central Intelligence Agency*, 56 CATHOLIC UNIVERSITY LAW REVIEW. 959, 972 (2007).

Report of CIA Inspector General, *Counterterrorism Detention and Interrogation Activities (Sept 2001–Oct 2003)*, No. 2003-7123-IG (May 7, 2004).

Rose, David, *Tortured Reasoning*, VANITY FAIR, Dec. 16, 2008, http://www.vanityfair.com/magazine/2008/12/torture200812?printable=true&currentPage=all.

Soufan, Ali, *My Tortured Decision*, NEW YORK TIMES, Apr. 22, 2009, http://www.nytimes.com/2009/04/23/opinion/23soufan.html?_r=3&ref=opinion.

Supreme Court of Israel: Judgment Concerning the Legality of the General Security Service's Interrogation Methods, 38 I.L.M. 1471, (Sept. 9, 1999); also available at H.C. 5100/94, The Public Committee Against Torture in Israel v. Israel (Sept. 9, 1999), available at http://www.derechos.org/human-rights/mena/doc/torture.html.

United Nations Convention Against Torture and Other Cruel, Inhuman or Degrading Treatment or Punishment, Dec. 10, 1984, 1465 U.N.T.S. 85 (entered into force for U.S. Nov. 20, 1994 ("Convention Against Torture" or "CAT").

U.S. Department of Justice, *Placing of United States Armed Forces Under United Nations Operational or Tactical Control*, 20 Op. Off. Legal Counsel 182, 185 (1996).

What Went Wrong: Torture and the Office of Legal Counsel in the Bush Administration: Hearing Before the S. Comm. On the Judiciary, 111th Cong. (2009) http://judiciary.senate.gov/hearings/testimony.-cfm?id=3842&wit_id+7904.

Young, Cathy, *Torturing Logic*, Reason, March 2006, at http://www.-reason.com/news/show/33263.html.

FEDERAL COURT OR MILITARY COMMISSION: THE DILEMMA

Bowman, M. E., *National Security and the Fourth and Fifth Amendments*, in John N. Moore and Robert F. Turner, eds., NATIONAL SECURITY LAW, (2005), at 1059, *et seq.*

Detention, Treatment, and Trial of Certain Non-Citizens in the War Against Terrorism sec. 1(a), 66 Fed. Reg. 57,833 (Nov. 16, 2001).

DOJ/DoD Press Release, Departments of Justice and Defense Announce Forum Decisions for Ten Guantanamo Bay Detainees, Nov. 13, 2009, http://www.justice.gov/opa/pr/2009/November/09-ag-1224.html.

E.O. 13492, *Review and Disposition of Individuals Detained at the Guantanamo Naval Base and Closure of Detention Facilities*, 74 Federal Register 4897, Jan. 22, 2009.

Garcia, Michael John, *Boumediene v. Bush: Guantanamo Detainees' Right to Habeas Corpus*, CRS Report RL34536 (2008).

Terry, James P., *Habeas Corpus and the Detention of Enemy Combatants in the Global War on Terror*, JOINT FORCE QUARTERLY (Jan. 2008).

Winthrop, William, MILITARY LAW AND PRECEDENTS 831 (2d ed., 1920) (describing the distinction between courts-martial and military commissions).

THE INTERNATIONAL CRIMINAL COURT AND THE TRIAL OF TERROR-RELATED CRIMES—A USEFUL VENUE?

Bolton, John R. Letter from Under Secretary of State for Arms Control and International Security, U.S., to Kofi Annan, U.N. Secretary-General (May 6, 2002).

Clark, Roger S., & Madeleine Sann, eds., THE PROSECUTION OF INTERNATIONAL WAR CRIMES (New Brunswick, NJ: Transaction Publishers, 1996).

Statement of the President: Signature of the International Criminal Court Treaty, The White House (Camp David), December 31, 2000.

Terry, James P., THE REGULATION OF INTERNATIONAL COERCION (Newport, RI: Naval War College Press, 2005).

HIGH SEAS TERROR AND THE ELIMINATION OF PIRACY

ANNOTATED SUPPLEMENT TO THE COMMANDER'S HANDBOOK ON THE LAW OF NAVAL OPERATIONS, 222–223 (1999).

Baumgartner, RAdm. Wm. Baumgartner, USCG, testimony of: *Hearing on International Piracy on the High Seas*, before the House Subcommittee on Coast Guard and Maritime Transportation, Feb. 4, 2009, at 6.

(u) cfmcc cent p 301133Z Dec. 08 (Subject: CTF 151 EXORD). Cong. Res. Rep. R40081, Ocean Piracy and Its Impact on Insurance, Dec. 3, 2008.

Cummings, Statement of the Honorable Elijah, Subcommittee on the Coast Guard and Maritime Transportation, Hearing on "International Piracy on the High Seas", Feb. 4, 2009, at 1.

Ellen, *Contemporary Piracy*, 21 CAL. WEST. INT'L L. J. 123 (1990).

Gartney, VAdm. Wm., *New Counter-Piracy Task Force Established*, www.navy.mil/local/cusnc, Jan. 8, 2009.

National Security Council, *Countering Piracy off the Horn of Africa: Partnership and Action Plan*, The White House, Washington DC, December 2008.

Petrie, *Pirates and Naval Officers*, NAVAL WAR COLLEGE REVIEW, May–June 1982, at15.

Pirate Washes Ashore with Cash, at http://news.bbc.co.uk/go/pr//fr/-/2/hi/africa/7824353.stm of January 12, 2009.

UNITED NATIONS CONVENTION ON THE LAW OF THE SEA, *opened for signature* 10 Dec. 1982, 21 I.L.M. 1261. Art. 15 of the CONVENTION ON THE HIGH SEAS, defines piracy in essentially identical terms. *See* 13 U.S.T. 2312, 450 U.N.T.S. 92, Geneva, 29 April 1958.

OUTSOURCING DEFENSE SUPPORT OPERATIONS IN THE WAR ON TERROR

CENTCOM Dec 05, Subj: (U) *USCENTCOM Policy Relating to Possession and Use of Arms by All DoD Civilian Personnel and All DoD Contractors and Their Employees Present Within Iraq and Afghanistan.*

DepSecDef Memorandum of 25 Sept. 2007, Subj: (U) *Management of DoD Contractors and Contractor Personnel Accompanying U.S. Armed Forces in Contingency Operations Outside the United States.*

DoD Inst. 3020.41, *Contractor Personnel Authorized to Accompany the U.S. Armed Forces* (Oct. 3, 2005). DoD Inst. 3020.41 requires the department to maintain by-name accountability of contractors deploying with the force, who are defined as systems support and external support contractors, and associated subcontractors, specifically authorized in their contract to deploy to support U.S. forces.

DoD Inst. 5525.11, *Criminal Jurisdiction Over Civilians Employed by or Accompanying the Armed Forces Outside the United States, Certain Service Members, and Former Service Members*, March 3, 2005.

DoD Deputy GC (International Affairs) Memo to SJA, USCENTCOM, *Request to Contract for Private Security Companies in Iraq*, Jan. 10, 2006.

GAO Report 07-145, *Military Operations: High Level DoD Action Needed to Address Long-Standing Problems with Management and Oversight of Contractors Supporting Deployed Forces* (Dec. 2006).

GAO Report GAO-04-854 MILITARY OPERATIONS: DOD'S EXTENSIVE USE OF LOGISTICS SUPPORT CONTRACTS REQUIRES STRENGTHENED OVERSIGHT (July 2004).

GAO Report GAO-08-436T, *Military Operations: Implementation of Existing Guidance and Other Actions Needed to Improve DoD's Oversight and Management of Contractors in Future Operations* (Jan. 24, 2008).

Gimble, Thomas F., testimony of Acting IG, DoD, in *Combating War Profiteering: Are We Doing Enough to Investigate and Prosecute Contracting Fraud in Iraq?* Hearing before the Committee on the Judiciary, United States Senate, March 20, 2007, at 9.

Miller, T. Christian, *Private Contractors Outnumber U.S. Troops in Iraq*, L.A. TIMES, July 4, 2007, at A-2.

MILITARY EXTRATERRITORIAL JURISDICTION ACT OF 2000, sec. 3261, Pub. L. 106–523, Nov. 22, 2000.

Solis, William, testimony of Director, Defense Capabilities and Management, before the Subcommittee on National Security, Emerging Threats, and International Relations, Committee on Government Reform in GAO Report, *Rebuilding Iraq: Actions Still Needed to Improve the Use of Private Security Providers*, GAO-06-86T, June 13, 2006.

Terry, James P., *Operation Desert Storm: Stark Contrasts in Compliance With the Rule of Law*, NAVAL LAW REVIEW, Winter 1993.

————. *U.N. Peacekeeping and Military Reality*, BROWN JOURNAL OF WORLD AFFAIRS, Winter/Spring 1996.

————. *Rethinking Humanitarian Intervention After Kosovo*, THE ARMY LAWYER, August 2004.

————.*"Operationalizing" Legal Requirements for Unconventional Warfare*, JOINT FORCE QUARTERLY, October 2008.

U.S. Air Force, *Performance Based Service Contracts*, Air Force Inst. 63–124 (Apr. 1, 1999).

U.S. Army, *Logistics Civil Augmentation Program*, Department of the Army Regulation 700-137 (Dec. 16, 1985).

U.S. Army, *Contractors Accompanying the Force*, Department of the Army Regulation 715–9 (Oct. 29, 1999); U.S. Army, *Logistics Civil Augmentation Program*, Army Material Command Pamphlet 700-30 (Jan. 2002).

U.S. Army, *Contractors on the Battlefield*, Department of the Army Field Manual 3-100.21 (Jan. 3, 2003).

STABILIZATION OPERATIONS

DoD Directive 1322.18, *Military Training*, Jan. 13, 2009.
DoD Directive 1404.10, *DoD Civilian Expeditionary Workforce*, Jan. 23, 2009.
DoD Directive 3000.05, *Military support for Stability, Security, Transition, and Reconstruction (SSTR) Operations*, November 28, 2005.
DoD Directive 3000.07, *Irregular Warfare*, December 1, 2008.
DoD Directive 5100.1, *Functions of the Department of Defense and its Major Components*, August 1, 2002.
DoD Directive 5111.1, *Under Secretary of Defense for Policy (USD(P)*, December 8, 1999.
DoD Instruction 2200.01, *Combating Trafficking in Persons (CTIP)*, February 16, 2007.
DoD Instruction 3000.05, *Stability Operations*, September 16, 2009.
DoD Instruction 5160.70, *Management of DoD Language and Regional Proficiency Capabilities*, June 12, 2007.
DoD Instruction 8220.02 , *Information and Communication Technology (ICT) Capabilities for Support of Stabilization and Reconstruction, Disaster Relief, and Humanitarian and Civic Assistance Operations*, April 30, 2009.
DoD Manual 4160.21-M, *Defense Material Disposition Manual*, August 18, 1997.
Deputy Secretary of Defense Memorandum, *Delegations of Authority*, November 30, 2006.
Sections 401, 2557, and 2561 of Title 10, U.S. Code.

ENVIRONMENTAL TERRORISM: FROM OIL FIRES TO FOULING GULF WATERS

Additional Protocol II to the Treaty for the Prohibition of Nuclear Weapons in Latin America, 14 February 1967, 22 UST 754; TIAS 7137; 634 UNTS 364 (1971).
Bevans, Charles I., TREATIES AND OTHER INTERNATIONAL AGREEMENTS OF THE U.S.A., 1776–1949, Dept. of State Pub. 8407 (Washington: November 1968).
Convention on the Prohibition of Military or Any Other Use of Environmental Modification Techniques (ENMOD Convention), signed in Geneva, May 18, 1977, entered into force, October 5, 1978; U.S. ratification, December 13, 1979; ratification deposited in New York, January 17. 1980.
General Order No. 100 (1863) signed by President Abraham Lincoln, in Dietrich Schindler and Jiri Toman, eds. THE LAWS OF ARMED CONFLICT (Leiden: Sijthoff, 1988).
Goldblat, J., AGREEMENTS FOR ARMS CONTROL: A CRITICAL SURVEY (London: Taylor and Francis 1982), 120–21.
International Military Tribunal (Nuremberg), *Judgment and Sentence*, AMERICAN JOURNAL OF INTERNATIONAL LAW, no. 41, 1947.
Interim Agreement between the Union of Soviet Socialist Republics (now Russian Federation) and the United States of America on Certain Measures with Respect to the Limitation of Strategic Offensive Arms, with Protocol, May 26, 1972, 23 UST 3462; TIAS 7504 (1972).
Regulations Annexed to Hague Convention IV of 1907 Respecting the Laws and Customs of War on Land, 36 Stat. 2259; TREATIES AND INTERNATIONAL AGREEMENTS SERIES (tias).
Treaty Banning Nuclear Weapons Tests in the Atmosphere, In Outer Space, and Under Water, 5 August 1963, 14 United States Treaties (UST) 1313; TIAS 5433; 480 United States Treaty Series (UNTS) 43 (1963).
Treaty on the Non-Proliferation of Nuclear Weapons, 1 July 1968, 21 UST 483; TIAS 6839 (1970).

Treaty on the Prohibition of the Emplacement of Nuclear Weapons and Other Weapons of Mass Destruction on the Seabed and the Ocean Floor and in the Subsoil Thereof, 11 February 1971, 23 UST 701; TIAS 7337 (1972).

DEFENSE OF CRITICAL INFRASTRUCTURE SYSTEMS FROM TERRORISTS: COMPUTER NETWORK DEFENSE (CND).

Brownlee, Ian, *The Use of Force in Self-Defense*, BR. Y.B. INT'L L. 183, 207 (1961).
Chairman of the Joint Chiefs of Staff Instruction 3121.01, STANDING RULES OF ENGAGEMENT FOR U.S. FORCES, Oct. 1, 1994, *as amended* Dec. 22, 1994, and Feb. 2005.
G.A. Res. 53/70, U.N. GAOR, 53rd Sess., U.N. Doc. A/RES/53/70 (1998).
Gertz, William, *Chinese Hackers Raid U.S. Computers*, WASHINGTON TIMES, May 16, 1999, at C1.
Gorelick, Hon. Jamie, Speech before the Corps of Cadets, U.S. Air Force Academy, (February 29, 1996).
Graham, Bradley, *U.S. Studies New Threat: Cyber Attack*, WASHINGTON POST, May 24, 1998, at A1.
Greenberg, Lawrence T. et al., INFORMATION WARFARE AND INTERNATIONAL LAW (Institute for National Security Studies: Washington) 1997.
Oppenheim, R., INTERNATIONAL LAW (London: Longmans: London (8th ed. 1955)).
United States Explanation of Vote After the Vote, re: G.A. Res. 53/70 (1998), *reprinted in* W. Gary Sharp, CYBERSPACE AND THE USE OF FORCE, (Aegis: Falls Church, VA 1999) at 189.
U.S. Department of Defense, Cyber Command Fact Sheet, May 21, 2010.
U.S. Department of the Navy, THE COMMANDERS HANDBOOK ON THE LAW OF NAVAL OPERATIONS (NWP 1-14m), para. 8.1 (1997).

THE LEGALITY OF ATTACK ON FOREIGN INFRASTRUCTURE POSING A TERRORIST THREAT TO THE UNITED STATES: COMPUTER NETWORK ATTACK (CNA)

CONVENTION (V) RESPECTING THE RIGHTS AND DUTIES OF NEUTRAL POWERS AND PERSONS IN CASE OF WAR ON LAND, signed at the Hague, 18 Oct. 1907, 36 U.S. STATUTES AT LARGE 2310-2331; 1 bevans 654–668; 2 AM. J. INT'L L., 1908 Supp., at 117–27.
DoD General Counsel, *An Assessment of International Legal Issues in Information Operations*, May 19, 1999.
Downs, Lawrence G., Jr., *Digital Data Warfare: Using Malicious Computer Code As A Weapon*, study published by National Defense University Institute for Strategic Studies (1995), at 58.
INTERNATIONAL TELECOMMUNICATIONS CONVENTION, Malaga-Torremolinos, 28 U.S.T. 2495, T.I.A.S. 8572 (1973). The Malaga-Torremolinos Convention was replaced by the 1982 INTERNATIONAL TELECOMMUNICATIONS CONVENTION, Nairobi, 6 Nov. 1982, 32 U.S.T. 3821; T.I.A.S. 9920 (entered into force for the United States January 10, 1986).
PDD 63, CRITICAL INFRASTRUCURE PROTECTION (1998).
Protocol I Additional to the 1949 Geneva Conventions (1977), 16 I.L.M. 1391, *reprinted in* Schindler and Toman, THE LAW OF ARMED CONFLICTS (Leiden: Sijhoff [1982]).
UN Charter art. 2, para. 4.. The Charter is codified at 59 Stat. 1031; TS 993; 3 Bevans 1153. Signed at San Francisco 26 June 1945. *Reprinted in* U.S. State Department Publication 2368, 1–20.
U.S. Space Command News Release No. 20–99, Oct. 1, 1999.
Whiteman, Marjorie, 5 DIGEST OF INTERNATIONAL LAW, Sec. 25, at 971–72 (1965).

THE WAR ON TERROR AND MEDIA ACCESS

Ackerly, William G., Analysis of the Pentagon's Press Pool Tests 10 (1987) (unpublished M.A. thesis, University of Kansas) (on file with the University of Kansas Library).

Ballard, Franklin, FAMOUS WAR CORRESPONDENTS 413–14 (Boston: Little and Brown, 1914).

Boccardi, Louis D., *Agreement on War Coverage Guidelines*, A.P. News Release, May 21, 1992.

Catto, Henry, Jr., *Dateline Grenada: The Media and the Military Go at It*, WASHINGTON POST, Oct. 30, 1983, at C7.

Chafee, Zechariah, Jr., FREE SPEECH IN THE UNITED STATES (Union, NJ: Lawbook Exchange, 1941).

Civil Liberties and the National Security State: Hearings Before the Subcomm. on Courts, Civil Liberties and the Administration of Justice of the House Comm. on the Judiciary, 98th Cong., 1st Sess. (1983).

Cloud, Stanley W., *Covering the Next War*, NEW YORK TIMES, Aug. 4, 1992, at 19.

Cohen, William S., Secretary of Defense, *Principles of Information* (Apr. 1, 1997) (public statement).

Combelles-Siegel, P., THE TROUBLED PATH TO THE PENTAGON'S RULES ON MEDIA ACCESS TO THE BATTLEFIELD: GRENADA TO TODAY 13 (U.S. Army War College Strategic Studies Institute, 1996).

————. *Operation Just Cause: A Military-Media Fiasco*, MILITARY REVIEW. (May–June 1995), at 77–85.

Gottschalk, Jack A., *Consistent with Security: A History of American Press Censorship*, 5 COMMUNICATIONS AND THE LAW 35, 35–36 (1983).

Greenstein, R., *Bridging the Mootness Gap in Federal Court Class Actions*, 35 STANFORD LAW REVIEW. 897 (1983).

Hearings on Governmental Information Plans and Policies, before a Subcommittee of the House Comm. on Governmental Operations, 88th Cong., 1st Sess. 15, 32, 34, 61 (Part 1), 269 (Part 2) (1963).

Hess, Stephen & Marvin Kalb, eds., THE MEDIA AND THE WAR ON TERRORISM (2003).

Hoffman, Fred, *Review of Panama Pool Deployment, December 1989*, in UNDER FIRE: U.S. MILITARY RESTRICTIONS ON THE MEDIA FROM GRENADA TO THE PERSIAN GULF, APP. C, at 4 (J. Sharkey, ed. 1991).

————. *Review of Panama Pool Deployment* (March 1990) (Report on file with the Pentagon Library, Washington, DC 20310).

Jacobs, Matthew J. *Assessing the Constitutionality of Press Restrictions in the Persian Gulf War*, 44 STANFORD LAW REVIEW. 675, 680 (1992).

Jeffries, John, *Freedom of Expression*, in NATIONAL SECURITY LAW 995 (Moore, Tipson, & Turner 1990).

Joint Chiefs of Staff, JOINT PUB. 5-02.2, ANNEX F, PLANNING GUIDANCE—PUBLIC AFFAIRS (30 March 1990).

Junger, Sebastian, WAR (New York: Twelve) 2010.

Kamenar, Paul D., *Media Restrictions are Necessary to Protect Troops*, LEGAL TIMES, Jan. 28, 1991, at 19–20.

Katovsky, Bill & Timothy Carlson, EMBEDDED: THE MEDIA AT WAR IN IRAQ xiv (Guilford, CT: Lyons Press, 2003).

Knight, Oliver, FOLLOWING THE INDIAN WARS: THE STORY OF THE NEWSPAPER CORRESPONDENTS AMONG THE INDIAN CAMPAIGNERS (Norman: University of Oklahoma Press, 1960).

Knightly, Philip, THE FIRST CASUALTY—FROM CRIMEA TO VIETNAM: THE WAR CORRESPONDENT AS HERO, PROPAGANDIST, AND MYTH-MAKER 337 (New York: Harcourt Brace Jovanavich, 1975).

Lewis, Anthony, *What Was He Hiding?*, NEW YORK TIMES, Oct. 31, 1983, at A19.

Lubow, Arthur, *Read Some About It*, NEW REPUBLIC, Mar. 18, 1991, at 23.

MacArthur, John R., SECOND FRONT: CENSORSHIP AND PROPAGANDA IN THE GULF WAR (Berkeley: University of California Press, 1992).

Mathews, Joseph J. REPORTING THE WARS (Minneapolis: University of Minnesota Press, 1957).

Metcalf, Vice Admiral Joseph, *The Press and Grenada:1983*, in DEFENSE AND MEDIA IN TIME OF LIMITED WAR, SMALL WARS AND INSURGENCIES, 169–70 (P. Young, ed. 1991).

Middleton, Drew, *Barring Reporters from the Battlefield,* NEW YORK TIMES., Feb. 5, 1984, at 36, 37.

Mott, Frank, AMERICAN JOURNALISM—A HISTORY: 1690–1960, 536–37 (New York: Macmillan, 1962).

News Policies in Vietnam: Hearings Before the Senate Comm. on Foreign Relations, 86th Cong., 2d Sess. 68 (1966) (Statement by Asst. Sec. of Def. Arthur Sylvester).

Pear, Robert *Military Revises Rules to Assure Reporters Access to Battle Areas,* N.Y. TIMES NAT'L, May 22, 1992, at 3.

SECDEF 101900Z FEB 03: Subj: Public Affairs Guidance (PAG) on Embedding Media During Possible Future Operations/Deployments in the U.S. Central Commands (CENTCOM) Area of Responsibility (AOR) (UNCLASS).

Shelton, Henry & Timothy Vane, *Winning the Information War in Haiti,* MILITARY REVIEW., Nov.–Dec. 1995, at 3, 5.

Special Report: The Battle for Grenada, NEWSWEEK, Nov. 7, 1983, at 66.

Stein, M., UNDER FIRE: THE STORY OF AMERICAN WAR CORRESPONDENTS 73 (1968).

Sturgess, Gary, *Media Powers Oppose War Rules but Shun Suit,* LEGAL TIMES, Feb. 4, 1991, at 2.

Terry, James P., *A Legal Review of U.S. Military Involvement in Peacekeeping and Peace Enforcement Operations,* 42 NAVAL LAW REVIEW. 79 (1995).

————. *An Appraisal of Lawful Military Response to State-Sponsored Terrorism,* NAVAL WAR COLLEGE REVIEW. (May–June 1986) at 61, 66.

————. *Law in Support of Policy in Panama,* NAVAL WAR COLLEGE REVIEW 110 (Autumn 1990).

————. *Operation Desert Storm: Sharp Contrasts in Compliance With the Rule of Law,* 41 NAVAL LAW REVIEW 83 (1993).

————. *Press Access in the Post Peacekeeping Era,* MILITARY LAW REVIEW (1997).

————. *Rethinking Humanitarian Intervention After Kosovo,* THE ARMY LAWYER (August 2004).

————. *The Iranian Hostage Crisis: International Law and U.S. Policy,* JAG JOURNAL (Summer 1982).

————. *The Vietnam War in Perspective,* NAVAL LAW REVIEW (2007).

————. *UN Peacekeeping and Military Reality,* BROWN JOURNAL OF WORLD AFFAIRS, (Winter/Spring 1996).

U.S. Central Command, Public Affairs Office, Guidelines for News Media (Jan. 14, 1991).

U.S. DEPT. OF ARMY FIELD MANUAL 100–5, OPERATIONS 1, 3 (June 14, 1993).

U.S. DEP'T OF DEFENSE, DIR. 5122.5, ASSISTANT SECRETARY OF DEFENSE FOR PUBLIC AFFAIRS (Mar. 29, 1996).

U.S. DEP'T OF DEFENSE DIR. 5400.13, JOINT PUBLIC AFFAIRS OPERATIONS (Jan. 9, 1996).

U.S. DEPARTMENT OF DEFENSE DIR. 5122.05, September 5, 2008.

U.S. Dept. of Defense, Report of CJCS Media–Military Relations Panel (Sidle Panel) (1984) (available in Pentagon Library).

Warren, James *In First Battlefield Test, Media Pool Misses Mark,* CHICAGO TRIBUNE, Jan. 7, 1990, Perspective sect., at 1.

Waters, Robert, *The Media vs. the Military,* HARTFORD COURANT, Dec. 23, 1985, at 1.

Index

About the Author

James P. Terry most recently served as the Chairman of the Board of Veterans Appeals in the Department of Veterans Affairs from 2005–2011. He previously served as Principal Deputy Assistant Secretary and Deputy Assistant Secretary in the Department of State from 2001–2005. Prior to that, he served for six years in the Department of the Interior as a member of the Senior Executive Service. James Terry was born in East Brookfield, Massachusetts, and received his undergraduate and graduate degrees from the University of Virginia. In 1973, he received his law degree from Mercer University and then completed the Master of Laws (with highest honors) and Doctor of Juridical Science degrees from The George Washington University. A career Marine Corps officer, he served twenty-seven years on active duty prior to retiring in 1995. Service included a tour as an infantry officer in Vietnam in 1968–1969 with the 3rd Marine Division and service as Staff Judge Advocate to the Commanding General, III Marine Expeditionary Force during the First Gulf War. He served as Legal Counsel to the Chairman, Joint Chiefs of Staff from 1992–1995. He has authored more than forty-five articles on coercion control and national security law, as well as the text, *The Regulation of International Coercion*, published by the Naval War College Press. The author resides with his wife, Michelle, in Annandale, Virginia.